Absentee Mothers

Absentee Mothers

PATRICIA PASKOWICZ

ALLANHELD, OSMUN   Totowa
UNIVERSE BOOKS   New York

For Joyce, David, and Chris,
that they may someday understand,
and
for Margaret,
who accepted society's verdict of guilt
and inflicted the final penalty by her own hand

Published in the United States of America in 1982
by Allanheld, Osmun & Co. Publishers, Inc.
(A Division of Littlefield, Adams & Company)
81 Adams Drive, Totowa, New Jersey 07512
and by Universe Books
381 Park Avenue South, New York, N.Y. 10016

Library of Congress Cataloging in Publication Data

Paskowicz, Patricia.
    Absentee mothers.

    Includes bibliographical references.
    1. Absentee mothers. I. Title.
HQ759.3.P37   1982   306.8'9   82-11492
ISBN 0-87663-411-0 (Universe)

82 83 84 85 86/10 9 8 7 6 5 4 3 2 1

Printed in the United States of America

Contents

Acknowledgments

I started college in my early thirties by enrolling in Mundelein's (a Catholic women's college) experimental Week-End College in Chicago. There, I met Rochelle Distelheim, a teacher who told me I could write, helped me groom my craft, and nourished my self-esteem. My advisor, David Orr, was a tactful dear. During our first counseling session, he ignored my mispronunciation of Camus as "Came us," but casually included the correct "Cah moo" during our subsequent conversation—all without so much as a flinch or a grin. Mary Griffin and Jane Trahey responded so positively to this book's precursor, an article called "Even Medea Had Her Reasons," that they gave me a strong second wind when I needed it most. But perhaps my most important encounter at Mundelein was with Bill Hill, a bearded mountain of a professor, demanding and devastatingly consistent in detecting flaws in logic. Bill Hill forced me to think, for which I continue to be very grateful. He was also the founder of the Week-End College program which made it possible for a secretary, who had to work full-time, to become what she had to become. I cannot exaggerate what these people and their school meant to me and my writing this book.

Thank you, Roi Tauer, for your help in recruiting participants and for directing me toward Mundelein.

I want to give special thanks to Judy, Marge, Pat, Kate, and Jane, my therapy group "sisters," who gave me part of themselves so that I could persevere in my work. To use Sister Sledge's famous lyric, "We are family."

I feel that close, as well, to the one hundred women who were willing to look inward at events that most found terribly painful. They cared enough for those who might be helped by their experiences to endure the process of taking part in this study. I admire their courage and give them my most sincere gratitude.

To my sister Vicky, who found many absentee mothers for me, taped television talk shows for me, and never doubted for a minute that I would finish and find a publisher, I express my deep love.

To my sister Joyce, who withstood the awkward side effects of having recruited an absentee mother friend for me, I also give my heartfelt appreciation for the psychic shoring of love.

I wish to give my appreciation to my good friends Dr. Raymond Mitchell (Ph.D. in public health) and Wendy Bock Mitchell (M.A. in psychology) both for their loving support in friendship and for their generous help with the psychological aspects of my project. Dr. Nathalie Ostroot (professor of sociology at Grand Valley State Colleges in Michigan), who also fulfills the dual role of friend and consultant, has been monumentally generous with her time, her expertise, and her affectionate encouragement. My gratitude to her will never diminish.

Peter, who has always been my cousin and more recently has become my husband, deserves gratitude of a higher order for the confidence he has had in me, for his financial provision which allowed me the luxury of writing full time, and for his amazing courage in facing my "author's wrath" as Number One Editor.

Finally, I want my children, Joyce, David, and Chris, to know that the enthusiasm and pride they have shown for their mother and her book have been vitally uplifting and a real balm in the midst of what could have been an impossible project if they had reacted differently.

Poem on page 173 is from William Carlos Williams, COLLECTED EARLIER POEMS OF WILLIAM CARLOS WILLIAMS, copyright 1938 by New Directions Publishing Corporation. Reprinted by permission of New Directions.

Introduction

It is not a garment I cast off this day, but a skin that I tear with my own hands . . . Yet I cannot tarry longer.

—*Kahlil Gibran*, The Prophet

Late in 1969, I left a nine-year marriage and the three children my husband and I had had during that marriage. My departure was the culmination of years of agonizing, years of internal struggle with the seemingly unresolvable conflict between conscience and dire personal need. When at last I made the decision in favor of my own survival, I did so with the certain belief that I was the only woman in existence despicable enough to do such a thing.

My children, a girl and two boys, were only seven, five, and two. Their smallness and almost total dependence combined to create for me an indelible vision of betrayed vulnerability. Over and over again, I would see Chris, my toddler, standing in his crib in a wet and soiled diaper, waiting for me to come and change him, looking toward the bedroom doorway with the full expectation that I would come through the doorway at any minute.

Or I would relive the day my brown-eyed David walked so confidently down our pebbled driveway toward the little bus on his first day of nursery school, so ready, at four, to take on his "responsibilities," while his own mother was contemplating running away from hers.

The night before I left home, my daughter, Joyce, had been listening from her darkened bedroom, her father and I assuming her to be asleep while we talked in the living room. She heard her

1

father ask me what I would do differently if it were possible for the two of us to begin again. She heard me say that I would not have children. What horrible pain this must have inflicted on my poor little girl. How could she possibly understand that my statement in no way meant that I did not cherish her and both her brothers?

These and similar visions haunted me. When they were not in my immediate consciousness, they lived under the thinnest layer of self-protection, which would tear at the slightest reminder of my crime. I did love my children desperately, yet had found it impossible to continue my attempt at mothering them. Why? What was wrong with me? What had been wrong with my marriage? And how was I to survive the murderous guilt?

Froma Sand has said that "trauma has a partner in ignorance."[1] In 1969, I knew virtually nothing about myself or how I had become that self, nothing about the individuals with whom I had been attempting to live a life, nothing about the community around us or its impact on us. My education had concluded with a high school diploma and never received the supplementation it might have had, through independent reading and introspection if nothing else. I thought psychology was for college students and movie stars; it certainly had nothing to do with real people. And sociology and anthropology were blurred into an exotic picture of statistics and jungle villages unrelated to any practical understanding of behavior. It is no wonder that I had not a glimmer of insight regarding the emotional conflict I had been experiencing my entire marriage, nor any hint as to why I had so often felt rage toward my children. Neither should it be surprising that I had no real understanding of the almost hysterical need to flee both my husband and my nurturing responsibilities. What I did know, intuitively, was that I *had* to "get out." And that, if I did not, I would in all certainty die. In retrospect, I know too that I might have hurt my children if I had remained.

So there I was, feeling just slightly less evil than Medea, unable to justify my desertion to either myself or anyone else and beginning what was to be a long, harsh, and uninformed period of both self-imposed and societally imposed punishment. Not until the fall of 1974, when I began a belated effort to further my education, did I start feeling that perhaps I deserved to continue living.

The first significant event that led me to write this book occurred during one of my children's weekend visits. I had picked them up from their home in Indiana and brought them to my home in

Illinois, a procedure that had developed into our semiregular bi-monthly routine. The four of us were swimming in the pool that was part of my apartment complex. The children began playing with a young girl who was also in the pool. They all came splashing over to me, very excited. "Mom, Mom, this girl is here visiting her mother too! Her parents are divorced and she lives with her *father*, just like us!" (The uniqueness of our arrangement had been forcefully impressed on all of us by then.) Beneath my casual "That's interesting" reply, there was a distinct reaction of disapproval, even of repugnance. I hoped I would never run into that girl's mother, for I was sure I would not like her.

As soon as I realized what I was feeling, I also recognized what the people around *me* had been feeling. I knew for the first time that *I* was capable of the exact sort of insensitivity toward "deviants" that had been crushing me ever since I had given my husband custody. I felt terribly ashamed.

But very quickly my shame was overshadowed by fascination. There were other women who did not live with their children! Were they very much like me? How many of them could there be? Why would an isolated "deviant" like myself respond so negatively to a person who had veered from society's prescription for mothers in very much the same way as I had? Dwelling on these questions and those which they naturally spawned over a period of some months, I began to see the psychological and sociological implications of my plight. And I realized that telling my story might help others like myself.

I wrote a seven-thousand-word article in which I attempted to describe my experience with marriage and motherhood and to explain why and how I came to relinquish custody of my children to their father. I called the article "Even Medea Had Her Reasons." The piece was never published, but it did circulate among a fair number of friends, acquaintances of friends, and so on, and very much to my surprise I started receiving letters and phone calls from those who had seen the narrative—friendly, sympathetic, and interested letters and calls.

The following year, while in France, I met Nathalie Ostroot, an American absentee mother *and* a sociologist. She gave me the encouragement I needed to undertake a book: not just my own story, but the story I felt sure absentee mothers had in common. I wanted to write it for absentee mothers, to provide whatever emotional support finding one another could give, and for our children, to help them understand. I also hoped to take the first step in promoting a wider understanding of absentee mothers among those who may be able to help them in a professional capacity and among the general public as well. What I ask of the general reader is fairness: not to prejudge without a hearing. Nathalie offered to act as a technical consultant where necessary and assured me that the rest was a matter of common sense, personal experience, and the ability to write clearly.

My first step was to create a set of about 150 questions intended to gather both quantitative data and qualitative responses during interviews with the absentee mothers I hoped to find. The questions were designed to obtain demographic information about absentee mothers, to learn the motivation/causation behind their maternal status, and to elicit the emotions experienced by these mothers before, during, and after relinquishing custody. I wanted to learn who noncustodial mothers were (if they had much in common that might differentiate them from custodial mothers) and whether their unorthodox situations could be attributed to anything other than general societal change. I was interested in whether there were factors in a woman's childhood or marriage that might contribute to the likelihood of her becoming an absentee mother, and I hoped to gain a sense of whether relinquishing custody of her children could be considered a good option for the future divorcing mother (and, to a limited degree, for her children).

When I returned to the United States in August of 1979, I started interviewing absentee mothers I had been able to find through word of mouth (termed "snowballing" in sociologic method). It soon became clear, however, that I would not be able to finance the travel and other expenses involved in conducting approximately one hundred personal interviews. Neither was I able to locate any source of grants. At this point I decided to proceed through the use of questionnaires.

When snowballing began to falter, I started placing ads at random to seek additional participants, with the knowledge that this was an accepted practice among sociologists and would result in what is termed a "convenience sample." This method does not necessarily result in a technically representative cross-section of the population, but it is nevertheless considered a valid method for gaining meaningful information toward the creation of representative empirical data. Thus, I found the rest of the hundred absentee mothers on whom this book is based through *Ms.* Magazine, *The*

New York Times, the *Washington Post,* the *Chicago Tribune* and *Sun-Times,* the *Los Angeles Times,* the *San Francisco Chronicle,* the *Oakland Tribune,* various free community newspapers, an association newsletter, and a number of organization bulletin boards.

The sample of absentee mothers thus attained consists of one hundred women from twenty-seven states; four participants live outside the United States: three in Canada and one in England, but only one of the four is not American. She is Canadian. Ninety-six of the mothers are Caucasian and four black. Based upon their type of employment, fifty-eight may be considered middle class and forty-two working class. The median age of the sample is thirty-five and a half, while the median educational level is two years of college. A most interesting distribution of religious preference is displayed in the group, especially when compared to the population at large. The most significant element of this religious makeup, I believe, is that 43 percent of the sample have no religion; only 7 percent of the American population hold no religious preference. (See Appendix: Demographics.) I have changed the names of all persons from the sample, as well as persons to whom I refer in my personal accounts (with the exception of my children and my sisters).

All respondents who completed a questionnaire fit the following definition of *absentee mother,* a term I created expressly for the purpose of this book:

One will be considered an absentee mother if she is a woman who has relinquished custody of her natural offspring after having lived for a time with that child or children. The term will apply whether or not it was the mother's wish to relinquish custody and whether the mother relinquished custody to the father of her children or to any other person, persons or entity. It will include mothers who plan the separation from their children to be temporary, and mothers who have relinquished and subsequently resumed custody.

The definition will necessarily exclude adoptive mothers who have relinquished custody and mothers who have given up babies at birth.

At this point, I will defend my creation of the term *absentee mother* to those few who have seen its use as pejorative. I understand and sympathize with the objection to the term; it does conjure up notions of dereliction of duty, and I do not mean to give the impression that I agree with those notions in my use of the term, but I have several good reasons for using it nevertheless.

My primary purpose for using *absentee mother* to describe a woman who has relinquished custody of her child or children (and keep in mind that I am one of these women myself) is that it attracts attention.

Another reason I am using the term is that its lurking negative implications accurately depict the way most of society sees us and, indeed, the way many of us see ourselves. The contents of the book, I hope, will highlight the inequity of that common perception, thus creating a dramatic and symbolic contrast between the title and the rest of the book. The title represents the way we are seen; the book intends to represent the way we are.

I would also emphasize, however, that the term *absentee mother* in its literal sense means nothing more than a mother who is not present in the child's home. Even *absentee landlord* means no more, literally, than a property owner who does not live on the property. We have simply come to assume that that automatically makes that person a bad landlord (just as many assume that absentee mothers are bad mothers). No one feels negatively about the absentee voter or the absentee ballot. It may be possible to accomplish the same nonjudgmental use of the term *absentee mother*. However, the term *noncustodial mother*, which is certainly unobjectionable, may be more widely accepted in the end.

Now I will clarify specific aspects of the absentee mother definition that have been questioned, namely, the exclusion of mothers who relinquish babies at birth and adoptive mothers who relinquish their adopted children in divorces.

Any woman who has given birth to a child or obtained a child but does not live with that child could be reasonably referred to as an absentee mother, and the exclusion of these women may seem arbitrary. However, the mother who relinquishes custody of her child at birth, although she experiences many of the same problems as the women to whom I refer in this book, is not in the same position as the mother who establishes a relationship with and initially accepts responsibility for her child. A mother who gives up her baby at birth does not live with the child's reaction to what she has done. In no way do I mean to dismiss the difficulty experienced by these women. I simply mean to explain my perception of relinquishing custody at birth as being, overall, a different experience from that of the absentee mothers in this book.

I included a reference to adoptive mothers in my definition of absentee mothers only in an attempt to be technically complete, and I excluded adoptive absentee mothers from my study, not because I believe that adoptive mothers necessarily feel differently than biologic mothers toward their adopted children, but because I believe that questions raised on this subject would bring up distracting side issues. The Group for the Advancement of Psychiatry has noted, "There are opposing views on whether or not the process of natural pregnancy is indeed central to the experience of parenthood. Those who hold to a biological view of parenthood, at least in terms of emphasis, feel that the natural parents are the real parents and that the adoptive parents cannot ever fully feel a total sense of parenthood!"[2]

Only two adoptive absentee mothers turned up while I was gathering my sample. One of them called me, after receiving the absentee mother definition by mail, to protest the exclusion. I deeply regret that, for this woman, my "logical" decision added to the sense of discrimination and prejudice that adoptive parents are apt to experience.[3] I certainly had no such intention. In fairness, I have to admit the possibility that my decision could have been subconsciously influenced by a painful situation that is commonly the lot of absentee mothers. My ex-husband and his wife have always insisted to my children that I am not their *real* mother because I do not live with them or fulfill their daily needs. Many women in my study are faced with rival claims to motherhood.

I now feel that, if I could begin again, I would not exclude adoptive absentee mothers. The side issue would have proved relatively minor, and in the essentials the problems experienced by these women are similar to those of other women who have relinquished custody of their children. (Their problems may, in fact, be compounded because they are adoptive mothers. For example, they may confront a deeper sense of guilt and unworthiness, since they have been faced with putting their children through the trauma of maternal withdrawal for a second time.)

There remains but one element of this book that seems to call for explanation: my decision to use a good deal of autobiographical material. One reason was the discovery that, in many respects, I have proven to be typical of the average absentee mother found in my sample. Therefore, it appeared that, since I was not comparing my sample of noncustodial mothers to a counter-sample of custodial mothers, comparing them to myself could act as a good centering device. In addition, the totality of self-knowledge (with which even the most conscientiously completed questionnaire could not compare) would allow me to enrich the study with intimate detail perhaps otherwise unavailable in certain areas. I hope this has resulted in a more readable work.

1

As Others See Us:
Stereotypes of the Absentee Mother

> Garcin: And, by the way, how does one recognize torturers
> when one sees them? . . .
> Inez: They look frightened.
> Garcin: Frightened! But how ridiculous! Of whom should they
> be frightened? Of their victims?
>
> —Jean-Paul Sartre, No Exit

One day in the late spring of 1980, I was turning my television selector carelessly and stopped at a Phil Donahue Show in progress. I recognized the woman being interviewed as a newspaper reporter who had written an article I had read a couple of months earlier. She was an absentee mother, and I soon learned that it was in that capacity that she was appearing on the show. She had evidently related her story to Phil and his audience, and she was now answering questions.

It was apparent that neither Phil Donahue nor the absentee mother had been prepared for the response of the virtually all-female audience. There was anger and hostility. There was self-righteousness. It was as if the absentee mother had been convicted of a crime and was now being stoned with words. Women were rising and making statements. No one was asking questions. "You didn't have to have kids if you didn't want 'em!" one middle-aged woman spat. "*I* could never do that. *I* love my kids too much," a younger woman said. Her self-satisfaction was palpable. "You shouldn't have done it. There's no excuse."

The relative absence of questions was significant, because it demonstrated the absence of a desire to understand. People are normally curious about and willing to understand situations that do not threaten them. It was all too clear that these women, most of them mothers no doubt, were frightened by the absentee mother. She represented—as do all absentee mothers—the universal childhood fear of abandonment, and she represented the part of every mother which does not like being a mother yet constructs defenses against admitting it. The emotional and immediate response of the audience members was to judge and attack the absentee mother in an attempt to "destroy" the source of their discomfort.

The absentee mother had apparently expected a discussion of her unusual custody arrangement. She found herself, instead, in the position of defendant. Donahue did his best to soften the crowd's barrage and to help his guest deal with it, but it seemed that her ability to respond effectively had been derailed by the hostility displayed. I turned the show off when it looked as though she might break into tears. I sat there pondering the fact that this woman was an absentee mother whose children had decided to live with their father after two years of living with her. As far as I could tell, the woman was being condemned for allowing her children to go and for her admission that she "was often sorry [she] fell into motherhood, for which [she] had no natural talent." I could not help but wonder how that audience would have responded to an absentee mother like myself, who had herself initiated the separation from her children.

Almost a year later, Phil Donahue aired another show in which mothers relinquishing custody were the topic. His guests this time were three absentee mothers. No solitary crucifixion would be possible. I waited expectantly for a more understanding response than I had witnessed a year earlier. After all, times are changing quickly. We are all becoming more flexible and broad-minded. But the condemnation was as harsh as a year earlier. The audience erupted into spontaneous group moans of disapproval whenever one of the mothers spoke. It was an extraordinary display of censure and bile.

Although the absentee mothers in my study have also experienced such negative reactions from women, they have noticed a difference in response toward them between women who are mothers and women who are not. One of these absentee mothers, named Alice, did not understand it.[1] "Surprisingly, the few who empathized with me were not mothers themselves," she says.[2] In a sense, neither did Jane understand her experience with the same phenomenon: "I was accused of being everything bad my relatives and friends could think of," she said, and in something of an understatement added, "They responded badly." But then she remembered another response: "Except for one friend who had not married or had children. She didn't understand marriage or motherhood, but she understood pain." In large measure, childless women are not threatened by absentee mothers and are thereby more readily able to befriend them.

Verifiable evidence of public attitudes toward absentee mothers is a rarity. I have been able to locate no studies that deal with attitudes toward the absentee mother, so to a large extent, my assertions will be based on my own personal experiences and those of the hundred absentee mothers who took part in my project. I recognize that my data are necessarily skewed, but by no means do I dismiss their meaning and validity.

For further support of my perception of social views of the absentee mother, however, I look to some of our popular entertainment. I do this based on the commonly held belief that books, films, songs, and other popular entertainments are reflective, to a fair extent, of our attitudes. These entertainments, in turn, also influence our views. So there is a sort of circular motion of influence. The process is not reducible to a formula, and many sometimes contradictory effects are felt simultaneously. This ambiguity may be seen in references made by two absentee mothers to *Kramer vs. Kramer*, a film which was very well received in 1979. Sherry felt the movie was a positive vehicle for bringing absentee mothers out of the closet, for "loosening attitudes" by making "the subject quite popular." In stark contrast to Sherry's reaction, a second absentee mother, Marta, told me that *"Kramer vs. Kramer* brought out some ugly reactions from acquaintances. They all missed the absentee mother's pain and seemed compelled to denounce her over and over again."

In spite of the ambiguities of communication, we cannot deny the interaction between our perceptions and our popular forms of entertainment. It is obvious to most of us and generally accepted that we are influenced in meaningful ways and to significant degrees by these creations, and more important, to my mind, these creations reflect us.

The Kramer vs. Kramer *Syndrome: The Absentee Mother as Self-Centered Bitch*

Avery Corman's *Kramer vs. Kramer* became a best-selling novel and then a successful film.[3] Although the book and film revolve primarily around the development of a warm relationship between father and small son, the book presents one of the prevailing views of women who leave their children: the absentee mother as self-centered bitch. It draws the absentee mother as a monster: immature, narcissistic, weak and spoiled, selfish, cold, frivolous and cruel—a picture real absentee mothers have had drawn for them personally by relatives, "friends," employers, neighbors, and total strangers. Margaret, for instance, told me that people she met in casual circumstances often made it clear by their line of questioning that they thought "I preferred to shed all responsibility and to live only for myself." Joyce related that both her own family and that of her husband viewed her relinquishing custody in the same way. "They thought I was terrible and that I was doing a selfish, irresponsible thing." Phrases like "running out" and "copping out" were commonly hurled at the absentee mothers I have come to know.

Thanks to Meryl Streep's sensitive insistence and the cooperation of the producer, the director, and Dustin Hoffman, the film does not portray Joanna Kramer in the same way as the book does. The book has been described as "the anti-feminist backlash novel."[4] The film is an improvement over the book primarily because it portrays Joanna Kramer's pain—at least visually. Unfortunately, the viewer is not given any insight into Joanna's reasons for leaving. We see her leaving, we see that it was difficult for her to do so, and later, we see her watching her son from a distance with anguish in her face. And the portrayal is moving, but I found myself constantly wondering, "Why did she leave? Why didn't she take her son with her? Why did she come back? *Who* is she?" She is someone we never get to know and, therefore, someone we cannot understand. I feel that the *Kramer* film, although well intentioned and finely made to the extent that it concentrates on the father/son relationship which develops, merely *avoids* the absentee mother. It does not replace the book's horrid portrayal with a full, realistic one, but with a suffering enigma, probably because those involved simply had no idea who the real absentee mother is.

Joanna Kramer, the absentee mother in Avery Corman's novel, is a vicious caricature embodying, one must assume, all the prejudices of its author—unless the creation is a cynical attempt to snare a certain kind of prejudiced audience. As a characterization, the person of Joanna is not worth discussing. A brief description of this Frankensteinian concoction is illuminating, though, because it reflects all the bits and pieces that make up the popular stereotype of the self-centered bitch.

The hatchet job on Joanna Kramer begins on page one where the reader is shown that she does not appreciate her supportive husband during labor and delivery of her child. In response to Ted's solicitous attempts to help with her timing and breathing, Joanna blurts at him, "Fuck you!" Her further obscenities establish her as a woman who hates motherhood from the outset, especially in contrast to the popular LaMaze attitude toward childbirth, which insists there need not be pain and should be fulfillment. We are repeatedly made aware of Joanna's "insensitivity." When Ted tells Joanna of how close he felt to her at the moment their son was born, "holding her at the very moment of birth," she responds rather distractedly, "I don't distinctly remember your being there."

The woman in the first Phil Donahue audience who was anxious to emphasize the absentee mother's free choice of motherhood made a point that is also made about Joanna Kramer. Joanna Kramer finished college, went to New York City to live on her own, worked prosaically as a secretary, and had dozens of affairs, including several with married men. She was almost thirty when she met Ted. Weary of the single life, she decided in favor of marriage and a child. What acceptable excuse could there be for turning her back on such a well-informed decision?

We are filled in on Joanna's spoiled childhood and pampering in marriage. By the end of the first year of little Billy's existence, Joanna Kramer is telling Ted Kramer that "being a mother is boring. Nobody admits it."

In the film of *Kramer vs. Kramer*, the viewer receives the suggestion that Ted is obsessed with his career and has little attention to give his wife, but in the book he continues to be the ideal husband.

Billy is two when his mother announces that she is "losing interest in Billy," as if he were a trinket. She wants to get a job, but Ted disapproves, mostly for Billy's sake, but also because he feels the amount of money Joanna would bring in from a secretarial job is ridiculously small. Billy is enrolled in an expensive nursery school, and Joanna devotes herself to tennis and to its attractive fringe benefits—a beautiful tan and the attention of men who ask her to play. A cleaning woman is hired, and then a financial crisis arrives. Joanna responds to the crisis like a pouting child, refusing to give up any of her luxuries. She finally exposes herself to the black core, however, when she, Ted, and Billy are on a "dull" vacation at the beach. Three-year-old Billy is being a nuisance, complaining about having nothing to do, until his mother finally screams, "Go swim, then!"—knowing that he cannot. Ted's response is ours: "Jesus, Joanna!"

It is shortly after Billy's fourth birthday party that Joanna Kramer decides to leave her husband and child. The birthday itself acts as the catalyst to her decision—the effort to make every detail just the way Billy wanted it, the grating chaos that only an apartment full of toddlers, ice cream and cake, and games can create. The party acts as a gross magnification of Joanna's daily misery, proof that she is living a life she can bear no longer.

Joanna's first inclination is simply to leave a note for Ted, but she decides that she owes him "a brief question-and-answer period." She makes and serves dinner as usual, puts Billy to bed, then simply tells Ted that she is leaving him. "I don't get it," he says. "You don't have to," Joanna hurls back.

In *Kramer vs. Kramer*, it is suggested that Joanna's narcissism has been encouraged, indeed justified, by the feminist movement. She has read articles that said other women found motherhood taxing or boring. She has learned that women must be their own people. She has latched on to these grand discoveries and used them to excuse her questionable behavior. But Joanna can scarcely be said to implicate feminism, because her understanding of it is so obviously superficial. Blaming feminism for Joanna Kramer leaving her family is like blaming Christ for the Jonestown massacre. The night she leaves, she tells Ted, "Feminists will applaud me." This equation of feminism with absentee motherhood firmly implanted in the reader's mind, Corman has Joanna deliver the most damaging blow of all. Expressing outright what people usually assume to be absentee mothers' feelings, she says to the boy's father, "I . . . don't want Billy."

Joanna's flight is made to seem all the more inexcusable because of her indifference to a career before marriage and the belittling of her earning potential after marriage. We are led to feel that if Joanna had gone off to some lofty profession or an exceptionally humane occupation, her decision to leave her child with his father could be seen in a less unfavorable light. In the film of *Kramer vs. Kramer*, one of the story details that was changed from the book was the sort of work Joanna did after she left her family. The film has her move to California, where she obtains a high-paying job—making more than Ted—as a commercial artist. We see a talented, able woman who achieves her full potential and earning capacity. She is more than a secretary, after all. The producer evidently introduced this to retain a little sympathy for Joanna. It is not enough justification in the long run, however. (As we will see in the third stereotype discussed later, the absentee mother is damned as well if she does have a career.) In the *Kramer* book, Joanna also ends up in California, but her life consists of playing tennis and working behind a car-rental counter. This is a loaded deck. Joanna's own mother says to herself, in dazed summary, "She left her family, her child, to go to California to rent cars." You can almost hear the bewilderment in her voice.

In my own case, I recall my sister-in-law and a friend questioning me expectantly after my divorce and relinquished custody. They were incredulous that *all* I was planning to do was return to secretarial work, the only work for which I was qualified, and go to school. They kept asking why I wasn't going to try something exciting or glamorous like modeling, something that could begin to explain relinquishing my children.

Joanna Kramer is portrayed as a floundering person with little self-awareness. She does not understand who she is or why she has left her family and has not learned about herself in her seclusion. The absentee mothers in my study almost invariably knew exactly why they have divorced and relinquished custody. If their motivation is not immediately clear to them, time normally gives them the answers. Joanna Kramer, by fighting to regain custody only to refuse it after she wins, displays her self-ignorance and uncertainty. She also subjects her little boy to the hurt of maternal abandonment for a second time.

Although this vacillation is not at all typical of the real absentee mother, Joanna's confusion does demonstrate the tragic ambivalence most absentee mothers feel and suggests the debilitating effect it can have on their emotional health, as well as that of their families. Joanna's final phone call to Ted shows a new side of her. In the courtroom she was tailored, composed, and able to convince everyone (including herself) that she was ready to resume care of her son. Her phone call letting Ted know at the last minute that she could not go through with taking Billy is from the subterranean Joanna. "I can't make it . . . I just can't make it." She had tried to regain custody because of the pressure to do what society says a mother *should* do, but she learned it was not something *she* should have done.

The novelist makes it clear, however, that the absentee mother must suffer for her crime. When Ted and Joanna meet in a bar upon her return to New York, Ted uses the tab for their drinks as metaphoric material. "Who pays the bill for this? Do I? Do I get stuck again?" (*Stuck* seems a strange choice of word from someone who is blaming someone else for not wanting custody.) Joanna ignores the implication and says she will pay. Ted's reply is menacing in its overtones. "Yes. That's right. You'll pay."

One can easily imagine the popular response to something like magazine photos of Margaret Trudeau—the most visible of those self-centered, shallow bitches—disco dancing or sunning on someone's yacht. How dare she stop living with her three little sons and proceed to live the playgirl's life? In her autobiography, *Beyond Reason*, Trudeau quotes her interviewer on the "Good Morning America Show" on June 4, 1977: "Now, Margaret. You talk with such love about your children. You always say Justin is a prince, Sacha very brave, and Micha an angel. I have to ask you a question that must be on the mind of every one of our twelve million viewers this morning. Have you abandoned your children?"[5]

The perception of the absentee mother as self-centered and frivolous, and therefore unreliable, has an impact on the absentee mother in her work environment as well as her social and familial environment. Pamela, one of the mothers in my study, relinquished custody of her eighteen-month-old son in 1978; she was working at a school for the mentally retarded at the time. She was forced one day to reveal the fact that she had given her husband custody of the boy after five months of trying to parent on her own. Her supervisor's face changed abruptly; she reached for words. She finally stammered that she just wasn't sure what something like that would mean in a school. They needed to be certain they had only the most reliable personnel. "They didn't actually fire me," Pamela told me, "but they made things difficult until I left."

In the early years of my own absentee motherhood, a job interview for me always included lengthy questioning about my child custody arrangement. In two instances, I learned that job offers had not been made because of my status as an absentee mother. From what I was able to draw with great difficulty from the interviewers, they each had the vague feeling that they would not know what to expect from "a person like you." One prospective employer was insistent that I submit to a psychiatric evaluation, which he admitted he had never before requested of an applicant. My refusal convinced him that I had a lot to hide and that he was right to suggest the evaluation. Experiences of this nature leave little doubt that the absentee mother stereotype exemplified by Joanna Kramer does, in fact, exist in the minds of many.

Passionate Anna Kareninas: The Absentee Mother as Sexually Promiscuous

My husband and I were divorcing after almost nine years. I was giving him custody of our three children. He was talking about it to whoever would listen. He told me his brother-in-law's opinion of what was happening: "Hell, she just wants a taste of some fresh meat!"

I saw my father a few months after the separation. I had been too upset and confused and self-conscious to see him before then. He was tender and nonjudgmental, but he wondered why I had left my family. "Are you in love with another man?" he asked softly.

It is ironic that two responses could be so different yet so alike. Crude and demeaning in one case. Sympathetic and loving in the other, yet each making the most common assumption of all about absentee mothers: we leave our husbands and children either in heat for anything male or in the grand passion for one particular man.

In my own case, my husband grabbed at this explanation as if it were his absolution. His alcoholism, which he could not admit to, had been a terrible problem almost from the beginning of our marriage and had worsened over the years. I hated him for torturing me with his implacable drinking and the horrors it produced, and he must have hated me in my constant cold anger, which had made his affectionate wife into that stiff female body in his bed. I finally decided to leave him in 1966. I told him about my decision. Then we found out I was pregnant for a third time. I stayed for three more years.

The drinking got worse, and with three children instead of two the strain increased. In late November of 1969, I decided once again to leave. There was one difference. I had met a former schoolmate at our class reunion that month, and we were attracted to one another. He knew of my decision and was willing to help me carry it out. I needed the help. The man had nothing to do with my decision. Nevertheless, my husband used him as a convenient out in the matter of fault. He convinced even himself that I was leaving him and the children for another man. That was much simpler and more comfortable than the truth. Even I succumbed to the charm of its simplicity. When my father asked if I had left for another man, I just said yes. It was too hard to go through all the truth again. I could do it later. My father died without my ever erasing that lie, and I died some because of it.

I must point out that the clear picture I have just outlined of my marriage and the reasons I left it is a picture I have been able to see only in retrospect. When it was all taking place, I was primarily alarmed and confused. I had not then been able to recognize that I was married to an alcoholic, for instance. From what I had been able to gather, he was a typical husband. All husbands went out regularly with the boys and came home drunk; it was just part of being a man. All husbands spent evenings and weekends in front of the TV drinking beer. So I felt guilty for leaving him. I had failed at being a tolerant wife. Worse still, I was breaking the solemn vow I had made before God to stay with him until death. This misplaced guilt contributed heavily toward my going along with the explanation my husband had latched on to so eagerly. I felt guilty, so I acted guilty. What difference did it make precisely what I was guilty of? The guilt I felt and the guilt put on me were different, but they were equally unjust and produced the same end product: an "innocent" absentee mother who cooperated with her accusers.

The best example of a "guilty" absentee mother cooperating with her accusers is Tolstoi's Anna Karenina.[6] She is the archetype of a particular kind of absentee mother. In the novel revolving around her, we also find many examples of the type of social response the absentee mother often experiences.

Anna Karenina's inclination toward sexual passion is suggested to the reader at our first meeting, when we are told through Vronsky that "her whole person was radiant with the overflowing spirits of youth, which she tried to hide; but, in spite of her, the veiled lightning of her eyes gleamed in her smile." When we are told that the Karenins' family life is not pleasant, that the relation between husband and wife seems false, we begin to anticipate in what way this unhappy wife will satisfy her need for love. She has returned Count Vronsky's immediate interest in her by "caressing" him with her smile, and Vronsky hurriedly sets out to manipulate the proper social contacts that will allow him to encounter the Karenins regularly. The subsequent numerous encounters give the handsome and wealthy military man the opportunities to tell Anna of his love for her. On her part, "She made no advances: but her heart, as soon as she saw him, instantly felt the sensation of fullness which had seized her the moment that they met for the first time . . . this joy, she knew, betrayed itself in her eyes, in her smile, but she had not the power to hide it." Thus, Anna and Aleksei Vronsky allowed their love for one another to "form the ruling passion of [their lives]," and they began a new life "with a sentiment of moral decadence."

Aleksei Karenin, Anna's husband, is, understandably, the first to punish Anna for her passionate liaison. He sees her as "without honor, without heart, without religion, a lost woman!" and "in the depths of his soul he desired that she should be punished." So he refuses to free her from their marriage.

No one sympathizes with Anna in her dilemma: married to one man but in love with another, unable to obtain a divorce but afraid of losing her son if she should leave her husband without one. "It seemed to her that every thing [around her, even the] sky and the foliage, was without pity for her." Yet she cannot give Vronsky up. Neither can she blame herself, because she equates her love with life itself. "I cannot repent because I breathe, because I love . . . God has made me so . . ."

Much turmoil follows while Anna continues living with her husband and seeing Vronsky. She gives birth to Vronsky's daughter, then becomes so ill that she is expected to die. As she lies close to death, Karenin forgives her, and Anna forces Vronsky to ask Karenin for the same forgiveness. Vronsky, in despair, attempts suicide. Finally, though, both Anna and Vronsky recover; Vronsky resigns his commission and they leave with their infant (but without Anna's son) to live together in Europe.

The social price for their passion is exacted regularly from then on, but much more so upon Anna than upon Vronsky, for only women acquaintances snub the couple, while Vronsky's male acquaintances see his relationship with Anna "in the right light." Serozha, Anna's eight-year-old son, is told that she is dead. When Anna and Vronsky return to Russia, she is refused permission to see her little boy. "This . . . wounded Anna to the bottom of her soul." One countess, Lidia Ivanovna, reflects the consensus when she refers to Anna and Vronsky as "those repulsive people." In a fit of bravery one night, Anna attends the opera only to have the woman in the adjoining box abruptly leave, loudly proclaiming that it "was a disgrace" to sit near her.

Society shuts its doors to Anna, but she and Vronsky think that at least their relatives and friends will understand. Such is not the case, however. When Betsy, a cousin to both Anna and Vronsky, comes to call, "Her manner was entirely different from what it used to be. She seemed to make much of her courage [in coming], and insisted that it was a proof of her fidelity and friendship towards Anna. After talking for about ten minutes on the news of the day, she got up, and said as she went away, "You have not told me yet when the divorce is to be. Grant that I throw my bonnet over the mill, but I guess few will do as much, and you will find that others will turn the cold shoulder so long as you are not married." Betsy does not call again. When Vronsky tries to arrange for his sister-in-law to socialize with Anna, she tells him that she does not allow herself to judge Anna, but that nevertheless "we must call things by their right name . . . I cannot receive her."

Anna is tormented by this ostracism, describing herself at one point as "a person dying of starvation" who experiences her brother's wife, Dolly, as "a banquet" when Dolly pays her a brief, belated visit. Vronsky tells Dolly that "in society it is hell! . . . you can't conceive the moral tortures Anna endured at Petersburg." The worst pain of all, though, was the feeling that her son would grow up despising her, not knowing that he was one of the two people she loved most in the world. Anna does finally resolve her terrible pain. She throws herself under a moving train.

Although few absentee mothers leave, as did Anna, in the throes of sexual passion, many are accused of doing so. Sylvia, one mother in my study, told me that her employers considered her a "wanton woman." Sylvia had been married for sixteen years. She had borne and cared for six children. She *liked* having and caring for her six children. It was her husband who wanted a divorce, because he had found a nineteen-year-old to replace his forty-year-old wife. He also wanted custody of his six children, who had composed most of Sylvia's life during their marriage. Sylvia was so bewildered and hurt by the bomb that had exploded in her life that she gave her husband his divorce and his six children with no struggle. She just removed herself from the scene.

None of the details, though, had any impact on the way Sylvia was perceived. They may have been unknown in some instances or discounted in others, but Sylvia was the mother of six children who did not live with her and therefore Sylvia was a wanton woman. It is so automatic an identification, one might liken the absentee mother to a prepunched computer card being fed through the social machinery. It is as if society has only so many columns available for information and so reduces every entity to two columns: entry and response. Absentee mother, wanton woman.

Carla was "fired on the spot" when her boss learned she would not have custody of her three daughters. His wife insisted. Cornelia, another absentee mother in my study, says that attitudes at work were the hardest by far to deal with. Four of her five sons live with their father. It is what they wanted. Yet Cornelia, an assistant professor, feels harassed in her work environment. "Although my students and friends totally accept it," she says, "the department and other colleagues are watching and waiting to see if I'm 'immoral' and keep asking when I'm going to get the boys. . . . They obviously think that I've done something wrong to end up without my boys."

Wilma experienced the same sort of instant judgment. She had been married for nineteen years and initiated a divorce when she learned of her husband's numerous affairs. She felt humiliated and hurt beyond repair; she felt she had to leave, but her two teen-aged sons wanted to stay with their father, in the same house, neighborhood, and school as always. So Wilma left without her sons. Most of Wilma's relatives "made me out a bad person for leaving my sons with their father. They wouldn't believe my sons wanted to stay." Some of her friends' husbands began making "indecent propositions." Only two women remained her friends. She told me that she got funny looks from new people she met. "It got so that I wouldn't say I had children to strangers, because I didn't feel like explaining the details over and over again," she said.

One experience of my own highlights the view of absentee mothers as promiscuous. I had been hired over the protest of an elderly personnel director because the research manager for whom I would be working was impressed with my test results and work experience. The personnel director made a point of letting me know at every opportunity that he considered me a slut and that he resented my presence among decent people. He made pointed remarks at the lunch table. He stopped at my desk frequently to question whether my attire was appropriate for the office. One day he complained to the plant manager that my boss and I were spending suspicious amounts of time in his office with the door closed. With no opportunity given to my boss or me to defend ourselves, it was ordered that I exchange positions with another secretary or, more accurately, that I exchange bosses with her. I resigned in outrage.

It goes on and on. One woman's father-in-law called her "unspeakable names" when she moved out of the state in which her daughter and husband lived. Another woman relates that new acquaintances respond to her "like a whore." The mother of three children, aged ten, five, and four, had become suicidal under the pressure they created for her. When she relinquished custody to their able and willing father, she was told that there were those who "wondered about her character" and took her explanation to be "a story." The young mother of a nine-month-old boy took her son with her when she left his father but became more and more agitated with the infant until she began seriously to fear that she might hurt him. Her husband was fifteen years older than she and a licensed practical nurse with experience in pediatrics as well as in the care of newborns. He gladly and capably took custody of the boy, but the mother's friends thought she "just wanted to be free to run around." She "was a complete outcast for months" among her relatives and very often strangers "say things that make [her] feel like a heel." Lorraine, who was physically prevented from taking her four-year-old and six-year-old sons with her when she left her husband was, nevertheless, also made "an outcast" and was told "even animals don't leave their babies." Laverne says that most people assume her children have been taken from her by the court and sometimes make jokes like, "That's funny, you don't *look* like a rotten mother," or upon first hearing of her noncustodial status, "Oh, really? I'm available if you'd like to fuck around."

Autumn Sonata: *The Absentee Mother as Cold-Hearted Career Woman*

Images of the new, ambitious woman created by the feminist movement and sustained by the advertising industry are, undoubtedly, the largest contributing factor to the cold-hearted career-woman stereotype of the absentee mother. However, prominent absentee mothers have also contributed to it. Celebrities are larger than life, and therefore their actions affect us out of all proportion to reality. So it is not difficult to understand we might read about a movie star like Shirley MacLaine, who has been an absentee mother (her daughter is now grown), and come away with the impression that she is representative of absentee mothers. One famous absentee mother has much more impact on the public than hundreds of unknown absentee mothers.

Shirley MacLaine has been married to Steve Parker, on paper only, for twenty-six years; they had a daughter together. The girl spent most of her childhood with her father in Japan. When an interviewer asked MacLaine recently if little Sachi hadn't ever wanted a "real mommy," Shirley responded: "In comparison to her friends, she might have wanted one. But she didn't have one. So she grew up knowing that. Spending twenty years with a husband and child would drive me into the ground. I would not be able to breathe."

Someone looking for a historical specimen of unfeeling absentee mother and career woman might be well advised to turn to George Sand, a woman who smoked and wore trousers in the nineteenth century, a woman who told her husband just the way it was going to be: "I want an allowance and I shall go to Paris forever; my children will stay at Nohant." She proceeded to do just that and produced constant scandal along with her sixty novels, twenty-five plays, an autobiography, and countless essays.[7] However, women like Shirley MacLaine and George Sand are not available for sustained scrutiny. They leave us with some facts, with an image, but they probably do not move us as forcefully as a fictional version of cold-hearted absentee mother would. A good fictional character will pour it all out for us, will not only reveal herself as far as she knows herself but will reveal her unknown self as we watch her, follow her, and listen to her for submerged revelations.

The fictional characters who represent the first two stereotypical views of the absentee mother were of a different order than the character who represents the absentee mother as cold-hearted career woman. Joanna was two-dimensional. Even Anna Karenina is readily seen in the singular sense of one overwhelming drive: sexual passion. The third character is much more complex. Indeed, to the extent that her complexities are presented, she becomes less an actual stereotype because stereotypes are innately superficial. By going beyond the obvious aspects of personality and the emotional responses to them (which will form our stereotype and typical reactions to her), we begin to see the larger issue. The larger issue, in the metaphoric form of the relationship between an absentee mother and her two daughters, is the relationship between the absentee mother and society.

Charlotte Andergast, of *Autumn Sonata*, at first glance is a woman who has coldly turned away from her family to pursue her career as a concert pianist.[8] However, her creator, Ingmar Bergman, goes beyond this surface perception to reveal the complexity of her motivation and the source of her flaws. In the process, we are presented with a character who possesses characteristics of all three absentee-mother stereotypes. Charlotte Andergast is narcissistic; she is ruled by passion for another man; and she is dedicated to the point of obsession to her musical career. So, in the review of pertinent scenes of the screenplay *Autumn Sonata*, we will see a number of things at once:

1. The stereotypical view of the absentee mother as cold-hearted career woman (with Charlotte's daughter, Eva, representative of society)
2. The characterization of the absentee mother as narcissistic and sexually "immoral"
3. The revelation of deeper motivation than ambition or fulfillment on the part of this career woman/absentee mother
4. The explanation for this absentee mother's narcissism, sexual "immorality," and cold-heartedness (which suggests that society look past their stereotypes)
5. The feelings of hatred engendered by the absentee mother (with Eva remaining representative of society)

6. The understanding, forgiveness, and acceptance of the absentee mother, which are possible and desirable.

Charlotte Andergast is not an absentee mother who became such by the most usual route of divorce, and her absentee-mother status is not a static situation. She spent almost her children's entire childhoods leaving them repeatedly for one concert tour after another. In the eyes of her daughters, she was an absentee mother even when she was at home—through her emotional withdrawal. There was, however, a period of eight months when she had left her husband for another man and left the girls with their father. She was an absentee mother in the stricter sense during this period.

Autumn in the Swedish countryside is the backdrop for a parsonage neatly kept and in good taste. Viktor is the parson and the first person we meet in his role of narrator. His wife, Eva (played by Liv Ullmann), is writing a letter to her mother, inviting her to come for a visit; it has been seven years since they saw one another. The prevailing atmosphere is impossible to ignore: two understated people in a quiet, extremely neat, joyless environment.

We see Charlotte (played by Ingrid Bergman) for the first time as she arrives at the parsonage. She hesitates at the trunk of her car before removing her luggage. We know she feels doubtful about being here. We also know that Eva is seeing her hesitation from a window. Eva rushes out and gives her mother a very enthusiastic welcome, doing all of the talking and calling her "Mother, darling!" We sense already that Eva's words of endearment must be in great contrast to her actual feelings.

Next, we are in the room that has been prepared for Charlotte. Mother and daughter sit together on the bed. Now Charlotte is doing all the talking, but in subdued tones. She is telling Eva of the last days she spent with Leonardo, who has died recently. He was her friend for eighteen years, her lover for the thirteen years they lived together. Eva listens with apparent sympathy. The recounting is sensitive, but Charlotte's conclusion makes us wonder about the depth of her feeling for the man. She so readily comes to a superficial summation. "I can't say I go around grieving. . . . Oh yes, of course, he's left a gap, but it's no good fretting." Her concern turns abruptly to winning Eva's affirmation of her good physical appearance after seven years. Eva reassures her. As with

Joanna Kramer, this absentee mother's negative makeup is quickly established. We already have reason to suspect that she does not love deeply and that she is narcissistic.

Charlotte's unpacking begins, accompanied by a litany of complaints. Her suitcase is dreadfully heavy, her back is giving her hell from the long trip, she must have a board under her mattress. Then it is back to checking her appearance. Eva breaks into tears. But when her mother notices and is solicitous of her "pet lamb," Eva says that she is crying only because she is so glad to see her mother. We know Charlotte has hurt her daughter's feelings by her total self-absorption, her lack of curiosity or concern for Eva after all this time. We also notice that Charlotte is now using the same sort of exaggerated endearments as Eva.

That night, we learn that Charlotte always has trouble sleeping. She drinks decaffeinated coffee, and at bedtime takes pills, but she still prepares for long hours of wakefulness with biscuits and mineral water, tape recorder and cassettes, two detective novels, earplugs, and a bandage for her eyes. We wonder what is on her conscience.

Little things keep emphasizing Charlotte's flaws. She feels magnanimous when she offers Eva *two* pieces of her Swiss chocolate. She confuses Eva with her sister, Lena, in her remembrance of which of them liked candy; this confusion of siblings is an indication that she has not been an attentive mother. Like a selfish child, she is glad when Eva refuses the candy. "Good, all the more for me." She continues to say things she does not mean. She tells Eva that Viktor is delightful but really feels he is a bore. By the time Eva leaves her mother for the night, Charlotte's false relationship to her daughter is plain, and we wonder how it came to be that way.

We learn from Charlotte reminiscing to herself that a man once attempted suicide over her and the knowledge gives her pleasure. When she is alone in her room, she takes out a little "accounts" book, and we learn that Leonardo has left her millions of francs. She also has a nest egg of her own. She wonders aloud what she will do with so much money and decides to buy Viktor and Eva a new car. It will cheer them up. A few minutes later she changes her plan. She will buy *herself* a new car instead and give her old one to Viktor and Eva.

A little later we see Charlotte in bed with her eyes closed, and the door suddenly opens. She is frightened. Helena, her ill second daughter (who lives with Eva), launches herself into the room and hurls herself on top of her mother. She is heavy and strong. There is a short struggle, then Charlotte wakes. It is a dream. The meaning is obvious. The heavy responsibility of her crippled daughter, the demands that her existence make, have been flung in her face by Eva. Eva's caring for her sister emphasizes that her mother is *not* caring for her, that when Helena's care was left to her mother, her mother put her in a nursing home.

Charlotte is so upset by the nightmare that she leaves her room and settles in the living room. Eva, who heard her mother call out when she woke from the nightmare, joins her downstairs. She offers to keep her company if she would like to talk, but Charlotte claims she cannot remember the dream and tells Eva to go back to bed. As Eva turns to go, however, her mother calls her name. "You do like me, don't you?" she asks Eva. "Why, of course. You're my mother," Eva replies. Charlotte pushes Eva for an answer which is not an evasion, to which Eva responds with her own question. "Do you like me?" Charlotte says that she *loves* her. But Eva delivers a heart-stopper when she tells her mother that that is not true. And she smiles when she says it. Charlotte protests the accusation as absurd. She asks Eva if she accuses herself of not loving Viktor (for Charlotte has learned that Eva does not, indeed, love her husband). The difference, Eva points out, is that she has told Viktor how she feels whereas her mother *pretends* to love. This scene presents the major thrust of the charge that absentee mothers are cold-hearted, that they do not love their children. Eva, as well as being Charlotte's daughter, represents society's position against the absentee mother.

Charlotte asks what it would mean if she were "in good faith," if she were genuinely convinced that she loved her and Helena. Eva asserts that it is impossible that her mother believes that. Charlotte attempts to prove it by asking Eva to remember the time she broke off her career and stayed home. Eva throws this supposed proof of love back at her mother, saying it would be hard to decide which was worse, when her mother stayed home and played wife and mother or when she was off on tour. Either way, she made life hell for all of them, including Eva's father, Josef. The absentee mother is, indeed, damned one way or the other, and this suggests part of the real absentee mother's argument: that a mother at home with her family who does not wish to be there is no blessing.

The mention of Josef angers Charlotte. She does not feel Eva knows anything about the relationship between her mother and father. They were happy together. Eva charges that he was as cowed and compliant as everyone else around Charlotte. The absentee mother with a career is mannish, which can be seen in her dominance over those around her. To Charlotte's claim that she would have done anything for Josef, Eva says, "Oh yes. You were unfaithful to him." Charlotte denies this. She was not *unfaithful*. She was *in love* with Martin and went away with him for eight months. We feel the absentee mother is trying to vindicate herself with mere semantics.

The point for Eva was the suffering she and her father endured because of her mother's eight-month absence. The rage in Eva is there to hear and see, just as society's anger is so evident to the absentee mother. Charlotte looks at Eva with quiet astonishment, seeing something she had not seen before. "Eva, you hate me," she says.

Eva is not so sure that *hate* describes what she feels toward her mother. She is confused about what she feels. She has thought she would be able to look at her mother and her childhood dispassionately after all this time, but she realizes now "that it's all a muddle." Anyway, there is no point in talking about the past. It won't change anything. And it hurts too much. But Eva's mother does not want to drop the matter now that it has come out. She charges Eva with making all kinds of accusations only to withdraw, leaving the accused with no opportunity to defend herself.

Eva relents and stays with her mother. She begins relating her primary childhood memories. These memories are a heartwrenching view of the effect an absentee mother can have on her child.

As a child, Eva saw her mother as beautiful, exemplary. But she felt ugly and was always afraid that her mother would notice her ugliness. The only thing Charlotte ever said that hurt Eva, though, was that she should have been a boy. Eva cried for a week after that, in private because she knew her mother hated anybody's tears but her own. Eva saw her mother as aloof. She would shut herself up with the piano, and she was not to be disturbed. When Charlotte did open that door and allow Eva entrance, Eva would talk to her mother but she could see her mother was not listening. She was always somewhere else. Eva felt herself to be like a doll, played with at times but to be put aside the rest of the time.

Nothing was as bad, though, as the days when Charlotte's luggage would appear at the foot of the staircase and Eva would hear her mother talking on the phone in a foreign language. Eva would panic when this happened. She would pray that something drastic would happen to keep her mother from leaving: that all the planes would have engine trouble, that there would be an earthquake, that grandma would die. "But you always went."

Eva's mother would kiss her and hug her, but she did not see her. She was already on her way. Eva used to think: "Now my heart will stop, I'm dying. . . . Only five minutes have passed, how can I bear such pain for two months?" A few days before her mother was due home, Eva would get feverish with excitement. She worried that she might really get ill, and she knew that her mother was afraid of sick people.

Little Eva loved her mother's voice, but she did not understand the things she said, which did not match the tone of her voice or the look in her eyes. She knew just by the tone and the look that her mother hardly ever meant what she said. "The worst of all was that you smiled when you were angry. When you hated Father you called him 'my dearest friend,' when you were tired of me you said 'darling little girl.' Nothing fitted." We know from earlier observation that Eva, too, is guilty of using inappropiate words to fit her real feelings, just as she accuses her mother of doing. She imitates her mother in spite of herself. Eva ends with the feeling that any attempt at communication with her mother is doomed to futility. "Your words apply to your reality, my words to mine. If we exchange words, they're worthless."

Charlotte feels she must, nevertheless, say *her* words, to get them over with. Charlotte's words begin to cast some reality on the life of a career woman who is also an absentee mother. She tells about the strain of touring, her constant back problem on tour, always risking humiliation in performance, *feeling guilty* for not being with her husband and little girls. There was a point when the guilt was so bad that she called Josef from Hamburg. She had decided to stop touring and was going to stay home with them. And she did. And they were happy, weren't they?

Eva shakes her head, no. Charlotte is confused. She remembers Eva saying that things had never been so good. (We have caught Eva saying things she did not mean again.) Eva simply had not wanted to disappoint her mother, so she had lied. Charlotte is incredulous. She asks what she did wrong.

Charlotte did too much. She felt she had neglected Eva in the past and so used all of her pent-up energies to rectify the matter. Exercising together to correct Eva's stoop; braces for her teeth; a skin specialist for her acne; sewing dresses for her without asking what she liked; giving her books to read and then discussing what she had read—they were always over her head. Then there was a psychiatrist when Eva showed signs of being troubled. But he did no good. Eva was convinced that the real Eva was not lovable. That was why her mother worked day and night to change her. She was fourteen. Then her mother left with her lover, Martin. She used to leave for her career. This time she left for a man.

Why had Eva never before said anything?

I never said anything before because you never listen. Because you're a notorious escapist, because you're emotionally crippled, because in actual fact you detest me and Helena, because you're hopelessly shut up inside yourself, because you always stand in your own light, because you have carried me in your cold womb and expelled me with loathing, because I loved you, because you thought I was disgusting and unintelligent and a failure. And you managed to injure me for life just as you yourself are injured. All that was sensitive and delicate you bruised, everything alive you tried to smother. You talk of my hatred. Your hatred was no less. Your hatred is no less. . . . You kept saying that you loved me and Father and Helena. And you were an expert at love's intonations and gestures. People like you—people like you are a menace, you should be locked away and rendered harmless.

After hearing Eva's raging hatred and heartless perception of her mother I was left wondering, do my own children feel anything like it? The children of other absentee mothers? Most of us do not yet know the full extent of what our children feel, but the treatment we have experienced by society carries a message almost as harsh as Eva's.

Eva hides her face in her hands as soon as she has finished. Her words have done their work. Charlotte begins, quietly, to speak, asking Eva if she remembers her grandmother, Charlotte's mother. Eva remembers being afraid of her, feeling her to be overwhelming both mentally and physically. But grandpa was kind.

Now we gain insight into Charlotte's flawed emotional makeup, something that is not done for the absentee mother in *Kramer vs. Kramer* in anything but a superficial way. We learn that Charlotte's parents were distinguished mathematicians. They were totally preoccupied with their science and with one another, good-humored but detached from their children. Charlotte cannot remember ever being touched by either of her parents, not even in punishment. The depth of her deprivation is cuttingly clear in her own words: "I was completely ignorant of everything to do with love—tenderness, contact, intimacy, warmth . . . [I feel as if] I'm not alive. I've never been born. I was squeezed out of my mother's body. It closed and turned at once to Father. I didn't exist."

In motherhood, then, Charlotte was being asked to give something she simply did not have. One who has not been loved has no love to give. Eva is moved; she hears something else about her mother she had not known.

Three years ago Charlotte was hospitalized for food poisoning, had come close to death. She tells this haltingly. Following her physical recovery she fell into a serious depression. Leonardo was with her through the whole thing. He talked a great deal. Charlotte listened. In the end, he was the source of Charlotte's insight, although she experienced his "lessons" as difficult, as if she were in first grade and he were teaching an adult subject. Charlotte tells Eva: "At last I formed a picture of myself; I've never grown up—my face and my body age, I acquire memories and experiences, but inside the shell I'm, as it were, unborn." We begin to understand and sympathize with Charlotte.

Mother and daughter are silent for a few moments. The few moments are all it takes for another realization on Charlotte's part. She realizes aloud that she has always been *afraid* of Eva. Eva does not understand. Rather astonished herself, Charlotte says she thinks she always wanted Eva to take care of her, to comfort her. It did not matter that she was just a child. Charlotte could see that Eva as a child loved her, and Charlotte wanted to love her too. But she couldn't. She was afraid of Eva's demands. "I didn't want to be your mother. I wanted you to know that I was just as helpless as you, but poorer, more frightened."

Poor Charlotte. She can hardly believe the things she has said. She is bewildered. She begs Eva to be kind to her, for "it hurts so!"

But Eva shows no mercy. "Look at me Mother. Look at Helena. There can be no forgiveness." (I hear the echo of the woman in the talk show audience: "There's no excuse!")

Charlotte argues, though, that she has never deliberately done anything to hurt them, so how can Eva blame her like this? Eva admits her belief that her mother, indeed, has not done any of these things deliberately, but that does not matter. She must face her guilt, like everyone else. Eva uses the word *guilt* as if it were the word *punishment*. One day, Eva threatens her mother, Charlotte will be forced to face just how guilty she was. "Guilty of what?" Charlotte asks. "I don't know. Guilty," Eva responds. This statement is revealing and meaningful in its emotional unreasonableness. Pathetically, Charlotte asks one more question. "Irrevocably?" Eva does not respond. The absentee mother waits for an indication that she may hope. "Won't you come here to me? Won't you put your arms around me? I'm so horribly afraid. Darling, won't you forgive me for all the wrong I've done? I'll try to mend my ways. You must teach me. We'll have lots of long, long talks. But help me. I can't go on any longer, *your hatred is so terrible.* I haven't understood. I've been selfish and childish and anxious. At least touch me! Strike me if you like! Eva dear, help me!"

Eva does not move. Suddenly, Helena starts screaming from the hallway. Both Eva and Charlotte run up to her. Eva gets to her first, but Helena pushes her sister aside and puts her arms out to her mother. Her mother rushes to her and gratefully buries her head in her crippled daughter's lap.

The next morning, Charlotte places a whispered phone call to her agent asking him to send her a telegram to the effect that she has to be somewhere or other immediately. She has to get away, but needs an excuse. Eva overhears the phone call, but there are no further exchanges between them. Charlotte leaves as soon as she is able.

The film ends with three images which speak to us profoundly. Charlotte on a train with her compatriot and agent, Paul, carrying on a monologue that etches her isolation, her insecurity and self-doubt and clearly indicates that she is retreating into her work, as always, for some vindication of her worth and for protection from any further encounters with self-knowledge.

Then there is Eva out-of-doors displaying a gloom equal to the murky gray surroundings, regretting that she had so frightened her mother, fearing she will never see her again, fleetingly considering suicide. She too feels alone; she is not able to love her husband and is therefore separate from him. She retreats further to her fantasized relationship with her dead son, an area in addition to her husband where one might look for *her* guilt.

And, finally, there is the image of Helena. She is told by Viktor that her mother has left. She breaks into a violent fit. She lets out inhuman shrieks, bites her lips until they bleed, convulses, foams at the mouth. She has been deserted again.

No one gains from the persecution of the absentee mother. But there is an epilogue. A letter written by Eva to her mother and read to us by our narrator, Viktor.

I have realized that I wronged you. *I met you with demands instead of with affection. I tormented you with an old soured hatred which is no longer real. Everything I did was wrong and I want to ask your forgiveness. Helena's insight is much greater than mine. She gave, where I demanded. She was near you, when I kept my distance. Suddenly it dawned on me that I was to take care of you, that bygones are bygones, that I will never let you go again. I will never leave you alone again. I've no idea whether this letter will reach you, I don't even know if you will read it. Perhaps everything is already too late. But I hope all the same that my discovery will not be in vain. There is a kind of mercy after all. I mean the enormous chance of looking after each other, of helping each other, of showing affection. I want you to know that I will never let you go again or let you vanish out of my life. I'm going to persist! I won't give up, even if it should be too late. I don't think it is too late. It must not be too late.*

Absentee mothers hope for a response of this tenor from their loved ones and from the people with whom they attempt to maintain a humane and productive society. A breathtaking film, *Autumn Sonata*, demanding of the viewer and therefore valuable. It will haunt every female who is either a mother or a daughter, and more so every absentee mother and child of an absentee mother.

It is clear that Ingmar Bergman did not create *Autumn Sonata* in order to study an absentee mother per se, but rather to study the mother-daughter relationship, one of the most powerful and problematic relationships existing and one which plays some role in the creation of absentee mothers. However, in the process of pursuing his goal, Bergman did create a meaningful portrait of an absentee mother. His portrait, in its honest portrayal of one complex individual, has, unfortunately, the tandem effect of creating a stereotype of the absentee mother as a cold-hearted career woman. The fault lies, of course, completely with the public. Audiences see selectively. Passive viewers can come away from a thoughtful film like *Autumn Sonata* with a simplified version of what they saw.

The absentee mother in *Autumn Sonata* is a woman who admits she has not been able to love her children. The fact that she has not really loved the men in her life either is an additional indicator of her cold-heartedness. Charlotte's emotionally deprived childhood might be largely dismissed by the public as merely an excuse. To some extent that could be considered a valid point, for as an adult, some schools of thought have it, Charlotte had the responsibility of dealing with whatever psychological problems prevented her from functioning well as an adult. Furthermore, if one is identifying more strongly with the daughter, it would be typical either to ignore or forget the extenuating factors on the mother's side.

Neither can there be any doubt that Charlotte is narcissistic. She is keenly aware of herself at all times: her aches and pains, her travels, her music, her food, her insomnia, *ad infinitum*. She is so self-centered that she is unable to remember faces of even those persons with whom she interacts on a regular basis. Charlotte wants to be loved, but she has nothing with which to reciprocate. It is difficult to admire even her concert work. Viktor comments after listening to both Eva and Charlotte play the same piece; "I think Charlotte's *analysis* is seductive, but Eva's *interpretation* is more moving." Can a woman who cannot love express love in her music? Besides, she has not pursued her work for its sake so much as she has been compelled to pursue it, using it as a shield from the demands of emotional involvement.

Although Charlotte admits her failings in the end and expresses a desire to change herself and to make up for everything, I believe most viewers come away from *Autumn Sonata* feeling distinctly negative about the absentee mother. The handful of people I have asked about it were unanimous in that respect. They thought the mother got everything she deserved from her daughter.

It appears, however, that there is an element in our society which views the stereotype of the absentee mother as cold-hearted career woman in a positive light. Some *employers* are more than happy to find, hire, and promote absentee mothers. The reason, of course, is obvious. An absentee mother lives in a child-free environment that makes her more completely available to the demands of a career. An absentee mother, then, may be considered as appealing in the job market as a male. Some employers evidently ignore the socially negative judgment put on the absentee mother because she is useful to them. Five of the women in my study relate that they encountered favorable responses in the marketplace to their status as absentee mother. Four of them express it in similar terms:

My employers felt it was very advantageous. They didn't have to worry about my losing time because of sick children.

Actually, it was helpful because they knew I could be dependable and didn't have to worry about emergencies at home.

That's how I was able to get a job in Chicago so fast. The fact that I did not have children living with me who might get sick or need more attention than my job helped.

My employer was delighted. He doesn't like children and thought it would give me more job flexibility, which it did. I now travel for the company occasionally.

One of these five absentee mothers encountered outright admiration from her employers:

They were impressed by my "masculine" approach to the matter and my "masculine" acceptance of responsibility. [She was providing child support payments to her former husband.]

Unfortunately, ninety-five absentee mothers did *not* meet such reactions to their parental status.

The Absentee Mother as Heroine or Alter Ego

Although absentee mothers, in general, meet with any one or all of the three negative suppositions discussed so far, there are instances in which she is surprised with an opposite assumption about her. This sort of elevated view of an absentee mother can be almost as disconcerting as the deprecatory characterizations.

I remember a woman who attended college classes with me. She had three children, an unhappy marriage, held a full-time job, and was trying, part time, to earn her bachelor's degree in business administration. She was invariably in a state of breathlessness, a truly harried person. She was present at the reading of an essay in which I had described my decision to relinquish custody. The last word was no sooner uttered than this young mother leapt to her feet and shouted, "I wish to hell *I* had enough nerve to do that!" Oddly enough, I did not feel good about it. It frightened me. "My God," I thought, "is it possible for me to be seen as an inspiration? Can what I've had to do be seen as encouragement to other mothers to do the same? Am I going to be responsible for a mass maternal exodus?" This was an exaggerated response, but I still sometimes worry about being perceived as a promoter of absentee motherhood. What I really am is a defender of those women who have already become absentee mothers and an advocate of identical custody options for men and women.

In reality, of course, a matter of this magnitude is not terribly susceptible to promotion. One day, shortly after I had moved to Berkeley, a neighbor named Beth came running across the street from her house to see me. She was crying uncontrollably. I could not imagine why she had come to me. "Is it true? Is it true?" she blurted with difficulty. "Is what true?" I asked, completely bewildered. "That you left your kids. Two people have told me that you have kids and you left 'em." "Yes, that's true," I said. She put her arms around me and burst into a new seizure of crying on my shoulder. At the same time, she was saying, "I have to talk to you. I have to talk to you."

Beth was a divorced mother of two. She was working for her bachelor's degree in anthropology. Her two boys were in the very early grades at school and required a lot of time and energy. Beth's school work was demanding, and she placed a great deal of importance on being an excellent student, because she had not done well in college as a teen-ager. It was essential to prove herself—both to herself and to the university administration. This was the day that the stress had reached a climax. "I've been thinking about bringing the boys to their father," she said quietly, with her head lowered. She felt ashamed. "Should I do it? How did *you* do it?" I did not know if she was asking about legal technicalities, logistics, or emotions. She meant emotions. I told her the whole story, the good and the bad, but I had the distinct feeling that my story was merely a minor strand in the braid she was weaving in her mind. For about two hours we talked about what kind of man her ex-husband was, about what she wanted in life, about our children. She felt better and rose from the easy chair to leave. "I couldn't really give up my boys," she said. "That's not what I want. But I think you had a lot of courage."

A handful of the women in my study have met with similar supportive attitudes from other women. Marie expresses her experience with this: "Society pointed its finger at me; however, there seemed to be a glint of admiration here and there." Sometimes a woman will just say to one of us, quietly and aside, "I can understand it." That sentiment is probably the most soothing. As one of the hundred said, "I don't need approval from anybody. I just want them to understand." At another time or place, an employer or a teacher might say that she thinks we did the right thing or might congratulate us on our ability to be so honest in such a difficult situation.

Dolly Oblonsky, Anna's sister-in-law in Tolstoi's novel, clearly understands Anna's motives and is perhaps a little envious of her. Dolly is the mother of eight and the wife of a philanderer. While out on a short trip alone, a rare occasion, she says to herself, "Everybody is alive and enjoying the world. . . . I alone seem like a prisoner set at liberty for a moment. . . . And why do people blame Anna? If I had not loved my husband, I very likely might have done what she has done. She wanted to live; and has not God put the demand for that into our hearts?"

It appears that a minority of women see the absentee mother as a woman of strength enough to fulfill her God-given needs, a woman to be admired, or even to serve as a model for their own fantasy lives.

The Absentee Mother as Reformed Offender

Judging from impressions I share with some of the absentee mothers in my study, it is possible under certain circumstances to redeem oneself from the condemnation that ordinarily accompanies absentee motherhood. The circumstances are simple enough: remarriage, mothering another child, activity in community affairs that is tantamount to mothering, or the achievement of adulthood by your surrendered offspring. It should be noted, however, that any of these circumstances other than mothering another child will probably bring only partial, and quite likely minimal, absolution.

In the case of Anna Karenina, for instance, if Anna had legitimized her position with Vronsky, she would have been reaccepted, at least partially, into society. The infant she and Vronsky had had together would, in that case, also have been transformed from evidence of sin into a reaffirmation of motherhood. Marriage would, to a large extent, have canceled the original crimes of adultery and child abandonment by means of re-creating the original condition, that of legalized husband, wife, and child. That this social reacceptance would have occurred is made very clear throughout the book. Anna's brother, Oblonsky, strongly advises divorce for this reason and attempts to convince Anna's husband to initiate it and Anna to encourage it.

Gina, one of the absentee mothers in my study, told me that people accept her absentee motherhood better since she has remarried and had another child. Even before she and her new husband became parents together, her status as an absentee mother was more acceptable, not only because she was married but also because she had a stepson living within the household. (Interestingly enough, she had married a man whose former wife was an absentee mother.) She also believes that the fact that she devotes full time to her domestic duties and is active in community affairs helps account for her new acceptability.

As an absentee mother named Jane related, immediately following her relinquishing custody, friends responded to her with suspicion and awe. Many were afraid of her. She was considered wild and crazy. Someone who defies the powerful, commonly held belief that children belong with their mothers and only their mothers represents a threat to the social order. Remarriage and/or a second family indicates reclamation of a lost soul, regained sanity and therefore predictability, and eliminates the social danger. It is also as if, with her first action of becoming an absentee mother, a woman is saying to the community, "You fools, your way of doing things is all wrong and stupid to boot." When her life takes a turn toward doing things their way again—marrying rather than merely living with a man; having another child of her own or committing herself to the care of a stepchild; or admitting the worth of a community by becoming active in one of its organizations—it is as if the absentee mother is admitting she was wrong after all.

My own experience, as well as that of others, supports this theory. For the first seven years after my divorce and relinquished custody, I remained single. I became an agnostic. I became involved with a married man. Then I lived for a while with a man to whom I was not married. I became politically active in several liberal causes. Finally, I moved cross-country from the conservative Midwest to California, land of rebellion. In my own eyes, I was merely asking questions and growing. But to others, I believe, my way of life was threatening. It was seen as a continuing craziness. My former husband and his new wife refused to speak to me during those years. Visitation of the children was made as troublesome for me as possible.

Four years ago, I remarried. Out of nowhere, things became easier with my former husband. Suddenly, the children were considered old enough to fly by themselves; matters could be negotiated rather than dictated. It is clear to me that my remarriage has conferred a new label of respectability, in spite of the religious and political positions I hold. In society's eye, I have reaffirmed their way as the right way, at least in part measure. Near-complete redemption will not occur unless I have another child or take up some other child-related activity. Religious belief and unquestioning patriotism, like whipped cream and a cherry, would complete the re-creation.

The Absentee Mother
versus the Holy Mother Ideal

The more perfect the "good guy," the blacker the "bad guy" appears. This is why I wish to conclude this chapter with a discussion of society's vision of motherhood. It is as a direct result of society's romanticized expectations in the realm of motherhood that absentee mothers are seen in such starkly drawn dimensions. When one envisions fairy-tale characters, confrontation with human beings is a terrible shock. A recent advertisement for a book of poetry (many similar examples could be readily found) effectively displays the fact that society's, and therefore our own, expectations of the mother go beyond even the extreme of human perfection.　　　　　　　　　　　　　　　　　　　　　．

Mothers Are a Gift of Love, by Helen Steiner Rice: A timeless treasury of heartfelt verse honoring God's special creation—the warmth, compassion, devotion and steadfast godliness that keeps Mother perpetually in the hearts of her loved ones.

This blurb is so astonishing in its deification of motherhood that it hardly requires much scrutiny to recognize it. What is perhaps less obvious is the impact that this holy view of motherhood can and does have on all of us, usually at a subconscious level, making all of us victims of impossible expectations, whether we are mothers or not. This is so because, although mothers are clearly the primary victims, the children and husbands and other disappointed loved ones are victims too in having to suffer inevitable disillusionment.

One may readily see the necessity for providing a special mother's niche in Creation upon the realization that obligation comes with identified status, not with individual personhood. We do not expect any or every person to run the country, only the person we identify as the president. Elevated demands can be made upon elevated ranks. The highest honor presupposes the heaviest obligations.

The characteristics of warmth, compassion, and devotion attributed to motherhood, cited singly or in a less rapturous context, would not be objectionable, and it is certainly true that especially good emotions and motivations may come with the experience of pregnancy, birth, and nurturing. As these terms are used here, however, they simply fortify the vision of mother as saint. A saint is expected to smother her human needs and deny human limitations. With her "steadfast godliness," a mother is someone you can count on even in the face of cataclysm. The capitalization of the word *Mother* seems to elevate the breed from minor to major god. And from divinity, we proceed logically to immortality: "Mother is *perpetually* in the hearts of her loved ones." Alas, in my ears I hear all those thousands of abandoned elderly mothers in their chorus of bitter warning: "Don't expect any gratitude."

In light of this virtual caricature of maternal virtue, we can see clearly how the mother who ceases to live with her children is bound to be cast in the sternest of terms. The idealized vision of motherhood also explains the few positive responses absentee mothers encounter. The more extreme and firmly entrenched a social role, the more fertile territory it makes for rebellion. Perhaps the absentee mother should be grateful she is seen as merely self-centered, cold-hearted, and/or promiscuous. Living amidst the current mood of reactionism, one does not have much trouble imagining a new law that might accuse us of ungodliness in the face of motherhood, or a punishment that would correspond with the severity of the crime. Meanwhile, we may take some small comfort from the fact that absentee mothers are "merely" confined to the cells of demeaning and hurtful stereotypes.

2

In Response to Society:
The Real Absentee Mother

Charlotte: *In your awful hatred you've formed a picture of me,
but is it true? Do you seriously think it's the whole
truth?*

—*Ingmar Bergman,* Autumn Sonata

Voluntary and Involuntary
Absentee Mothers

One factor is common to all three of the negative stereotypical
portrayals of absentee mothers. Joanna Kramer, Charlotte Andergast, and Anna Karenina all left their children, rejected them,
one might say, in favor of someone or something else. It was *their*
decision to relinquish custody.

Among the hundred real absentee mothers who completed
questionnaires for me, those who chose to relinquish custody
represent only one of three types of absentee mother, although
admittedly the most numerous type, at seventy-five. Two additional types of absentee mother should be recognized: those who
have had separation from their children imposed on them, one
group by the courts, the other group by their own children. Twelve

41

of the women lost custody of their children through legal judgment; thirteen were told by their children that they wanted to live
with their fathers. The fact that these twenty-five women wanted
their children to live with them is supported by the fact that twenty
of them took their children with them at the point of separation
from their husbands. Not until later did the separation of mothers
and children come about. They are clearly not the rejecting
mothers society has cast the absentee mother to be, but in the way
they are perceived and treated they are lumped together (and this
point must be strongly emphasized) with absentee mothers who
relinquish custody.

Robin experienced the loss of her children in *both* ways simultaneously. Divorced for three years, she lived with her three daughters, who were then sixteen, thirteen, and nine years old. She told
them she had decided to remarry; they were to have a stepfather,
and the five of them would be moving a long way to his job:

*They were not happy about it, but were getting used to the idea when
their father said they could stay with him. I decided the older girls were
old enough to make that decision; however, I felt my nine-year-old
daughter belonged with me. We went to court. I lost. The judge simply
said that my youngest should stay with her sisters. I did not want to
relinquish custody, but I would not refrain from entering into a second
marriage for them. I felt rejected by them, but two days after the court
hearing I married as planned, put my furniture into a rented truck, and
moved to Kansas. Ever since then, my former husband has said that I
abandoned my children.*

Leslie had also been divorced for three years before her ex-
husband challenged her custody of their then five-year-old son:

*My former husband had remarried "the first woman who would have
him," just as he had told me he would do. They did not plan to have any
children, so our son was the only way for them to have a "complete
family." The court hearing was a circus. I have never heard as many lies as
I did in those four days. It was the most humiliating, embarrassing,
traumatic experience of my entire life. I have no respect for our court
system, and I would advise any mother to do anything rather than face
this experience.*

As Glenda learned, one does not always have a choice. She was
the mother of a two-year-old boy and a newborn girl, in a three-
year-old marriage:

My husband had become a stranger. He would leave for months or weeks at a time, and he started beating me whenever he did come home. He just didn't want to be married to me anymore.

She divorced him, but eight months later he forced himself into her troubled life once again:

I was working full time as a waitress at night and had to hire babysitters. My ex-husband and his friends were calling the Welfare Department daily to report that I was neglecting the children. The Welfare Department would send someone out and find the charges were false. At the same time, my mother was dying of cancer. So I started taking care of her, her house, my children and my house during the day and working at night. I got very little sleep. I lost a lot of weight. Still, the Welfare people continued investigating me. My brother, who worked at the same place as I did, could see how much this was upsetting me and called the investigator to ask her to leave me alone. He must have alienated her. The next thing she did was to call my ex-husband to suggest that he press neglect charges against me which he did. In court, my ex-husband had several people whom I had never seen before speak against me. The judge did not think the children were neglected, but he gave custody to my ex-husband because he was remarried and his wife stayed home all day and night.

In the cases revolving around a child's decision, it is often easy to identify with their reasons for remaining with their fathers. More often than not, their decisions are based on their desire to maintain the status quo as much as possible. Lea's thirteen-year-old daughter, for instance, had attended seven different schools through the eighth grade. Her father remained in town at the time of the divorce, and her mother moved three thousand miles away to a new job. The girl chose to stay with her father.

Sometimes the children are manipulated, as were Celeste's four boys (aged thirteen, twelve, ten, and nine). One year after their parents' divorce, the boys went to spend the summer with their father. At summer's end, they did not want to return to their mother's home:

I took the boys from Nebraska to California for the summer. Their father got them involved in activities they did not want to leave, gave them expensive gifts which had to be left at Daddy's. Only my oldest was able to fight a way out. He lives with me.

Whatever the basis for the child's decision, it usually hurts the mother. As one such absentee mother remarked:

*I always knew that the apron strings would have to be cut sometime, but it
was a rude awakening to find my son's timetable meant that it would take
place when he was only nine years old.*

Absentee mothers like these, who have had their nonresident
maternal status imposed upon them, nevertheless find that their
treatment in social circumstances is very nearly identical to that of
the absentee mother who relinquishes custody. No refined, reasoning climate surrounds an absentee mother once it is known that
she does not provide the daily care for her children. The particulars
of how it happens that a given mother does not live with her
children are either never known or ignored, wiped out by the
power of an instant negative judgment. That judgment comes
much more quickly than the most anxious absentee mother can
manage an explanation, and it tends to interpret all explanations as
excuses. If a mother has lost her children in the courts—declared
unfit—dare she reveal this, whether or not she was justly declared
so? No, of course not. If it was an unjust decision, her explanation
sounds defensive, meant to cover the truth. If it was a justified
decision, no extenuating circumstances will save the woman from
vilification. So the woman who has lost custody will either avoid
the topic altogether or lie. The assumptions and judgment are not
affected by anything she can say, so why bother trying to make
people understand? More incredibly still, the absentee mother
whose children make the choice to live away from her is also
blamed. A mother minus her children is so highly suspect that no
explanation serves. Many mothers in these two categories hear
responses to their explanations such as "Oh, that's awful," or
"That's a rotten shame," meant to convey understanding and
sympathy, but which are often recognizable as mere humoring
devices to help save face until the subject can be changed. Or they
may encounter the reverse, a great deal of curiosity. The curiosity
is laced with subtle charges: "But don't you miss him?" "How
could you let him go?" One absentee mother who had one of her
three sons leave to live with his father phrased one important
response rather humorously: "My mother acted as if I had sold him
in a raffle drawing." One way or another, however, this minority
group of absentee mothers is learning to cope with the treatment
they receive. Says one, "I no longer feel I owe people all the
answers they want." Says another, a bit less politely, "What the
hell do they know about it?"

Once, when I was introduced to someone as an absentee mother, the person to whom I had been introduced was visibly disconcerted. Nervously, she said, "But we all know there are *different kinds* of absentee mothers, don't we?" "Do we?" I asked.

Absentee Mothers Who Voluntarily Relinquish Custody

The reasons absentee mothers decide to relinquish custody are not usually simple or clear-cut. Contributing factors appear in various combinations and in varying degrees of intensity. In an effort to make the absentee mothers' motivations as clear as possible, I have categorized each mother in my study who has relinquished custody as having done so for one reason more than any other. But it should be understood that only in a minority of instances has an absentee mother in this study relinquished custody for a single reason.

It must also be stressed that, although the word *decision* is used in connection with mothers who relinquish custody, the word needs to be taken in a diminished sense, because a large number of these absentee mothers perceived no element of choice in their custody arrangements. The thought I probably heard repeated most often was, "It was not my *wish* to relinquish custody; I had *no choice.*" Indeed, the word *relinquish* itself connotes reluctance. So it is that, in many cases, a mother's "decision" to give custody to the father is merely a technical description of what has occurred.

In none of the seventy-five sets of interwoven motivations was there a single reference to boredom. One woman in the entire hundred used the word to describe the reason she left her marriage; it had nothing to do with her custody arrangements. That is why the character of Joanna Kramer is so irritating. Her motivation is artificial and seems to be a deliberate misunderstanding of the absentee mother. Charlotte Andergast, on the other hand, is infused with more valid implications, as the development of careers has played *some* part in *some* of the custody decisions of real absentee mothers. Surprisingly few absentee mothers in my study, however, cite careers as motivating factors in relinquishing custody. As for the stereotypical Anna Karenina motivation, *not one* absentee mother among the seventy-five who relinquished custody left her husband and children for a lover, although some left their husbands for another man.

EMOTIONAL PROBLEMS

It was 1967. I had been married for six years of what was to be a nine-year marriage. I had three children. The last of four live-in relatives had departed. My husband's drinking continued to worsen despite his repeated assurances that he would stop.

Tired to the marrow, I could not sleep. Bill reeked of beer. The children's rooms reeked of urine. What was I doing wrong? Mountains of soaked linen every day. If I slept, there would be no time to think. But I *had* to think.

It's getting hot in here. What's happening to my life? Who's controlling it? Who's using it? I have absolutely nothing to say about how my days or months or years are spent. They're just used against my will. I've tried. I try so hard to go on. But these are the only days I'll ever have, the only ones. Do I literally owe them my life? Am I really supposed to submit? I promised to be a mother. But can I continue to submit? Can I keep my promise? All the air is being used up. I'm breathing as fast as I can, but I can't get what I need. What is it I need? . . . . I have to get to the window!

Something hurt in my throat, but it got out when I opened the window. I would throw my head out the second-story bedroom window, and the tears would get out.

One night I knelt at my husband's knees and told him about my nocturnal panics. I felt I would die if I did not get some help. Maybe he could help. I told him about my days. How hard I tried to be a good mother, to fulfill our babies' every need, to care for them in all the ways I had always wanted for myself. Then I started to cry again. Nobody ever loved *me* when *I* was little. Nobody ever took care of *me*. There was never a hug, never a word of praise, never anything that resembled a sign of affection. But my body became adult anyway. And my body created babies. And now I had to give my babies what they needed. But all the while the real me, the kindergarten me, was screaming, "When is it *my* turn? When do *I* get loved and cared for? I *want my* turn! Somebody *owes* me my turn!"

I thought that when I married I would have my turn, my own Daddy to love me and take care of me. But I had babies. And all the while I was giving my babies what they needed, I was full of anger at them. I knew they did not in any way deserve it, but I felt it anyway. Sometimes it was just simmering, smoldering in my harsh tone of voice or gnarled facial expression, but sometimes it erupted into fury. Once I slapped my one-year-old Chris on his tiny rear end and, as if he were a doll in a slow-motion film, he flew halfway across the room. I was astonished at what I saw. I could not believe what my hand had caused. I gasped in horror of the terrible power which had released itself through my arm and hand. I picked my baby up and held him and kissed him, and we both cried together. After I put him to bed for his nap, I became overwhelmed by fear of what was in me, and by an all-encompassing shame. I closed myself into the upstairs bathroom and buried my face in a thick towel and begged God to forgive me. But I never told my husband about the incident.

My husband said I should talk to our pastor. Maybe he could help me. I told him that I *had* been talking with him, in the confessional, for years. And before him, there were other priests, young and old, at the other parishes to which we had belonged. They all advised me in the same way; I was to continue my battle against selfishness. It was a strong human fault, but God would help me overcome it. My husband felt that he could certainly not improve upon the advice of priests. They must know best. It was just a matter of perseverence. Or maybe I should stop taking the Pill; he had heard that some women reacted to it strangely. I sat up as if struck by lightning. He got the message. So, really, it was just a matter of perseverance. The positive-thinking seminar he had just attended had convinced him that there were no limits to what one could accomplish with will power. I wanted to ask him if he was going to use it to stop drinking, but I talked about emotional illness instead. He felt extreme disgust for people who were supposed to be emotionally ill. I picked myself up from the floor and resolved not to be weak or lazy anymore. But my resolve was no match for the evil strength of my soul. It was a resolve much weakened by fruitless injunction, by years of repeated assertion and defeat.

The suffocation seizures began happening during the day as well as late night. I started having nightmares in which I did ghastly things to my children, in which I stabbed my husband over and over again. I dreamed repeatedly of desperate unsuccessful attempts to win my father from other women. I did not understand any of this, but I began to feel that I would either have to kill myself or face the real possibility of inflicting grave harm on someone else—probably my innocent babies. I had to get out of there. What could I do? I tore away at myself for another year. But, finally, I made the decision to leave. I made the decision to protect my children from my emotional illness and to save my own life, for I felt in some way that I was dying.

Eighteen of the seventy-five women in my study who relinquished custody did so out of serious emotional stress similar to my own. That amounts to almost one-quarter of us who were making more than a custody decision. We were, in some cases, recognizing the danger we posed to our children and removing that danger, and we were running from our own deaths. We shared a sense of impending doom. We saw no other choices, but we despised ourselves nonetheless. The mother of a boy who was only four months old when she relinquished custody says:

It was either run away or kill myself! Anything at that point for a little rest and understanding. I loved my baby. I wanted him away from me at a time when I was emotionally unstable. I recognized that I had needs but no one to help. I was afraid I would hurt him or end up hating him. I wanted him to have the best life had to offer. I still love him, I still care and I still want the best for him. I was not the best.

The mother of a four-year-old girl, who had just begun psychotherapy:

I was terribly upset then. I had stopped eating because of emotional despair. If I didn't get out, I felt I would have died.

Over and over again, these women echo the theme of dire emotional distress:

I felt I was running away, but I knew I would die if I did not.

I felt I was dying and to leave was my only way to live.

When not referring specifically to death, they use words like *self-preservation* and *survival* to express the powerful need to get out.

Melissa took her nine-month-old son with her when she left her husband in spite of the fact that the baby's father had been fulfilling a large share of the boy's needs.

His father did everything for him, right down to giving him his bath. I very rarely even fed my son when I was with his father.

But Melissa began to feel frightening things toward her baby when she was on her own with him:

I knew my feelings were not reasonable, and I was afraid of hurting my son in a fit of rage. I used to put whiskey in his milk so he would be sure to sleep all night. One night after I bathed him and put him to bed with a bottle, he started crying. I was watching T.V. and ignored him. When he finally stopped, I could barely hear a funny little noise. I went to see what it was, and he had thrown up all over the bed and floor and himself. I picked him up to put him on my bed, and he vomited again—on me, my bed and everywhere. By this time, I was crying, screaming, shouting and slamming things around as I ran him another bath, started changing clothes and sheets and cleaning up the mess he had made. He was sitting in the bathtub and started crying again when I hadn't settled down any. I turned to look at him and realized he hadn't done anything babies don't do. His pathetic crying made me catch myself, and I began trying to comfort him. Then I discovered that the poor child had a fever and was teething. That was when I decided he'd be better off with his father. The next day, I asked his father if he wanted him. He said yes and asked when he could get him. I told him, "Today. You can have him today."

Several of these desperate mothers were alcoholics, one a drug abuser, and all had either attempted or seriously considered suicide, had nervous breakdowns, or been under psychiatric care. Some of the psychiatric histories are staggering.

Sarah, a black woman, had three nervous breakdowns during her four-year marriage, the first when her daughter was just a month old. The second time, the baby was only six months old. Sarah left her husband and little girl while they were all living with her mother-in-law. Then she sank into a nonfunctioning state for a year before returning to her family. She was well for only one year before she collapsed again, and she once more removed herself from the household. Sarah may be locked into this emotional rollercoaster for a long time to come. The last time I heard from her, she was beginning to feel better again and was talking about returning to her husband and daughter.

One tortured woman had made four attempts on her life as a child, twice before age twelve, once at twelve, and once at fourteen. Her marriage at eighteen lasted for only two years. It could not have surprised anyone when, as the single mother of an infant, she tried once again to kill herself. The ferocity of her attempt was certainly evident in the multiple means employed: pills, alcohol, and, for good measure, a razor blade on both wrists. She could not understand how she had survived:

I had taken four prescriptions' worth of pills, half a bottle of rum, and both my wrists were cut up. I remember falling against the wall. I was smiling and saying "Oh, sweet Jesus, help me." Then I realized that I had not cut one wrist deeply enough. I made a second cut downward, and the two together formed a cross. I remember thinking how ironic that was.

But she did survive, and she allowed her son's father and grand-mother to keep him:

It was a shock to realize that they loved my son as much as I did, or at least almost as much. I looked around me—the ranch, the openness in which he could run and play, in which he could have a dog—and I compared that to what I could offer him: a room, me gone all day working, a series of babysitters, my emotional instability. I knew then that love was not enough. I could show my son how very much I loved him by allowing him to stay here, in this sunshine, in this freedom, in all the love he would come to know because I had left him with a whole family. I am consoled by the fact that I know I love him and loved him enough to allow others to give him what I could not. And, slowly, that dark chasm of my past is being filled with a soft light, and with it comes the peace I have so long sought, peace from my anguish, peace from myself in despair.

Liz, the mother of an eleven-year-old girl and a fourteen-year-old son, had been in psychotherapy for fourteen years before leaving her husband and children:

I had really had it with them and leaving was the most emphatic thing I could do to save myself.

A mother of six had entered therapy sometime after learning of her husband's continuing four-year affair. Then her mother died a short time before Christmas.

I asked my husband to accompany me to California during vacation to try to work things out. We'd always been fond of the Carmel-Monterey area. But "matters" would not allow him to leave, so I went with my daughter. She visited friends in San Francisco, and I drove down the coast . . . My husband had agreed earlier to talk to the therapist about my problem as soon as he had time, but he hadn't had time yet. The night I arrived in Carmel, I sat on the beach feeling that I would be better off dead and I

*dwelled on killing myself then. I knew what I had to do but felt I didn't
have the strength to issue an ultimatum to my husband and to follow
through with leaving him if he refused to give up his mistress. What
stopped me from killing myself was the sudden realization that my
children would be told that I was a coward.*

Even so, this mother felt that relinquishing custody of her children
to their father when she did finally leave him "was the only thing
[she] could have done at the time because [her] physical, financial
and emotional condition could not have supported them."

Belinda left her eleven-year marriage with her two children and
temporarily moved in with her mother and stepfather. There was
nowhere else to go. A month passed. The strain of the divorce, of
caring for a seven- and a nine-year-old, of continuing to be dependent, of never having privacy, broke Belinda one night:

*I had been intensely depressed for some time out of fear of the future.
What would I do? How could I support myself and the kids? That evening
the children would not go to sleep, and I could not get any time alone. My
mother and stepfather were out. I became hysterical and went into the
bathroom and gulped twenty-eight Valium tablets at once. I ended up in a
psychiatric unit for sixteen days . . . The children and I were in a very bad
emotional state . . . and my husband brought suit for custody. I was told
that it could drag out for an entire year. I felt that it would be better for all
of us if I gave my children up.*

It should be clear from these stories that some women should
never become mothers, that others could do well as nurturers if
they were simply given sufficient support, and that there are
certain conditions under which even the most maternally talented
woman cannot fulfill the unrealistic responsibilities imposed upon
her in conjunction with motherhood. Perhaps Julie's words, in a
broad sense, summarize the experience of most absentee mothers
whose emotional problems led to their relinquishing custody of
their children:

*I was so unhappy that I was making my son's life miserable. Whatever
good I was bringing to the mother/child relationship was also laced with
poison because it was so oppressive to me . . . I also knew on a very deep
level that by relinquishing custody I was saving my life; that, had I stayed,
I would not have helped anybody. Had I stayed, I either would have
continued to die a slow spiritual death or I would have literally died. Or
gone crazy. Or done terrible, destructive damage. Surely, that would have*

been worse for my son. I feel grateful that I had the strength and the support to let that go and to stop the self-destructive behavior that was called mothering.

Indeed, what we continue to call mothering could be more accurately described, in the light of society's expectations, as imposed blood letting. In the case of single mothers, especially, there seems no limit to the supply of blood. The single mother is to comfort, clean, dress, feed, support, love, and entertain her children around the clock and the week and the year. She is to largely ignore her own needs; to avoid the company of men for the sake of preserving her children's morals and not having her own challenged by the court. And then, if she is lucky, if she is good enough at total self-sacrifice, she will be given the privilege of continuing to carry the entire and very real burden of raising her children. Certainly there are joys associated with a mother's responsibilities, but these joys do not necessarily nullify the problems involved. The fact that most mothers, single and otherwise, choose or manage the responsibilities of parenting is a monument to their moral, physical, and loving capacities, but I believe that the extremity of the demands made on a mother should vindicate those who relinquish custody from the suspicions of immorality, character weakness, and dispassion. Mothers, like all other human beings, have limitations.

FINANCIAL REALITIES

The Bible teaches that woman brought sin and death into the world, that she precipitated the fall of the race, that she was arraigned before the judgement seat of Heaven, tried, condemned and sentenced. Marriage for her was to be a condition of bondage, maternity a period of suffering and anguish, and in silence and subjection, she was to play the role of a dependent on man's bounty for all her material wants.
                                                    —The Woman's Bible, *Part I*

Everybody knows it. Nobody denies it. Men make more money than women. On a national average, for every dollar a man makes, a woman makes fifty-nine cents. Men dominate management and certain professional positions and are paid more than women performing the same tasks. For every one of the seventy-five absentee mothers in my study who relinquished custody, financial reality played a part in her decision.

In 1979, the median annual income of single mothers was $7,000; if her children were all under the age of six, it was $4,500. In 1981, almost two million single mothers were living on incomes below the poverty level. And as for alimony and child support, one figure for each of these categories should demonstrate that male complaints are exaggerated. Less than 4 percent of divorced women collect alimony, and the average yearly child-support payment as of 1978 per family was $1,800. The further impact of this meager figure is felt when one learns that only 35 percent of single mothers collect child support at all and that only 49 percent of those receiving payments collect the full amount awarded.[1] This is unfair and injurious to single mothers and their children, yet the huge majority of divorcing mothers still prefer to have custody. Whether this is evidence of intense maternal affection, innocence, or masochism is arguable, but I believe that the eighteen absentee mothers in my study who relinquished custody primarily for economic reasons have an impressive case with which to justify their decisions.

I was not surprised to find that the two women in the hundred of the study who had the most children, six each, fell into this category. Single mothers with one or two children are in difficult circumstances. Imagine a mother on her own with six. Jane, one of these mothers, has a master's degree in special education, which makes her one of the better-educated women in this study as a whole and more so among those who have relinquished custody primarily for financial reasons. (In the entire group of one hundred, the average level of education was two college years. See Table 3 for details. Among the women in the "financial realities" category, that average was one year lower.) As a teacher, the mother of six earned only a modest salary. In this case, the father was equally well educated, but in business for himself. Jane summed the situation up concisely:

My husband was in a position to care for the children without lowering their standard of living.

But she confesses that she had also hoped to prevent his marriage to his mistress.

The second mother of six has only a high school diploma and worked as a cashier at the time of her marriage. Her ex-husband, on the other hand, has a bachelor's degree and is in banking management:

As the divorce was imminent, my husband and I talked about what would be best for the children. He had been the sole breadwinner in our sixteen-year marriage except for the one year before our divorce when I worked half-time as a department store sales clerk. So, naturally, he knew he could take care of them. I looked at a divorced friend who had custody of her children, and I saw how drastically their lifestyle had changed, and I was scared to death to bring the same thing upon my children. Of course, my husband reinforced all my fears at the time. I had no lawyer; there was no money. My husband told me his lawyer could take care of my questions as well as his. When I asked his lawyer about joint custody, he told me there was no such thing. I was so naive, I took his word for it. I no longer feel I ran away, but for years I did.

The ex-husbands have more desirable employment in terms of income than do the absentee mothers. Four of the custodial fathers who have custody as a result of financial realities own businesses, two are in middle-management, and one is in an entry-level corporate position; two are Ph.D.s (one a professor, the other in a well-paid area of research). The three men who are blue-collar workers make solid wages in unionized positions. One of the fathers is an architect, and one is an air traffic controller. Another two are in stable, decently paid public service jobs, one a postal service worker and one a fireman. Only one of these men holds a low-paying job. He is a security guard. But his former wife, who gave him custody of his two boys, makes even less. She is a full-time college student.

Compare these fathers' jobs with the ones the mothers held when they made their decisions to relinquish custody: seven were clerical workers; three were teachers; three were sales clerks; two were nurses' aides; one was a paramedic; and two were wait-resses.[2]

Among these eighteen women is an absentee mother unique among the entire hundred, although I have since come across another in her category outside of the study. She is what might be called a dual absentee mother: she has relinquished custody to two different fathers. There had been a first marriage and a first son, followed by divorce. The mother had kept her first son and remarried, producing a second son with the second husband. When the second marriage dissolved, however, the mother relinquished custody of both boys, each to his own father. I believe that the second marriage, second baby and, therefore, the second relinquishment would never have occurred if Clarice, the mother involved, had simply given up her first son at the time of her first divorce.

Clarice first married at seventeen; she remained in the marriage for four years. Her response to single mothering at twenty-one, most especially to the financial aspects of it, was to remarry after one month. "I remarried for security only," she says. "There was no love."

Her second marriage also ended after four years. This pattern of escape is not uncommon for women in general; most of us are not raised in preparation for independence, and it often takes many years of repetitious behavior to recognize what is happening and perhaps still more years to address it.

Clarice addressed it at the point of her second divorce:

The reasons I relinquished custody of both children at the time of my second divorce were primarily ones of financial and emotional strain . . . At the time I made the decision I was, to say the least, emotionally distraught. I felt I had no other alternative, and I didn't want to see my children suffer any more; both had been through enough . . . I was unskilled, emotionally immature and completely without help or guidance.

I believe a large portion of the emotional strain Clarice was feeling then was related to the confrontation, once again, with the fear that she would be unable to attain self-sufficiency, intensified by the existence of two children for whom she would have to provide. She must have known, subconsciously, that she was ready to hold her ground this time, but that she had to start from zero if she was to have a good chance for victory. She saw her dilemma in the light of strain due to the divorce and financial realities; I see it as having been one of postponed primal assertion. None of us can be adults until we have made this assertion, and if too many negative factors are attached to a minimally developed emotional structure, we may never be able to do it. At any rate, Clarice's statement of her goals can be seen to reflect both views of what her dilemma meant, since personal and financial well-being are, after all, closely related and often accomplished in conjunction with one another. In her words:

I want to get an education and, in the near future, become independent and self-sufficient.

She is clearly well on her way to achieving her goals, having earned a bachelor's degree and begun graduate work in psychology. However, a larger hope has not yet been fulfilled:

I would like to see women in general feel good, if that's possible, about making similar decisions. The only way that can be a reality is if the topic comes out of the "closet." No one, man or woman, wants to be separated from his or her child. Unfortunately, there are many types of circumstances which make it necessary. Men are not condemned in these circumstances. Women in the same circumstances should also be free from condemnation.

Mention of condemnation seems a natural bridge to the type of absentee mother who may be the most strenuously denounced of all absentee mothers—the mother who relinquishes custody to someone other than the father. There are nine absentee mothers of this type among the women in my study; two relinquished custody primarily for financial reasons.[3]

Lorisa married at nineteen because she was pregnant. Her husband was only seventeen and worked as a gas station attendant. She was a nurses' aide. The couple had a baby boy by Caesarean delivery and separated by the time their son was one-and-a-half. Lorisa *had* to leave her boy-husband:

He beat me regularly. I didn't know it then, but he was becoming mentally ill like his mother. He was so hard to live with; I did all the compromising and trying.

Lorisa's ex-husband is currently an institutionalized mental patient.

In spite of her difficult position following the divorce, Lorisa enjoyed her little boy. She tells us:

He was a really neat kid, full of life and interested in everything. He was very lovable.

But three years of trying to get by were very destructive to her spirit and energy. She was unemployed most of the time, unable to obtain work that would have paid enough to provide for child care:

My divorce had nothing to do with why I gave up my child, except that it sentenced me to welfare. There was the constant, day-by-day struggle within the welfare system . . . no way out of the situation, desperation, getting "high" to cope, wanting to commit suicide as a way out, seeing what inner-city life was doing to my child.

Lorisa did not have the option of relinquishing custody to her son's father which most of the absentee mothers in this study have had.[4] Lorisa gave up her five-year-old boy for adoption:

I couldn't live that kind of life anymore. My son needed more than I could give, more than just love can provide . . . I don't even remember driving home from the agency the last time I saw my son. I cried without control, and I felt a horrible emptiness. I tried to lose myself in my work and my friends. I knew I had done the right thing, but I still hurt so bad, and the loneliness was overwhelming.

Lorisa remarried four years after she gave up her son, but she has not had another child. She is physically unable to do so, but she would not become a mother again even if it were possible. Her first experience was too traumatic, and the pain lingers even though Lorisa's son had met his adoptive parents beforehand and had liked the idea of living with them:

I still cry occasionally, and I still miss him. He is in my thoughts daily . . . I have had some problem with depression and emotional pain. I have lost part of myself, but I will always love him.

Lorisa participates in a group created to support mothers who have given children up for adoption. They also work toward the amendment of current adoption regulations, which Lorisa sees as

terribly inhumane. My son and I can't have contact with one another. I still care about him, and I have a great need for news of him. I worry about how this separation will affect his life. I think adoption the way it is now is beneficial only to the adoptive parent.

   Perhaps that is why the second absentee mother in the "other-than-father" category to whom I have referred chose a foster home for her children instead. Foster care is considered temporary, and it offers the relinquishing mother or father almost unlimited contact with the child(ren).
   Clara was sixteen when she married, with a tenth-grade education. Her twenty-three-year-old husband had thirteen different

jobs in the first year of the marriage, and things did not get much better. Four children, two boys and two girls, were born. One of the children was diagnosed as having severe dyslexia caused either by genetic defect or brain injury. Clara's husband drank too much; he abused her, both by beating her and regularly raping her. After five years, Clara left him.

She needed time to recover from the years of abuse, financial anxiety, and constant childbearing, yet she had no resources. She placed all four of her children in a foster home. They were three, two, one, and four months old at the time. Letting them go was "bad, heartbreaking" for Clara. She says that she "almost went over the edge." But she had no choice. Her only living relative was a brother, from whom she was alienated. Her acquaintances did not think that putting her little children in a foster home was a good idea, but as another absentee mother said in a similar situation, "Nobody did anything to help me keep them." So Clara became an absentee mother, and the situation remained static for almost two years. By that time, she had remarried. A few months after the remarriage, she brought three of her four children back to her and their new stepfather. The fourth child, the retarded child, she decided to leave in foster care and, to that extent, she remains an absentee mother. Her current marriage is a happy one, she has had another child within it, and enjoys working as a secretary. Marriage was virtually the only option available in a society where women work as hard as men in the work force, and more so out of it, but do not earn anywhere near the same wages.

VALID SELF-REALIZATION

The seventeen absentee mothers for whom personal freedom was the primary contributing factor in relinquishing custody are, obviously, the group upon whom most of the negative stereotypes are erroneously built. Thus, I feel the need to introduce their cases with a brief delineation of the basic issues involved in the debate over their custody decisions: a person's undeniable need for and right to self-realization and the biased perception and treatment of mothers regarding child custody. Unless the former is admitted and the latter changed, all absentee mothers will continue to be damned for their supposedly frivolous efforts to fulfill personal potential.

The concept of self-realization has gotten a bad reputation because the term has been loosely used for the past decade to describe behavior that would be more accurately described as self-gratification. Thus I use the term *valid self-realization* to set my meaning apart from the crass perversion some have made of the original assertion of self-realization as an essential good.

About a decade ago, the concept that individuals owed themselves some attention was seemingly discovered for the first time. Generations of flinching at the mere mention of self, with its intimations of selfishness, took their toll. Individuals, especially women, started asking questions. As is the way with "new" discoveries, self-realization proceeded to monopolize the attention of an entire culture for years. It got out of hand and lost its original meaning. Enthusiasm for all its genuine merits ran wild. I remember reading somewhere an actual exchange between a psychologist and her client. The client was a young woman who was complaining that her hectic life contained too many parties, too many lovers, too many vacation trips. When the psychologist asked her why she did not simply stop doing so many of these things, the girl responded with, "You mean I don't *have* to do everything I want?"

We have largely lost sight of what is actually meant by self-realization and in so doing we have trivialized it, robbed it of its essential nature. Self-realization is *not* doing everything one wants. Self-realization is *not* the abandonment of responsibility. Self-realization is *not* excessive self-love. It *is* beginning to do the things one *must* do, not to satiate one's senses, but to realize, discover, and develop one's self beyond mere physical existence. It is the managing of responsibilities *simultaneous* to fulfilling the primary responsibility to oneself. Individuals exist in advance of whatever responsibilities they may incur. Self-realization involves the belief that it is not only all right to love oneself, it is *essential*. Self-realization is not, therefore, an extreme philosophy that rejects anything difficult or unpleasant, but rather a moderating philosophy that saves individuals and their society alike from the destructive extreme of denying the self altogether.

Demanding that the mother bear the entire responsibility for childrearing in *every* case of divorce and penalizing her with societal condemnation if she does not is evidence of just such a destructive extreme. We do not blame the seed for developing roots or the bud for blooming. Why should we point at mothers who even more needfully turn their faces to the sun? They have not abandoned their responsibility to their children. They do not cease to exist for their children; they simply cease to live under the same roof. When divorce occurs, when joint custody is either not workable or undesirable, children must live with one parent or the other.

The first thing that struck me as I studied the absentee mothers whose major goal was valid self-realization was the exceptional degree of creative and socially oriented occupations among them. Even those who do not work in the arts and crafts or socially oriented positions hold salaried positions, in contrast, for instance, with the majority of women in the "financial realities" category, who are hourly workers. Among the eighteen women who relinquished custody for primarily financial reasons there is a preponderance of unpromising work situations requiring repetitive tasks: fourteen of the eighteen are in clerical work, waitressing, hourly labor, or the like. The exceptions in that group are the three teachers and the paramedic. Among the seventeen absentee mothers who relinquished custody for the primary goal of personal freedom are six women who work in arts or crafts: theater stage manager, some work on set creation; woodworker in business for herself; composer-musician, currently working in a rock band that uses her own music; locksmith in business for herself; dance instructor; and producer of television commercials. Three women work in innovative social services: administrator of a "center for independent living," an organization that educates and assists disabled persons toward self-sufficiency and attainment of their civil rights; administrator of a private, religious primary and secondary school; and resident house manager of a shelter for abused women and their children. One woman works in a traditional social service as a nursing supervisor. Two women are full-time students working toward social service careers: a graduate student, sponsored by a fellowship, currently studying hospice care in England, with plans to enter law school; and an undergraduate majoring in psychology with plans to pursue graduate work and then specialize in assistance for incest victims. Four women earn their livings in salaried administrative positions not related to arts, crafts, or social services: sales administrator; research administrator; claims representative; and director of meetings and conventions.

Many of the women also have serious avocations, such as political activism, singing in light opera, painting, and photography. One is a published writer and an active feminist. The average educational level in this group is one year higher than among the sample as a whole and two years higher than among the eighteen "financial realities" mothers, but that alone does not reveal the more precise educational differences. The absentee mothers who relinquished custody for primarily financial reasons did so in employment situations that made their decisions thoroughly reasonable; in comparison, the women who relinquished custody primarily for reasons of personal freedom have proven to be more aggressive and successful in obtaining more interesting and better-paid jobs, though with little more to offer as job candidates. The absentee mother who seeks personal fulfillment is evidently often successful in her quest (see Tables 4 and 5).

Sandy, one of the women in the "personal freedom" category, was actually a *former* absentee mother when the study was initiated.[5] The third, and oldest, of her three children had returned to live with her just one year before the study began. The other two children had returned four years earlier. This is one of the rare cases in which the transpiring events of interest are all very orderly and easy to follow: the participants had well-defined motivations and plans and then proceeded, almost exactly and with seemingly no squabbling, to fulfill the plans as stated. Sandy, whose twelve-year marriage had broken up by a mutual agreement, wanted to earn a college degree and find a good job. When she and her husband married, she was a high school graduate and he had completed one year of college. He earned a Ph.D. while she had three children, worked when she could as a typist, and attended some college classes when possible. She did not get very far, educationally, in twelve years. Her two boys and one girl were nine, ten, and eleven when their parents divorced, and it was their mother's turn to go to school. So Sandy's husband took custody of the children. She tells us what the following years were like:

I lived apart from my children for four years, during which time I earned my B.A. and got an administrative job. For the first two years, I lived in the same city as the kids, for the second two years I lived in [a town about twenty miles away]. During the whole four years I saw the kids a lot; they spent most weekends with me, and we often had dinner together during the week. There were also three or four times a year when we would spend one to two weeks together.

I was constantly frustrated during this time, because I always felt as if the children and I were "visiting" one another. I was not in touch with their daily lives, and missed the ongoing contact. However, I had neither the time nor the money to have them live with me, and their father had enough of both. At the end of four years, the kids were offered a choice of which parent to live with; the younger two came to me, and the older boy stayed with his father.

Although Sandy's arrangements worked well, even she found some difficulty in taking part in the study:

I found myself facing some painful memories. That part of my life is past and I don't care to go back and look at that other life anymore.

Marion, an absentee mother in the "personal freedom" group who has resumed custody since the study began, recalls 1970, the year her four-year marriage ended and her difficult struggle toward self-sufficiency began:

I had custody of our children right from the time of the divorce; they were one and two years old then. I wouldn't have considered leaving them. During the first part of my divorced life, the children and I lived in the same city as their father. I had a job which was very unpleasant; I bled chickens for a doctor doing research at a university medical center. I had to earn a living. When I wasn't bleeding chickens, I was washing glassware. After a year, I was fired from that job and got a much better job at another research facility. I didn't like that job either, but it beat bleeding chickens. After four years like that, watching my friends in medical school go off to interesting jobs, I began to feel that everything in life was somewhere else, that all that would be waiting for me at the end of my life would be a gold watch for doing a menial task I hated. So I decided to move to another city. My ex-husband kept the children for the summer so that I could get situated. As I left, he said to me, "I'll believe you can make it when I see it."
  Two months later, I asked him to send the children as promised. He not only refused, but allowed as how he had hired detectives in an effort to prove I was unfit and proceeded to sue me for custody. It was a horrendous experience, but I won.
  After that, I couldn't find a job, but I luckily won a college scholarship. [Marion was a high school graduate with no college.] *While I was in school, my ex-husband continued to try to get me to let him have the children. I refused steadfastly until three years later when I wanted to try to go to medical school. I relinquished custody to him temporarily.*

Marion's daughters were nine and ten years old at that point, and the younger one seemed glad to go. The older one cried as the car pulled away. The leave-taking was hard:

I almost died at that point. Instead, I ran to the car and hugged her one more time. Fortunately, I was still on campus and had a lot of emotional support from all sides from teachers and classmates. [Marion was attending a private women's college.]

One year later, when I had given up on medical school but had won the fellowship to study and travel with my children in Europe for a year, my ex-husband sued me again for custody. I won that one too. Hence, the children are back with me permanently.

Nevertheless, things might have been different, Marion might well have allowed her daughters to remain with their father and stepmother, if they had not developed into religious fanatics. Marion tells about her feelings:

Since the first custody suit, when I moved, I have wondered if I was selfish to want the children with me considering the financial hardships, when their father could do so much more for them. They could have benefited from the kind of home their father could provide, but during the second custody suit I learned how fanatical my ex-husband's religion was . . . He and his wife had provoked my older daughter to "speak in tongues," and they burned a colorful paper dragon I had sent the children as a present, telling them that it was a symbol of the devil. I might have let the girls stay if it hadn't been for things like that, because apart from my ex-husband's religious proclivities, he is a good father. He is attentive and loving. The children are crazy about him and, despite my misgivings about him, they love him dearly.

Marion does not intend to change the custody arrangements again:

I almost went crazy making the actual decision to let the girls go to their father. One minute I'd be convinced that letting the children go was the answer for everybody. Fifteen minutes later, I'd think I was the cruelest mother in the world to even consider such a thing. Immediately after the children left with their father and his wife, I went into a decline. I got my work done, but I also found that I wasn't any latent intellectual giant even without my children's interruptions . . . I have to say that the act of letting the children go to stay with their father was the most difficult decision I ever made. I knew I was risking the chance that their father might try to keep them permanently, but I also knew that it would be a terrible burden on the children to think that they were the reason their mother didn't even try to go to medical school when that was what she desperately wanted to do. As it turned out, though, the price was too high for me, and I couldn't pass chemistry.

Even so, the issue never seems to be completely put to rest. A mother never stops being aware of the things she is *not* giving her children, and Marion is no exception:

It sometimes still breaks my heart that I can't give them the kind of calmness a mother "should." My life is on the frantic side. Now, I'm hell-bent on going to law school. The children will survive, but I won't if I don't find some kind of meaningful work to do that will provide me with the lifestyle I want.

Still, Marion is determined not to go the common, convenient route of remarriage:

I could never depend on anyone to rescue me. I don't want to have to get married again. I think you have no alternative to marriage if you can't support yourself financially as well as provide yourself with self-sustaining interests.

There are women who seem, by some of their actions, to know that children will not be a positive experience for them; yet one also sees that they can be distracted from that knowledge. One such woman is Carol, who went through several situations involving her children before coming to a final resolution of her problems with mothering.

Carol became pregnant at seventeen by her high school boyfriend and gave birth to a baby girl, but she did not marry the boy or keep the baby. She gave her first-born daughter up for adoption—the first message to the psyche of a girl who would not like being a mother. Only two months after this birth and relinquishment, Carol, who had turned eighteen, married a twenty-seven-year-old divorced man who had custody of his two little girls, two and four years old. Ten months later Carol gave birth to another daughter of her own. Carol says there was no real choice in the matter of having children:

In a small town in the Midwest, women had children . . . The woman who was childless for long after marriage had lots of questions to answer.

When her baby was seven months old, Carol started college. She wanted to be a teacher. She says her husband tolerated it only because he anticipated the extra income it would mean when she finished school. He had not gone beyond high school and his job did not encourage or require creative thinking. Carol really enjoyed going to school, but her husband resented her interest in school and the attitudinal changes it prompted. He spent most of his spare time doing "man things" such as hunting and watching sports.

The marriage continued a little more than three years. Carol was expecting twins when she filed for divorce, and the two girls were born a month later. She left her marriage primarily because of the difference in personal growth between her husband and herself; her husband's two children and a brother of his who had lived with them for almost a year increased the overburden of responsibility. She no sooner lightened her burden by two stepchildren than they were replaced by her own twins. Still, Carol felt herself in an improved position from which to follow her own interests and lead a self-determined life. Indeed, remarkably, she continued going to school and earned her B.A. two years after her divorce. For seven years, she continued to care for her three daughters, but it was not done in a state of tranquility. Carol had started fantasizing about what it would be like to be free, and the fantasy grew for two years before she finally felt she had to do something about it:

Just like what had happened with my husband, I finally came to resent my children for the restrictions they put on my life. I could not follow my own interests and determine my own life patterns when their requirements had always to be considered and, ultimately, take precedence. There seemed to be a big world out there which I couldn't adequately experience as a mother.

Carol wanted to move to a city and felt that if she could leave the girls with their father for a year or so, things would work out for her. The girls' father, however, refused custody. A year after the divorce from Carol he had married a woman with three children from her previous marriage, and they had had two additional children of their own. This meant a total of seven children in the household. Carol's father, however, came to her rescue:

He volunteered to have the girls live with him and Mom, but only on the condition that they be given permanent legal custody until the girls were eighteen years old. Although I thought that I had been looking for a place to leave them for only a year or so, I took his offer without hesitation.

Carol was, at last, aware that she really did not want to be a mother, but she did not feel that she was running away from her children. Rather, she felt that she was running toward a new life that would not have been possible for her as a mother. She is only thirty-four, but she will not have any more children:

I have no desire ever to be involved with motherhood again. It is no more suitable for me now than it ever has been.

More than one-third of the women in the "personal freedom" group continue to feel that their decisions to relinquish custody were correct, but only one other absentee mother in the group, Paula, was as forceful in her expression of this feeling as Carol.[6] Paula says:

It has been six years since I made my decision, but I am still sure that I would not want that responsibility of children full time ever again.

In contrast, Marilyn kept her daughter for one year following her divorce, and went along with her former husband's failure to return the four-year-old girl after what was supposed to be a summer visit. She had obtained a job in advertising despite having only two years of college; it was an exciting job, and she began meeting a lot of people. She came to know who she was and that she could not only survive but prosper:

I have a very successful career. I travel a lot; my income is high. I am very comfortable. I just wanted enough time to do all this. I want my daughter back now.

Look at the strong difference in sentiment, before and after relinquishment, on the part of Cissy, another absentee mother in the "self-realization" group. She married at fifteen, having completed only two years of high school. Her five-year marriage produced one boy and one girl, who were two and newborn when Cissy accepted custody at the time of divorce. Here is how she felt after one month with custody:

I discovered that I would be imprisoned with my children and my husband would be free. There was no money, no help from anyone. I was nineteen with a two-year-old and a newborn. I resented what society was pushing on me. Why shouldn't I let my husband have the responsibility?

When I finally signed the papers, I knew I had made the right decision. When I look back at that day, I realize that I couldn't get away fast enough.

Now that Cissy has completed high school, is near completing college, and has developed plans for graduate work and a career in psychology, she is a different person, involved in fulfilling her potential and sure she is capable of doing so:

The day has arrived for regret. I am sorry I signed the custody papers. I would like to have my children with me now. I finally feel I have something to offer them. I could be committed to them in a way I could not have been when I was nineteen. I see now that it is possible to enjoy a family.

Six years have elapsed since Nora gave custody of her three-year-old daughter to the girl's father. She has not pursued schooling beyond her high school diploma, but she has obtained a salaried white-collar job as opposed to the clerk-typist jobs she used to hold. Perhaps more important, Nora has had the chance to pursue adult interests without any inhibitions of the sort a child imposes. She has had the chance to mature with the experience. Men are advised to sow their wild oats before committing themselves to a wife and family. Women are not so advised, but they probably should be. Witness Nora's words regarding herself before and after she had matured with independent and unencumbered experience:

Before, I was selfish and wanted to do things I never had a chance to do; a child would have inhibited me. I felt smothered and afraid and very unhappy. I didn't really know why, but I didn't like it or want to stay that way.

After, I became independent, found I could make it on my own and I now have a good husband, home and job . . . My former husband is remarried, but it doesn't seem to be working out. If he and his wife split up and he acts erratically again as he did with me when we divorced, I will take action to regain custody.

The haunting thought for the absentee mother, however, regardless of the positive effects she has garnered from relinquishing custody, is reflected in Jessie's flat conclusion:

The break was good for me, for my rehabilitation. It helped me gain my own identity, but I do not see it as having been good for my children emotionally.

That creates the fearful question with which each one of us lives. Have we harmed our children? It may be that what we have done was unavoidable or that our children have not been seriously damaged, but we do not really know yet. That is the hardest part of all, especially for the absentee mothers who have relinquished custody in their need for self-realization. Given their mother-as-selfless-saint indoctrination, the notion that a need of their own could rightfully take precedence over one of their children's is rarely fully accepted. I believe along with Simone Weil, however, that "the needs of a human being are sacred [and that] their satisfaction cannot be subordinated to any consideration whatsoever." One must, however, be as sure as possible, when delegating the responsibility for children, that one is moving toward fulfillment of a *need* and not merely toward pursuit of pleasure.

INTIMIDATION

> *What I consider my weaknesses are feminine traits: incapacity to destory, ineffectualness in battle.*
>
> —Anaïs Nin, The Diary of Anaïs Nin

Physically, men are stronger than women. This fact gives man an edge when male and female come into conflict, but the physical advantage, most often, is not needed or used directly. Physical advantage is merely the first ingredient of the aura of power, and therefore of intimidation, he is often able to establish over the woman or women in his life. Even though women today are more aware of the possibility of intimidation and are therefore on guard against it, it continues to be a prevalent problem. Fourteen of the seventy-five women in this study who relinquished custody did so in response to intimidation by husbands (and sometimes the husband's family as well).

Every one of the fourteen absentee mothers in the "intimidation" group initiated the end of her marriage, compared to fifty-three (62 percent) of the other absentee mothers in the hundred. (That is, each woman *wanted* to end the marriage; she did not necessarily file for divorce.) In none of the fourteen cases, in other words, was it the husband who wanted a divorce, whereas fourteen men (16 percent) in the rest of the study initiated divorces and seventeen (20 percent) of the marriages in the rest of the study were ended by mutual agreement. (Two women in the study never married or lived with the fathers of their children.) Where wives divorce husbands, as is the pronounced case among these fourteen couples, husbands very likely feel rejected and angry. An angry, hurt husband may also harbor a desire for revenge. The husband who feels injured is perfectly capable of seeking revenge by depriving his wife of her children; indeed, many women in the study accuse their former husbands of doing just that: demanding custody of their children for the sake of revenge. Whether or not revenge is the motivation of these particular fourteen husbands, however, intimidation is undeniably the means used to wrest their children from the wife/mothers who have become the enemy.

Beyond the male aura of power, I suspect that the fourteen husbands in this group had an additional factor in their favor when entering battle over their children: the guilt felt by their wives for having initiated divorce. The initiation of divorces, regardless of justification, creates a feeling of guilt: marriage is still considered a societal good, and the person who initiates the end to a marriage is still considered a villain. Guilt may well be an important factor in the cases where women become absentee mothers as a result of intimidation. One asks whether these fourteen husbands would have succeeded in their threatening methods, or if they would have even introduced them, if they themselves had initiated the divorces or the divorces had come of mutual agreement. If these wives were feeling guilty, justly or not, for having initiated an end to their marriages, they were more vulnerable to their spurned husbands' self-righteous intimidation.

One of the custodial fathers involved in this group was perfectly willing to use one of the most destructive sorts of intimidation to prevent his wife from taking custody of their seven-year-old son. He blackmailed her. His wife, Thelma, was a career officer in the military as well as being a lesbian. She had no chance of retaining custody, although she wanted to do so, unless she were willing to give up the military and could win custody in spite of her sexual orientation. The U.S. military has a strict policy of discharging homosexuals, and the courts have a record of refusing to grant child custody to homosexual parents. Although Thelma remains in the service and her ex-husband continues to hold custody, the last time she was in touch with me she was seriously considering either leaving the service and moving nearer her son or leaving the service and reconciling with her former husband just for the chance of being able to share a life with her little boy. Regardless of her decision, Thelma will continue to be the victim of blackmail.

In the same sense, each of the women who has relinquished custody as a result of intimidation continues to be a victim, since she continues to live apart from her child or children. One does wonder if the victim of physical intimidation does not feel her victimization more vividly and more lastingly than victims of more subtle forms. Perhaps the story of the one absentee mother who experienced physical abuse will help illuminate the issue. Darlene, a high school graduate in 1968, was married at eighteen to a nineteen-year-old mechanic. The couple had two children, a boy and a girl, who were three and eight at the end of their parents' twelve-year marriage:

The reason I wanted an end to my marriage was that my husband had come, over years, to manipulate me totally. He told me what to do and when to do it. I felt like a child. When I started resisting his control, he became physically abusive. I was very unhappy with the marriage, and I asked and then begged for a separation for two-and-a-half years, but he would not leave his house. The house was in both our names, and I had worked for six years, but everything, including the children, was his. He wasn't unhappy, so I was just going to have to live with things the way they were. He felt extremely powerful because I had no family. I had only one friend, a close friend from childhood, but she lived two hours away and we only got together three or four times a year. I didn't discuss what was going on even with her. That was one of my mistakes, but I was so embarrassed and really confused.

Darlene felt totally trapped by her husband's violence. If she were to leave with the children, he would surely find them, beat her, and take the children back, but even that risk was not really possible to attempt. Darlene had no car when her husband was at work, and no money. She felt immobilized by the situation:

When I began pressing harder for a separation, for him to leave, he became even more violent. Things began to occur every day and in front of the children. He even started slapping me across the face when I would say something he didn't like. I became extremely quiet and withdrawn, and I cried constantly. It was a terrible way to live. Things just kept snowballing. The slaps became punches, and so on. I felt utterly alone, as

if there was no one who gave a damn if he killed me or not. I feared that he
would actually kill me.

My best friend had been writing to me and sensed something was not
right because I was not responding. She showed up on my doorstep one
night demanding to know what was going on. Thank God! I was in
terrible physical condition, and I told her everything. Her husband tried
to talk to my husband but to no avail. Two weeks later, I went to stay with
my friend. My husband would not allow me to take the children.

The extent and effectiveness of this sort of intimidation are awe-
some. Darlene was afraid even to call the police or to obtain an
attorney. The man who was an abusive husband happened also to
be a good father, and Darlene says he never hit his children. So the
children remain with their father, but it is sad to hear Darlene's
feelings of loss:

My friend loaned me five hundred dollars to put down on a decent-
running car and helped me put things together a bit. I went back to work
and got my own apartment one block away from the house. This way, I
can keep an eye on the kids. I miss them terribly. Sometimes I don't see
them for months, and I see other kids their size and that really hurts. And
I feel like I'm missing out on so much. I didn't see them on Christmas; I
did call them, but now my ex-husband has changed the phone number
and won't give it to me. I walked over to their school the other day after
not seeing them for three months. They seem healthy and happy though,
so I keep telling myself it's best. I want to avoid any more scenes, not only
for myself, but for the children. But most people don't understand why I
don't just take the children.

Money adds power to the male's physical superiority and is an
integral part of the aura of power. Men consistently earn more
than women in general; when a husband has more income than
usual, his power over his wife increases accordingly.

Millicent's husband was a multimillionaire. His wealth made his
major threat against Millicent plausible. He swore to her that he
would have her declared insane and institutionalized if she attempted to take their four-year-old daughter with her when she
left him. He had also threatened to do her bodily harm, but it was
the other threat that had the biggest impact.

Millicent's husband was so authoritarian during the seven-year
marriage, and he sometimes dealt with other people so cruelly,
that it is not difficult to imagine his putting Millicent into an
institution for his own purposes. For instance, Millicent wanted to

study at college, but her husband was suspicious about her going to class at night. She withstood his harassment in this matter only long enough to complete four class hours. He controlled the credit cards. She was not allowed to have money on hand; if she needed something, she had to ask for the money to buy it. Millicent says that her husband's extreme possessiveness and jealousy almost drove her insane. She was not allowed her own friends. But the most forbidding of Millicent's husband's actions was what he did to an older couple who had been his wife's friends before their marriage. The man and woman had been like parents to Millicent, and she had introduced her then-fiancé to them. They advised Millicent not to marry "this man." She made the mistake of telling her husband about this advice. She later learned that her good friends had been financially ruined by manipulations her husband had instigated.

Hillary's husband was not rich, but he was violent and had a powerful friend, a doctor. When Hillary finally told her husband that she wanted a divorce, he thought she was out of her mind and, with the assistance of his friend, had her placed in the psychiatric unit of a hospital. She was released after three weeks, but when she left her husband six months later she also left her four children. The forced psychiatric commitment she had already experienced was proof enough of what her husband could do to her, and she knew the pride he had in his paternity. He saw his children as proof of his manhood, and he liked having them visible and in his company at the "right" times. Hillary told me of a shocking incident linked to his view of what it means to be male. He knocked her out one night with a blow to the head and raped her. Their fourth child was conceived that night.

Again, one can see that Hillary was not dealing with a man prone to empty words. He was volatile and dangerous. Even so, in retrospect, Hillary says, "I should have fought to keep my children."

This group of absentee mothers shares a profound feeling of impotence and a marked distaste for their perceived weakness. Society's crippling expectation is of a mother who fights to the death for her children regardless of circumstances. Their own human limitations convince these absentee mothers of their maternal inferiority. Given these feelings, even in women who face gross intimidation—physical violence, blackmail, and psychiatric confinement—imagine the feelings of absentee mothers who have succumbed to lesser intimidation. Several gave custody to their husbands when threatened with custody suits, two more gave custody when their husbands insisted that they would contest the divorces unless they were given custody, and four others simply did not test their husbands' defiant statements that they would not allow the mothers to take the children away. After months, sometimes years, of fighting and anguish, emotional depletion is usually the ultimate factor in the decision. Women became too tired to go on, too frustrated to keep hoping. Sometimes the children take their fathers' view of their mothers as being to blame for it all, and the mothers despair and walk away feeling perfectly justified. Later, though, they question whether they fought hard enough. They see themselves as having been too weak. They also continue to be "manhandled" by their ex-husbands, who make visitation as difficult as possible and any necessary communication unpleasant or downright cruel.

When Lena left her husband and their nine-year marriage, there was no question that their eight-year-old son would live with her. Of course, Lena was forced to go to court eight times over the next few years to obtain child support payments. Three years after the divorce, her ex-husband remarried, and he and his new wife kidnapped his son. Lena is convinced that they did it to eliminate the support payments. She was tired of going to court, so she tolerated the kidnapping and the new arrangement it brought about. It also turned out that the boy liked living with his father. Then the visitation hurdles began—the major one being a refusal to allow Lena a visit longer than a day. Her son's father wanted legal custody. If she would cooperate and sign the papers, he would stop giving her trouble with the visits. She held out for a year but finally went along. Not long after that Lena's ex-husband asked her to resume custody. She gives her view of why he did this:

He had succeeded in taking John away from me and now that everything was moving along somewhat smoothly, he wanted to stir it up again as was his way.

Lena's husband had also begun to realize some of the problems that often come with child care. His son was causing trouble at school and beginning to cause friction between his father and stepmother. It was not as simple as merely saving support payments. He became enraged when Lena refused to resume custody.

He picked up his entire household and moved twelve hundred miles away. Lena has not seen her son in a year, does not even know his address, and has recently enlisted her former father-in-law as an emissary.

Mona is an absentee mother who did not see her two sons for eleven years. When she left their father, they were four and six. All of them had been living with the father's family. Mona intended to find a job and an apartment and then come back for the boys. She did these things, but the family refused to let the boys go. Mona felt she had no choice but to submit, because she was only one against a large family of determined persons who made threats when she tried to take her children. When she finally was able to see her sons eleven years later, she learned that, on top of everything else, her former husband and in-laws had raised the boys to believe that their stepmother was their natural mother. Mona's sons were as bitter about this as Mona was.

Women who have become absentee mothers through intimidation and have remained so in defeat are left feeling inexcusably weak and deprived. Their anguish is expressed poignantly by two in a way applicable to all of them:

If in the same circumstances again, I would at least attempt to fight the whole fight . . . As it is, there are just frequent tears of bitterness.

I feel worthless. I want a puppy. I mother my boyfriend.

PROBLEMS IN SECOND MARRIAGE

> *Estelle: You must have had reasons for acting as you did.*
> *Garcin: I had . . . But were they the real reasons?*
> —Jean-Paul Sartre, *No Exit*

Four of the absentee mothers in my study relinquished custody of their children because their second marriages were not doing well. Three of them attributed the marital problems to the presence of their children, the strains of attempting to establish good relationships between stepchildren and stepfathers. The irony is that in none of the four cases did the second marriage endure even after the mother had arranged for her children's exit. (In one case, the mother did not expect the marriage to improve; she relinquished custody in anticipation of a second divorce.)

This group of four may be too small to hold much generalized meaning. The only apparent common denominator is that, in each case, their educational level is two years lower than the absentee mothers as a group.

Leona waited two years after her divorce to remarry. She had two children, a boy and a girl, who were four and five at the time of her remarriage. She expected her second marriage to succeed, primarily because her second husband was quite the opposite of her first. He was a quiet introvert who earned his living as a systems analyst, whereas her first husband had been a physically abusive tool-and-die maker. Nevertheless, the new marriage was disillusioning. Leona's new husband did not make her feel loved; he was not affectionate. This affected the children too. He did not show affection toward them either, although he did not actually mistreat them. A real shock was in store for Leona, however, when she began addressing the issue and contemplating divorce. Says Leona, "He was like a madman, and I was *petrified* of his anger and violence." She began to realize that she would have to leave and that it would be safest to remove the children first. She did not want to have to go back to her parents the way she had after the first divorce, so she started thinking about giving custody to her former husband. He was happily remarried. The children could be in a two-parent home with more emotional support and financial security than she would be able to give them. The children were nine and ten when they went to live with their father and stepmother. Leona was glad her children were in a stable home, that they did not have to live through another divorce and live with a single parent again, but her daughter refused to see her for two years.

Kitty and her husband of seven years were swingers, predominantly with one other couple. But Kitty's husband later wanted a divorce to marry the other woman in the quartet. Kitty did not contest the divorce. She took her two sons with her and promptly married the other man in the quartet. The marriage was a disaster, primarily because the stepfather abused the children. Kitty thought she might be able to make the marriage work were it not for the children. Besides, if she sent them to live with their father, they would no longer be subjected to their stepfather's beatings. The two-year-old and seven-year-old brothers went to live with their father and stepmother. Their mother's second marriage lasted for six more months.

Manette was twenty-six and divorced when she became pregnant and had her first child, a girl. Two years later, when she was twenty-eight, she married a twenty-one-year-old sailor who had great influence over her. Manette was already insecure about her ability to bring up her daughter and concerned about the fact that her little girl would never know her real father. Now, here was a *third* man in Manette's life who apparently would have preferred that the girl be somewhere else. He worked on Manette's feelings of inferiority, confirming her own belief that she was not well suited for raising the girl and pointing out their low standard of living and the unlikelihood of improvement. Manette at first rejected the thought of giving her two-year-old daughter up for adoption, but later decided her husband's points were real. In her words, "I considered only my husband's opinions and I disregarded my own feelings." Within a matter of months, Manette signed adoption papers. Three years later, her husband divorced her. He felt he would never make any progress, financially, while being married and supporting a wife. Manette had not been working outside the home but had been earning some money by babysitting. Manette regrets having taken such a permanent step as relinquishing her daughter for adoption. She is always thinking that if she had simply put her in a foster home, she could have taken her back when she was ready. Most of all, though, she hates the self who was so badly influenced by a man, and tries to take comfort in the vision of her daughter leading a happy life. Manette is still not in a financially sound situation, so maybe her little girl is better off anyway. That is what she tells herself.

From the time Eugenie was thirteen, she had hoped to get pregnant so that she could get someone to marry her and she could feel secure. At sixteen, she succeeded in creating a pregnancy, but when she told the father about it, he married someone else. Eugenie dropped out of school and gave birth to a son, whom she kept. She went back to high school while her mother and a cousin babysat for her. After one year, Eugenie married a twenty-three-year-old laborer. He was a good provider, always kept a job, always brought money home. The couple had a son and a daughter together in a marriage that lasted twelve years. The good provider also liked to fight and argue and drink heavily. Eugenie "got sick and tired of it."

For three years, Eugenie and her three children lived together with no man in the house. Then Eugenie married again. The children were a major problem in the marriage. Once, in response to the children's complaints about their stepfather, Eugenie's first husband kept the children with him for three months. The children liked living with their father. That must have planted a seed in the mind of Eugenie's second husband; when he and Eugenie had what turned out to be their last fight about the children, he took the two youngest to their father again, this time for good. Eugenie let him do it, but her marriage endured only one year more. It had existed for a total of three years. Her oldest son, who was born out of wedlock, continues to live with his mother. He is fifteen now. His fourteen-year-old half-brother and eight-year-old half-sister are pleased with the arrangements, as is Eugenie. She feels she has better relationships with all her children now than she has ever had because she is finally able to relax a bit and enjoy them.

Three of these four women are not sorry about relinquishing custody, in spite of the fact that the second marriages which prompted the changes have ceased to exist. Perhaps mothers in this category feel less guilt because they are able to project it onto their second husbands, or perhaps there is another element which has not been unearthed, a motivation which has not reached the surface.

FATHER THE MORE NURTURING OR ESTABLISHED PARENT

The day I brought my first baby home from the hospital, my husband showed me how to change her diaper. He was immediately comfortable with her, confident in his handling of her. I felt as though I had a fielder's mitt on each hand. Bill had a brother fourteen years younger than himself for whom he used to be responsible much of the time, so of course he was more at ease with his own newborn than I. I had a sister five years younger, but I also had a sister five years older; she had taken care of the youngest. My mother had refused to let me babysit as a teen-ager; she projected her own deficiencies onto me and felt it carried more responsibility than I was capable of handling. The doctor who cared for me during pregnancy and delivered my baby was a general practitioner, the family doctor. He gave me no preparation whatever, not even the suggestion that I attend prenatal classes or read a book. It never occurred to me to prepare for the baby in anything but the "supplies" sense. A mother taking care of a baby, I assumed (to the degree that I thought about it at all), was a natural, automatic thing. I do not know if this was more a reflection of the times (1961–62) or of a need to keep the reality of the baby suppressed as long as possible. I hated nursing the baby;

natural is the last word I would use to describe how it felt to me. It was awkward and filled me with constant doubt about whether the baby was getting enough. My full breasts were painful. I had to relieve them with a hand pump in the middle of the night. I could not sleep on my stomach for the pain in my breasts or stand for my husband to touch me there. Still, these things were probably not the worst aspects of nursing; they were the things I complained about out loud. The worst thing about nursing, which I kept hidden, was the terrible feeling of forced intimacy. It felt as if a foreign creature had invaded a thin shield which protected me and was imposing intimacy on me, insisting that I allow it to suck what it needed out of me, to suck out of me what I did not have. It was revolting. When the revulsion, physical discomfort, and anxiety turned into daily crying, I had the doctor dry the milk in my breasts, and I fed the baby with a bottle. I never tried nursing again with either of my other two babies. My bad experience has seemed to me since a metaphor for my unsuitability to nurturing.

Four women in my study relinquished custody of their children primarily because they felt the children's fathers to be the more nurturing parents, the ones who participated in parental activities and fulfilled parental duties more easily. None of these absentee mothers, however, voices as strong a resistance to nurturing as I experienced when I first became a mother. Their feelings about mothering more closely resemble the sort of muted enthusiasm that I came to feel gradually over the years of child care. As I learned the mechanics that led to self-confidence, as my babies developed personalities I loved, my initial rebellion against maternal intimacy was diminished, but my husband was still the more clearly happy about being a parent. By virtue of this factor alone, he was the parent with whom the children could better prosper. I always knew this, but Shelley, one of the four women in this category, did not reach the conclusion until she had lived with her daughter for four years after her divorce:

I tried to keep my child, I think, more out of a sense of duty than any great maternal drives. But I also felt like I had to do something for me: finish school. I wanted a professional career, not just a bunch of jobs. So I was trying to work full time, go to school on a two-thirds schedule and raise my daughter. I was doing a bad job of all three; I was spread too thin. In a way, I knew all along that something had to give, but I couldn't figure out what it was possible to change. I had to work; we had to eat. I wouldn't quit school; it was too important to me. And I couldn't give up my daughter because I was too afraid of the possible emotional effects on her, and me, for that matter. I was totally saturated with the training that said a child should be with its mother.

So I tried to keep her for four years after the divorce, but the strain gradually increased. She was becoming a tremendous behavior problem because she was desperately trying to tear my attention away from my text books and because I was never much of a disciplinarian. She was turning into an obnoxious child with temper tantrums and breaking things and so on. Still I persisted.

When she started first grade, I realized that our lifestyle had to change somehow. I had been taking her to school with me at night, after they finally opened a child care center for night students. Before that, it was a constant hassle finding babysitters and nurseries that were open at night. I missed a lot of semesters because no child care was available. This created more resentment on my part. Even so, I had always felt bad about her "living in nurseries." Nothing tells the story better than what our schedule used to be: I would pick her up after work at her daytime nursery, we would stop at MacDonald's or some other quick cheap place and eat in the car while driving to school. Then I would leave her in the school nursery until whenever I would finish classes, usually about 10:30 P.M. When she started school, I felt this would have to stop. She needed regular, early hours and decent meals.

With this and the behavior problems and the constant exhortations from my ex-husband to let her come live with him, I finally gave in and relinquished custody. He loves her and really is a better parent than I am.

Rita, the mother of two boys, made her decision about relinquishing custody at the same time as she did about her divorce. She had never felt there was a choice about having children because of her adherence to the "unrealistic religious principles" of the Catholic church. Both her children were conceived accidentally while she and her husband practiced the rhythm method of contraception. She describes her feelings on the matter of motherhood:

I never felt that I wanted to have a baby. I could have gone all through my childbearing years, not had a baby and not felt unfulfilled. I don't find babies or children particularly enchanting.

So it was appropriate that Rita's sons live with their father. He was the nurturing parent, and he had his parents available to help take care of them. In addition, Rita believes the boys' father needs them for his own emotional well-being; besides, Rita intends to pursue a career that means possible long irregular hours and travel.

The one woman in the study who relinquished custody primarily because her husband was in a much more established and regularly predictable job echoes Rita's intention to pursue a career. Candy was, in effect, sharing custody of her four-year-old son with her former husband for the year following their divorce. The boy stayed fifteen days of each month with each parent. Candy began to feel that the constant shuffling around was unwise. There was also the uncertainty of her working hours even during "her" two weeks. She worked as a crisis counselor; she never knew when she might be needed. Her ex-husband had a nine-to-five job. Further reasons for a change in custody developed as well. Candy was offered a promotion that would involve additional responsibilities and make child care ever more complicated. Her former husband had remarried a woman Candy describes as "a very warm, caring person who enjoys being a parent." The stability available to Candy's little boy in the care of his established father and stepmother was undeniably in his best interest.

Ellen had not wanted any children early in her seventeen-year marriage. Sometimes she felt clearly that she and her husband could have been happy together without children. They had a son and a daughter, both conceived in spite of contraception. When Ellen left her husband and gave him custody, the children were fourteen and ten. Ellen felt their father to be a better and more involved parent, as well as a better homemaker than she. In addition, she worked nights and did not deny her husband's accusation of being a workaholic. Once again, there seems to be every reason for the father to maintain custody of the children—apart from society's opinion. Ellen's comments on child custody are ideally appropriate to close this section:

I see so many women struggling to survive because they feel they are the only ones who can raise their children. Often they are too exhausted to give the child the attention he needs. Maybe my way would be better for them. In today's society, fathers still make more money than mothers on the average. Why not let the parent with the financial ability shoulder the primary care and the other parent contribute time and what money they can. I think mothers would be better about keeping up their visitation than many fathers are and that they would feel less need to "entertain" the kids. They would be able to spend time with the children doing routine things. I truly believe this would be the best approach for the children, the mothers and the fathers.

I personally do not advocate such a complete reversal of our present child custody traditions. Awarding custody based on *any* rigid rule is not right. That children always belong with their mothers for biological reasons or that children always belong with their fathers for financial reasons are equally foolish proclamations. I do feel strongly, however, that we must consistently apply common sense to the child custody procedure. Each divorcing family needs to be considered individually. Most important to my concerns, which are for the emotional health of the absentee mother, custody arrangements must be made and accepted without judgmental overtones. Injustice and unkindness do not help society deal with trauma; they simply create more trauma. On both the societal and the personal levels, everyone will benefit when the absentee mother is perceived in an unemotional and impartial manner. And for the absentee mother, there will be the monumental relief of no longer having to explain and defend her maternal status.

The Absentee Mother's Sexual Mores

In Chapter 1 I used *Anna Karenina* to represent the stereotypical view of the absentee mother as sexually promiscuous; her negatively perceived sexual behavior occurred while she was a married woman. In the process of determining the real absentee mother's sexual mores, however, I feel a more sweeping approach than scrutiny of marital behavior is called for. In my experience, the application of the term *promiscuous* tends to communicate a belief on the part of the labeler that promiscuity is a permanent character trait rather than a temporary behavior. By reviewing the sexual mores of the absentee mothers in my study before, during, and after marriage, I will address this fallacy.

BEFORE MARRIAGE

I used to believe in a God who expected certain behavior of me, and in the Catholic church, which told me what God's expectations were. Sexual intercourse before marriage was a mortal sin; if one died in the state of mortal sin, one was doomed to spend eternity in hell. As a sexually blooming adolescent and as a single young woman, I avoided sexual intercourse with all the determination that eternal damnation inspired. When I met my husband-to-be, I was a virgin and remained so until a few weeks before our wedding.

Twenty (21 percent) of the absentee mothers in my study also remained virgins until they met their husbands-to-be.[7] An additional fifteen (16 percent) remained virgins until the actual wedding night. Nineteen (20 percent) engaged in premarital sex only with a man they expected to but did not marry.

The premarital sexual activity of seventeen absentee mothers does not fall into any of the above categories, but I would not consider them promiscuous. One woman experienced sexual intercourse on only one occasion before becoming involved with her husband-to-be. Two women had twice before taken part in premarital sex before meeting their husbands-to-be. One woman had been to bed with the same man three times before becoming engaged to her husband-to-be. One woman had been sexually involved with another girl from the time she was thirteen until she was sixteen. At sixteen, she was raped by a cousin and had no sexual involvement thereafter until she married. Twelve (13 percent) absentee mothers describe their sexual activity before marriage as sparse.

There should be little argument in light of current sexual behavior and attitudes that the women to whom I have just referred cannot be considered to have been promiscuous in their premarital sexual behavior. Although the prevailing social *norm* (in the sense of a societal standard) for premarital coitus in the United States remains moderately restrictive, prescribing chastity until marriage, prevailing sexual behavior has influenced some liberalization of the norm.[8] In other words, although premarital chastity is society's formal ideal, there are few sanctions against the increasing numbers who act counter to the ideal, so that an informal, more realistic expectation has developed, according to which the absentee mothers discussed here are well within our culture's parameters for premarital sexual behavior.

It should also be noted that the premarital sexual intercourse of most of the women in my sample converges with the *subculture* standard of "permissiveness-with-affection." Among young unmarried persons, it is acceptable for two persons to be intimately involved if they are emotionally attached to one another.[9] Thus, the absentee mothers in this study have been twice found innocent of premarital promiscuity, first by use of general cultural norms and then by their subculture's norms. Most important for their own well-being, neither do they see themselves as having been premaritally promiscuous.

DURING MARRIAGE

The term *adulteress* is a damning label; it separates a "cheating" wife from society at large. A woman who is unfaithful to her husband by way of a relationship with one man whom she loves or cares about is not literally promiscuous, however. The synonymous identification of adultery and promiscuity is not arrived at through reasoning but is based on a subconscious, automatic retaliatory response to societally offensive behavior. It is similar to instantly assuming that if a mother relinquishes custody of her children, she must be lusting after men, the former being the repugnant behavior which triggers the latter defamation.

I myself, during my nine-year marriage, lusted only in my heart. Even this consideration of infidelity existed simply due to the anger I felt at my husband for drinking. I fantasized often of punishing him by having affairs, but the closest I ever came to really doing it was having a drink with a co-worker or exchanging letters with a former high school sweetheart. Whenever the opportunity for infidelity arose, I felt disgusted by it. I felt I would not be punishing Bill by it so much as I would be demeaning myself. And I did not feel any sexual desire for these men; I really still loved my husband, which only created all the more anger, frustration, and despair on my part.

Similar stories among the absentee mothers in my study, marital stories full of justification for infidelity, astonished me when I learned that fifty-nine (62 percent) of the ninety-five women being considered in this section had remained faithful to their husbands all during their marriages.[10] I felt this was a "good showing." Then I found that Alfred Kinsey's 1953 study, *Sexual Behavior in the Human Female*, showed that, by the age of forty, of the 2,480 women in the study who had ever married, there was a fidelity rate of 74 percent. This, obviously, would indicate a higher rate of infidelity (38 percent) among my absentee mothers than among married women at large (26 percent). However, there are factors that suggest Kinsey's study no longer accurately reflects American female sexual behavior.

First, the Kinsey study is almost thirty years old and continues to be used as the major indicator of female sexual behavior simply because no one has undertaken a study of its magnitude and structure since. It is still the best empirical data available. It is not likely, however, that sexual behavior among women has remained unchanged since 1953. (In fact, Kinsey's data was collected before 1953, and so reflects a data base perhaps closer to forty years old.)

A few later studies, although smaller and less representatively structured than Kinsey's, suggest that extramarital coitus has, indeed, been increasing among females since 1953. Bell, Turner, and Rosen of Temple University, for instance, conducted a study among 2,262 married women in 1975.[11] They found an increased incidence of extramarital coitus (when variant data was equalized with Kinsey's), and they stressed the fact that rates of incidence were clearly linked to age (among other things).

Bell cast his statistics in terms of the average age of his participants—34.5, (compared to 36 among the absentee mothers in my study). In Kinsey's study, we do not know the average age of the women who had been married at one time or another. Kinsey presents his data on extramarital coitus under the rubric, "by the time they were forty." Thus, in order to compare results between Kinsey's, Bell's, and my data on extramarital coitus, it is necessary to project the Bell and absentee mother average participant ages to Kinsey's reference age of forty. We cannot say what rate of extramarital coitus has occurred among my participants by the time they were forty, since some of them have not yet reached that age, so we project their ages and their mathematically predictable rate of extramarital coitus (as determined in the Bell study).[12] We are thus able to compare what Bell suggests is the current rate of extramarital coitus to Kinsey's 1940s rate and, in turn, compare the rate of the same behavior among my absentee mothers. When this projection of age is complete and the rate of extramarital behavior among specific age groups is taken into account, the rate of extramarital coitus in Bell's group is between 40 percent and 50 percent.

This places the infidelity rate of 38 percent among my absentee mothers lower than among the currently married women at large (if the Bell study is representative). In other words, it seems reasonable to assert that the absentee mothers in my study were at least as faithful as married women in general today.

In an effort to be more precise about the marital situations that encouraged extramarital affairs among my absentee mothers, I have considered specific mitigating factors that were present for thirty of the thirty-six women in my study who experienced extramarital coitus (see Table 6).

Among the six women in my study who were unfaithful to their husbands simply out of curiosity, the felt need for variation, or emotional confusion, four were involved with only one man (see Table 7). The absentee mother who was married for sixteen years had been intimate with one man, one time during the first fifteen of her married years; only in the last year of her marriage did she involve herself with others "a few" times. Her behavior was reflective of the emotional upset and confusion accompanying the ending of a marriage. The absentee mother who was married for nine years had a keen awareness of sexuality and felt the need for a highly active sex life. For the first three years of her marriage, her husband provided her with this. They had a "very active and pleasurable" sex life together. She was not extramaritally involved during those three years. When her husband reduced his level of sexual activity with her to "moderately active," she initiated "moderately active" extramarital activity. When sexual activity with her husband became sparse, she started participating in more extramarital coitus than ever and was finally exposed by a detective her husband had hired. For the next three years, this woman lived a celibate life within her marriage and without. In her words, "I didn't want anyone near me" during that time. When her repugnance for sexual activity dissipated, she ended her marriage.

Returning to the main body of absentee mothers, who maintained fidelity throughout their marriages, one observes women unhappy in their marital beds but faithful to a perceived duty to remain monogamous. The result is anger, cynicism, bitterness and, ultimately, divorce. It is interesting to read the individual sexual situations. The complaints include planned sexual activity ("I didn't feel that sex on Tuesdays and Saturdays was very spontaneous") and include sexual encounters too quickly ended or too prolonged:

Sex with my husband lasted all of two minutes.

My husband had read all the books that said foreplay was the most essential ingredient of sexual activity. This is not to say that he was very good at it but to say that a minimum of three hours before the actual act of intercourse would be involved with hugging and kissing—on the lips only. By the time we got to intercourse, I had become excited and unexcited and, frankly, exhausted more than once. After a full day, I did not want a three-hour sexual encounter.

There are also complaints of infrequent orgasm:

I thought sex would be great, but I experienced orgasm so rarely that I kind of gave up. I couldn't communicate my desires, and anger built up over the years so that sex was largely a mechanical duty "for him."

I had one orgasm in the entire thirteen years I was married. My husband and I must have been among the more ignorant adults around.

Infrequency of intercourse is also high on the list of complaints. One woman who described her rate of sexual activity as sparse was married to a professional military man. They were separated for very long periods of time, sometimes a year or more, yet she never became sexually involved with anyone else. Another woman, who had a very short marriage of one year as a result of infrequent intercourse, says that she and her husband had made love only three times in that year. "We couldn't communicate," she says. One wife whose sexual relations with her husband went from sparse to nonexistent explains:

During pregnancy and nursing, I had little sex drive and many infections, which made it painful; but then my husband stopped having energy for sex, as he put it, when he "began to assume responsibilities."

Another wife who experienced a very low frequency of sexual activity with her husband tells how it happened in her case:

My husband was very much the loner type, with many hobbies which isolated him from me: model railroads, tropical fish, voracious reading, etc. I always felt he was putting something between us. I was wanting more of a sexual relationship, but if I was obviously interested in sex he would be turned off. So I had to act disinterested and somewhere along the line, if I were lucky, he would become turned on and want sex. But it wasn't very often and it wasn't very satisfying. There just wasn't very much going on between us at any kind of emotional level. The mad, sexual passion part of the relationship ended with the marriage, literally. Interestingly, the sexual part of the relationship picked up just prior to my leaving and shortly after my leaving, but then it was too late.

The most dramatic case is of a wife who had no sexual intercourse for eleven years of her marriage:

My husband and I ceased having any sexual relations at all after the conception of our third child. In order to understand why I tolerated this, you have to understand that all my life I have been fighting a problem of extremely low self-regard. At first, I bought new nightgowns and things like that, but—nothing. For me, this was the ultimate rejection. I was too afraid to verbalize anything for fear of actually getting from my husband the answer I dreaded. Anyway, I had been brought up to feel that many marriages were like this, and since I had one I just had to accept it. Only many years later did I realize I had alternatives.

AFTER DIVORCE

Unfortunately, there is little data in the area of postmarital sexual behavior. Even Kinsey's study dealt only briefly with the sexual behavior of the previously married woman, and in a study conducted as late as 1970, the information used to draw previously undrawn conclusions is still anywhere from twenty-five to forty-two years old.

It is odd that our society prescribes the same sexual behavior for divorced and widowed women as it does for premarital women: total abstinence. Society has placed itself in a dilemma that cannot be resolved without devaluing the institution of marriage. Society's insistence that sexual intercourse is good and necessary only within the structure of marriage seems to me primarily oriented toward controlling the premarital situation: to prevent illegitimate pregnancy and to set marriage up as the only acceptable outlet to those of child-producing age. The same social control over the sexuality of the postmarried is not so essential. The postmarried have had the edge taken off their sexual needs through regular satisfaction and hormone stabilization; they are knowledgeable about birth control, and a large part of their social function within marriage has probably already been fulfilled: they have produced their children—legitimately. Society does not dare make the necessary distinction for fear that the approval of coitus outside marriage for any group might lead to every group asking, "Why get married?" The vision of mass rejection of marriage is frightening to Americans because they believe that their entire social structure rests on the foundation of marriage.

Combined with the fact that there is much less need to control postmarital sexuality, society also finds itself telling a person who has become accustomed to regular sexual release in coitus that the sexual "habit" is no longer an inalienable adult right. Society does not really *expect* the postmarried to return to premarital abstinence, but pretends it does, ignoring the dilemma rather than risking the changes necessary to eliminate it. Men face little if any strictures; women, as always, are subject to different expectations and responses. Society only partially accepts a woman's postmarital sexual behavior.

Even so, in the area of *post*marital coitus, women have been going contrary to the norm established for them to a larger extent than in other areas. The 632 white females in Paul Gebhard's study, "Postmarital Coitus Among Widows and Divorcees" (interviewed between 1939 and 1956), showed an 82 percent rate of postmarital coitus among divorcees.[13] But 82 percent is considerably less than the almost 100 percent male postmarital coitus rate.[14] For her inferior rate of assertion, the divorcée is recklessly decreed "promiscuous," while the divorced male receives a wink.

The incidence of postmarital coitus among my absentee mothers is 95 percent. In my opinion, this does not reflect a 13 percent higher incidence among my absentee mothers than among divorced women at large. Rather, I believe it reflects, once again, the age of the women in this study, as well as social changes. Data used to establish the 82 percent incidence of postmarital coitus among divorced women in general are a generation old.

It is interesting to note here that the difference found earlier between Kinsey's older extramarital figure of 26 percent and Bell's more recent extramarital figure of 40 percent (minimum) is 14 percent. Could it be that the 13 percent difference between the older Gebhard postmarital incidence and the postmarital incidence among my absentee mothers is a coincidental rate of increase? Conceivably not. I believe that my absentee mothers' higher rate of postmarital coitus may indicate changing behavior at large.

Further indication that my absentee mothers' postmarital coitus rate is typical and not promiscuous may be taken from the following:

(1) Gebhard's study discloses that "the largest proportion of divorced women having coitus occurs from ages thirty-one to forty." Of the 632 women in Gebhard's study, 36 percent were between the ages of thirty-one and forty.

(2) Of the 94 women under consideration in my absentee mother study, 49 percent were then between the ages of thirty-one and forty, a difference of 13 percent.[15]

This suggests that the difference between Gebhard's group postmarital rate of 82 percent and my group postmarital rate of 95 percent may substantially be due to the comparative overrepresentation of the most sexually active age group in my study, not a higher incidence of postmarital coitus among absentee mothers than among divorced women in general.

Another important factor in Gebhard's study suggests the rate of postmarital coitus among my absentee mothers may be misleadingly high. The Gebhard study points out that, among the women who had postmarital coitus and remarried, almost all experienced a portion of that sexual activity with their husbands-to-be. This tends to reduce the level of "wrongdoing" and the possibility of promiscuity. A typical period spent with a husband-to-be before marriage seems to be about one year. Exactly half (47) of the absentee mothers considered here have remarried. Nineteen of them remarried within one year, ten more within two years, which lends weight to the suspicion that many (at least) of those who remarried did not have numerous sexual partners in their postmarital sexual activity. I use the word *suspicion* because my data does not allow me to determine sexual activity levels more precisely. The absentee mother questionnaire, unfortunately, did not ask specifically for frequency of coitus or for numbers of partners. It has been well established, however, that women show a marked preference for sexual involvement with one man over a longer period of time than with a number of men for shorter periods.

3

The Full Pull of Gravity:
The Absentee Mother's Childhood

*It was all happening in a great, swooping free fall, irreversible,
free of decision, in the full pull of gravity toward whatever was to
be.*

—Laura Z. Hobson, Consenting Adult

Mothers Who Were Absentee Mothers

My own mother was an absentee mother. I never thought of it that
way before now, but she was. I was not the one who was sent
away, but my little sister, Vicky, five years younger than I, who
had been born after my mother and father separated. When Vicky
reached her first birthday, she was sent to live with my mother's
brother and his wife. It had been obvious even to a five-year-old
that, although everyone was invariably charmed by my little
round-faced, curly-headed sister, my mother felt her to be an
irritation, an additional burden atop her factory job and me. My
ten-year-old sister was not, as far as I could see, part of my
mother's burden; she cleaned and cooked and took care of the
baby. I thought she was a grownup. I think my mother thought so

too, but she was, nevertheless, overjoyed when my older sister chose to enter the convent at fourteen. My mother really wanted to be rid of us all.

Vicky lived with our aunt and uncle and their son of my age for only one year. By then, my mother's brother had started pressing her to let them adopt my sister. My mother confided years later that she really wanted to let Johnny and Eleanor do it, but "what would people say?" I remember, too, in the years following Vicky's return (and especially following my older sister's departure for the convent), my mother would periodically threaten to send us to an orphanage because she "couldn't take it any more." She discussed it with our parish priest, but he shamed her out of doing it.

I do not recall ever feeling dependent on my mother. The first day of kindergarten, for instance, I walked the five or six blocks by myself, found my way to the proper classroom, and was utterly amazed at the scene of mass hysteria I encountered there. I could not fathom why all my classmates were crying and clutching at their mothers' skirts, or why their mothers were so loathe to leave them. I was intrigued by the relationship. The only thing which intrigued me more and over a much longer period was that phrase of my mother's, that she "couldn't take it any more." What could be so hard about living with me and my sisters? Everyone said we were so good. For that matter, what had been so hard about her living with my father? He was so much fun. I concluded that she, too, was silly and made no sense. Not until I became a mother myself did I begin to understand what my mother had meant, not only about mothering but also about living with an alcoholic.

As those who have read Nancy Friday's *My Mother, My Self* may agree, daughters tend to be more like their mothers than not in many ways. Psychologists tell us that we relive our own infant and childhood relationships to our mothers when we become mothers ourselves. If our mothers felt negatively toward us as babies, it is likely that we will feel similar emotions toward our own babies. One might say that our reactions to maternity are preordained by our mothers' reactions to maternity. To the extent that we are unaware of this subconscious inheritance or incapable of neutralizing it when it is negative, we are more likely to be adversely affected, or even sometimes controlled by it. The pain or rejection and neglect that I harbored from my own childhood created within me a heartfelt resolve that *my* children would never have to feel that pain. But one day I, too, heard myself shrieking in my mother's voice, "I can't take it any more."

Eighteen of the hundred women in my study had mothers who were actually absentee mothers.[1] An additional eight had mothers who were absentee mothers in effect. That is, in one way or another, the mothers withdrew from actively raising their daughters in spite of the fact that they may have lived under the same roof with them. The mothers of another eight women in my group died while my participants were children. (The death of a parent is frequently experienced by the child as desertion.) A total of thirty-four participants (or in a few cases, their siblings) were raised, in part or in whole, by someone other than their mothers. That represents one-third of the group. In one case it was even possible to trace the pattern of absentee motherhood one generation further, to the grandmother of my participant. This participant, interestingly, is the "double" absentee mother who relinquished custody of two sons to their two different fathers. The discovery of this third generation of absentee motherhood was strictly incidental, so it is not possible to say whether the rest of the study group has any similar history. Let us look in some detail, however, at some of the circumstances that made absentee mothers of my participants' mothers.

When Manette was an infant, her parents divorced and her mother placed her in a foster home for four years. Manette did not say what prompted her mother to take this step; she may not know. However, as the mother of her own daughter years later, in a troubled marriage with a man who was not her daughter's father, Manette gave her daughter up for adoption. Was she, in part, rejecting her daughter the way she herself had felt rejected by her own mother?

Three of my participants' mothers were unable to raise their daughters due to mental illness. Eugenie's mother was "weak-minded" as she put it, incapable of caring for her seven children (by various fathers). There was no father present, so four of Eugenie's sisters and brothers were raised by various aunts, uncles and cousins; she and two of her siblings were raised by her maternal grandmother. Felice and Robin, in similar circumstances, were taken care of by their fathers. Felice's mother was mentally ill from the time Felice was eight, was not hospitalized, but drugged most of the time in the incapacitating way that is often avoidable now. Felice says that when not drugged, her mother was raving and did not get better until Felice reached nineteen. Robin's mother was at first only unassertive and markedly turned inward. When Robin was about ten, however, her mother became disoriented and confused. She lost her memory, and by the time Robin was fifteen, she had been diagnosed as prematurely senile, and died at the age of forty-eight.

To some degree, even today, mental illness is often perceived as a weakness, an inability to confront the rigors of the world. Such was certainly the case two, three, and four decades ago when my absentee mothers were growing up. Eugenie, Felice, and Robin, I believe, perceived their mothers' mental conditions as voluntary withdrawal, weakness. Thus it is noteworthy that all three relinquished custody of their children under coercive circumstances. When Eugenie relinquished custody of her three children to their father, her first husband, it was as a result of continual confrontation with her second husband, who refused to adjust to her children. In the end, she could not prevail. I believe she may have been identifying with her own mother's "weakness." Felice was one of the group discussed in Chapter 2 who relinquished custody in fear of their children's fathers and the threats they were making. She was intimidated into it, beaten in a contest of will and power. She was as ineffective as her mother had been in her contest of will with her own mind. Robin was ordered by the court to give her three daughters to their father.

Four of the absentee mothers in my study were adopted at birth and never knew their natural mothers. One of them later gave her child up for adoption. Another of these four felt twice rejected because her adoptive mother did not raise her either; household help did all the parenting. Darlene, a fifth absentee mother in my group, was also adopted, but not until she was eight years old. Her earlier childhood was a dizzying confusion of loss and hurt, as her mother had died when she was two and her father promptly deserted her and her two siblings. She and her sister and brother lived with an aunt for a year before her father reappeared, only to put the two girls in an orphanage while keeping his son (a powerful message about the value of being female). For the next five years, Darlene lived in the orphanage with her sister until she was adopted by a family, but then she had to leave her sister behind.

Jenny had six brothers and sisters and a mother who worked to support them all; her father was an alcoholic. When Jenny was eight years old, her mother put her into foster care where she remained for seven years with a foster mother she says detested her. The woman also hated Jenny's family, who lived on the same block all the while Jenny was in her care. Even though her real family was so near, Jenny was permitted to visit them only on special occasions. Christmas was the one occasion Jenny can recall that was lofty enough to qualify:

I was virtually a prisoner of the backyard, and it was unusual for any other kids to want to stay back there to play. I was not permitted to play "out front" with the neighbor kids . . . In my teens, I couldn't stay after school for sports and had to practically get an act of Congress to be allowed to go to a dance . . . My foster mother kept me only for the added income it brought, and her hatred grew worse and more apparent as she grew older and "talked to herself" out loud. I could hear her in another room preparing her accusations, criticisms and arguments . . . Finally, at fifteen, she somehow convinced the Welfare Department that I was pregnant, which was not true. They came to school and took me to a Catholic home for wayward girls. They never even told my parents I was there. Nine months later to the day, I was released to my grandfather, but that didn't work either. Then I moved in with an older sister for a while.

Eventually, Jenny came full circle and returned to her biological mother—until her mother got drunk one day and kept telling Jenny there was something wrong with her, that she couldn't get along anywhere, and that she couldn't afford to keep Jenny with her anyway. This blatant and repetitious maternal rejection had its impact. Jenny says she left and "became wild and promiscuous." She also became pregnant, unsuccessfully attempted suicide, bore a son, and gave him up for adoption after a year. She duplicated the action of both her natural and foster mothers. When her eventual marriage ended, she tolerated her husband's taking their son.

Just as the image of separated mothers and children was placed in my own subconscious by watching my sister being sent away by my mother, four women in my study also watched or knew of their mothers letting brothers or sisters go. The places these siblings were sent usually seemed vague to the sister at home, and the children involved were usually lost to one another forever. Gloria's mother had three daughters from a first marriage, Gloria's half-sisters. The four girls did not live together; two of Gloria's half-sisters lived with their father and had done so from the time of the divorce. Ilona's mother had given birth to a daughter out of wedlock but had kept the child until she met Ilona's father and became pregnant with Ilona. At that point, she gave her first daughter to the child's maternal grandmother to raise and married Ilona's father.

The other two cases of sibling relinquishment involve participants' brothers. Although I do not believe the gender of the relinquished sibling necessarily has much to do with the image implanted in the subconscious, to the extent that it does it is probably more a matter of degree to which the image has meaning rather than whether it has any meaning. Presumably a sister identifies more strongly with a sister than with a brother, and perhaps also more strongly with a full sibling than a half-sibling. At any rate, Clarice's parents divorced when she was an infant, and her only brother (she had no sisters) went to live with his father. Brother and sister did not meet again until they were both in their twenties. In Cissy's case, her mother relinquished a son by a first marriage to his paternal grandparents after her husband's death in the Korean War. What makes Cissy's case different from the other three discussed here, and from mine, is that she herself later experienced her half-brother's fate. When Cissy turned thirteen, she was sent to live with an aunt. The reasons for this are unclear, but Cissy's three younger sisters were kept at home, so there were no doubt elements of "why me?" involved in Cissy's reactions.

The hackneyed suggestion of things being easier the second time around may well apply to the mother's action. Once a person has done something, even something basically unpleasant, he or she is more likely to do that something again. And when eighteen of my absentee mothers, whose own mothers had relinquished them or a sibling, relinquished custody of their children, they proved that this phenomenon can be true of families as well as individuals (as has proven true regarding divorce, for instance). Further, as sixteen additional absentee mothers in my study seem to indicate, even skewed or mistaken perceptions of living arrangements or death of the mother can be turned into the next generation's reality of absentee motherhood.

Mothers Who Were Perceived as Absentee Mothers

"I feel I never really had a mother," Liz said. "She didn't know how to be a mother and she was very passive and never stood up against Dad for herself or us kids."

"My mother was never home; she worked," Belle told me. Her parents had divorced when she was five and her mother had remarried, but Belle and her two brothers and two sisters hated their stepfather. Even when Belle's mother was at home, Belle felt strongly that her mother was not available to her, that she gave of herself only to her new husband, not to her children. "I always felt we were in the way," she said.

Sonia was sent to boarding school when she was nine. Before then, she had a nursemaid whom she feels she was raised by. The nursemaid and her grandparents had lived with Sonia and her mother from the time Sonia was six months old, when her father had died. Sonia's mother was a professional woman and worked because she loved to work, not for financial reasons; there was family money. Sonia says, "I think she also loved me as long as she didn't have the full responsibility." But Sonia felt deprived when she saw her mother "around" only on weekends, and she was miserable in boarding school.

Katra describes her mother as a child, emotionally incapable of mothering, very much like the mother in *Autumn Sonata*.

It was devastating. There was no emotional support or concern—only rejection. She showed no interest in me whatever except when I wanted something from her; then her response was, "Go away!" Her anger and rage when I needed from her were unbearable. I believe I stopped asking or expecting anything from my mother when I was about three or four.

Katra's early resignation coincided with her parents divorcing and then additional proof of her mother's inability to sustain and nurture her children. The fatherless family of four moved in with the maternal grandparents who, it turned out, also perceived their daughter as a child. "My grandparents never considered my mother capable of doing anything in an adult manner," Katra tells us. A woman not perceived as an adult is not likely to be seen as a mother. Katra saw her withdrawn mother, who not only lived with her but remained out of the workforce for most of Katra's childhood, as no mother at all.

Holly's mother did not work outside the home either, yet Holly is also one of the absentee mothers in my study who felt as a child that she did not have a mother. Her parents married later than most, so Holly's mother was thirty-eight when Holly (who was followed two years later by a sister) was born. Holly feels that her mother's age was somehow related to her negative attitude toward parenting. Regardless of the actual reasons, Holly sounds quite sure that her mother had children only because it was a social expectation. Why else would she have them and then "relegate all the responsibility involved," as Holly puts it, to hired help? "She hired anyone who would work cheaply to raise us," says Holly, and although her mother expected Holly and her sister to be model children, the people to whom she gave the task of molding such children "weren't very bright and were totally inadequate."

One of the absentee mothers in this group of eight seems neither to perceive her mother as having been absent nor to feel anger toward her as the others do. I have included her because her mother sent her five hundred miles from home to a boarding school for two years. I believe the image is significant and that the way Gretchen refers to it indicates the way she understands it now rather than the way she might have experienced it then:

My mother was troubled by my changes; she could never relate to my wild energy. I think she was afraid for me.

This is a sophisicated analysis of her mother's action, and, in my opinion, not likely to have been the response of a high school sophomore who has been sent far away to an environment meant to control her "wiid energy."

The two remaining mothers who were perceived as absentee mothers were also single parents, one a widow, the other divorced. They were forced to hold jobs for financial reasons, but this does not seem to have had much impact on their daughters' feelings of abandonment. In one case, the girl perceived her grandmother as the person who attempted to fulfill her needs; in the other case, my participant and her mother lived with the mother's sister, whom the girl saw as the day-to-day parent. "My mother turned the responsibility over to her sister," Lilly rather sadly asserts.

Rollo May has pointed out a pronounced difference in emotional response to parental treatment between children of the lower classes and those of the middle classes.[2] Children raised in a lower-class environment appear able to tolerate with fewer emotional scars uncaring, distracted, or even abusive parents. May suggests that this apparent difference in perception of parental actions can be accounted for by an inherently different set of expectations held by the two classes of children. Among the eight participants who perceived their mothers as absentee mothers, three were raised in upper-middle-class environments, two in middle-class families, and three in working-class families. Those from the working class may have adopted certain middle-class attitudes to the extent that they were not totally segregated from the middle class. Their middle-class expectations, circa 1940s and 1950s, played an important role in their feelings of abandonment when their mothers were not primary and full-time caretakers.

The absentee mothers in my study, at the median age of 35.5, were raised in a generation when society expected wives and mothers to be full-time homemakers and home-bound mothers. Children are strongly impressed by such societal expectations. The women in my study who perceived their mothers as absentee mothers because they were working were responding to expectations of the time. I believe children's expectations of their mothers have changed and continue to change. Working mothers are simply the way it is now. Many mothers my age (the same category as my participants) still feel guilt when they go out to work because they are having a difficult time convincing themselves that the social values of their childhoods are no longer in place. But the children of these mothers, who have been socialized within the current set of values, apparently do not feel deprived because their mothers work. More than half of their friends' mothers work too. Assuming that children of absentee mothers do feel deprived even in the midst of today's eclectic culture, they are likely to be the last generation of children to feel that way about it if fathers with custody become more common. There is good reason, however, to believe that children of divorcing parents, while suffering a great deal due to the divorce itself, essentially feel it does not matter which parent has custody.[3]

Mothers Who Died

Few departures can match death for impact. It is abrupt even when preceded by protracted illness. It is absolute. Its impact is intensified by children's limited ability to perceive that they have no causative effect on the event. They ask themselves, "What did I do to make my mother die?" or "Why did my mother want to leave me?" It is difficult for them to comprehend that their mothers had no choice in the matter. Children also know that they are incapable of fulfilling their own needs and that they are suddenly bereft of perhaps the only person who was obviously committed to doing so for them. They concomitantly fear that the remaining parent, if there is one, will also disappear.

Eight mothers of women in my study died while their daughters were children. This is twelve times higher than usual.[4] Although it is always traumatic for a girl to experience the death of her mother, peripheral circumstances may heighten that trauma. These eight little girls drew bad cards. In six of the eight cases, the girl whose mother died was left the only female in the household: three of them were only children left with their fathers; the other three were left with brothers and fathers. This is one of the most difficult family constellations for a girl who has lost her mother to face, especially in her early childhood.[5] The median age at which my participants lost their mothers was seven. Remnants of the Oedipal experience may cause the girl to feel guilty; she has won not only her father but all the males in the household. She is also terrified by her perception that it is suddenly she who is to keep all of these males happy, by herself, without a model to give her cues. It is impossible, of course, for children to replace a parent, but they desperately try to do so. The years spent trying bring continual pain; their inevitable failure can effect their entire adult lives.

In one of the two cases where my participants had sisters when their mothers died, the sister was four years younger, so her situation was similar to the other six. Although the presence of a sister and the absence of brothers probably reduced the pressure for this girl, as the oldest girl she also was in a classic position to feel she must replace her mother and yet not be able to do so. Indeed, in a brief description of herself as a child, one senses her frustration at attempting to duplicate her outgoing, attractive mother.

I was unhappy and insecure and I felt I was unattractive; I was fat.

Her feeling of failure may have been confirmed when her father died just one year after her mother. She had failed so utterly that her father died for lack of what he needed.

Thus, the women whose mothers died may have carried two subconscious images that contributed to their becoming absentee mothers: one of the "deserting" mother, the other of inability to fulfill that same role of mother and wife.

Fathers Who Died or Were Absent

My own father died when I was, chronologically, an adult. Emotionally, I was a pathetic five-year-old. I had lost my father the first time when I was *really* five, when my mother "threw him out," as she loved to boast. That was the time in which my subconscious had chosen to stay. I was passionately in love with my father, refusing to see his faults, glorifying his every characteristic, clinging to a treacherous cliff of possibly false conviction and desperate hope that he *did* love me. Never mind that I rarely saw him, that he seemed oblivious to my existence after the divorce, that he had married again and had new children who held his interest. I held with ferocity the long-ago visions that proved how he really felt about me: the horsey-back rides to bed, our late winter suppers alone when I had waited for him to get home while my mother and sister had eaten earlier, the way he cried once while he held me on his lap. I was still in the full flush of attempting to gratify my Oedipal love when my father died at fifty-eight; I was thirty-one. The last time I saw him in the hospital, he was sitting up in bed. When I walked into the room, he turned to look at me and immediately broke into tears. I hugged him while he cried, and I felt that he was crying because he had to leave me in just a few days. I remembered that it was the very same reason he had cried the first time, when he and my mother were separating. He *did* love me.

That was two years after I had relinquished my children and left my husband in a blind lurch toward dealing with the child in me. But wonderful as the final visit with my father was, it did not mitigate my Oedipal complex. It seemed that now, when he had finally given me a sign, when he seemed on the edge of fulfilling my need for him, he had also withdrawn—now more profoundly than ever. I could not face his wake or funeral; to see him dead would have meant admitting he was dead.

In one of the very few studies that focuses on the absentee mother, a 1975 doctoral dissertation suggests that there may be a higher than usual level of Oedipal strivings among noncustodial mothers.[6] Based on the very generalized data having to do with the participants' family relationships, one group of absentee mothers displays some preliminary signs of marked Oedipal involvement: the seventeen women who experienced a parent's death while they were children. (There are also cases of possible Oedipal strivings among the participants whose parents divorced and mothers had custody, although the indications are not as marked in that category.) Evidentally, the loss of a father for an Oedipally unresolved girl, whether it is to death or divorce, heightens the girl's longing. It is less complex, after all, to idealize an absent figure. Nothing can inspire greater passion than a distant, seemingly unattainable love object. There is also evidence that points to exaggerated involvement with fathers on the part of girls whose mothers have died.

Fathers of nine women in my study died while my participants were children. Like the maternal death rate, this number represents a much higher than average occurrence among men of their generation—*ten times higher* in this case.[7] The median age of my participants at the time of losing their fathers was seven. Among the women who had lost their mothers, five out of eight felt that, overall, their childhoods had been happy. Among those whose fathers had died, only three of nine could say the same. This suggests that, among the absentee mothers who suffered the loss of a parent, the loss of a father might have had a more negative impact than the loss of a mother; but many additional factors would have to be considered before any such conclusion could be clearly confirmed.

I should point out that this group stands out from the participants in general as well as within itself. Among the whole group of one hundred, there is a nearly equal split between those who had happy childhoods and those who did not (fifty-two experienced their childhoods as unhappy, forty-eight as happy). Thus, the marked contrast between the two groups whose parents died is all the more suspicious. One is inclined to ask not only why there is a significant difference in perceived childhood happiness between those who have lost a mother to death and those who have lost a father to death but also why those women who have lost a mother express a meaningfully higher rate of childhood happiness than those who have never experienced the death of either parent. Electra's satisfaction leaps into mind. That women whose fathers died express a much higher rate of unhappiness than those who have never experienced the loss of either parent through death would not seem unreasonable or abnormal in and of itself. One would expect the same emotional difference among mother-loss participants, however; finding the opposite triggers the notion of Oedipal pathology.

The picture that emerges when they categorize the relationships they had with their parents further supports the suggestion of Oedipal strivings among the seventeen women under discussion. When the hundred participants are considered as a whole, positive and negative relationships with both mothers and fathers are, again, almost exactly even.[8] However, when the seventeen in the parent-death group are considered separately, a father-love/mother-hate dichotomy seems present for additional reasons. Perhaps the most significant point is that not one member of the group expressed ambivalance about her relationship to her father. No one described her relationship with her father as mixed or even neutral. Such clear-cut perceptions of a relationship are often reason to suspect some departure from reality, and, in the cases of *purely* positive relationships, the kind of paternal idealization that occurs in the Electra version of the Oedipal triad. Equally important here, three times more participants felt they had positively good relationships with their fathers than felt that way about their mothers. Only two women of the seventeen could say they had positive relationships with their mothers. Only three women said they had negative relationships with their fathers. Twice as many women in this group refused to respond to what sort of relationship they had with their mothers as failed to do so regarding their fathers. Were they avoiding negative feelings toward their mothers and the related guilt by ignoring the question? Were the others avoiding lingering incestuous feelings toward their fathers?

I believe the matter deserves further investigation, since the work accomplished to date is extremely limited. My study brings up the question for a second time in the course of only four airings. The other two bring up the question of Oedipal strivings but, unlike the 1975 paper, report no deviance.[9]

Divorced Parents

As children, the absentee mothers in my study lived with divorce to a staggering degree. The power of their parents divorcing almost assuredly had greater negative effects than the same occurrence would have on a child today, when one of every three marriages ends in divorce. Now the primary source of pain comes from the personal aspects of the situation; social disapproval has diminished. Raised during a two-decade period that produced anywhere from a low of 8 divorces to a high of 18 divorces per 1,000 marriages, however, the women in my study come from different circumstances indeed.[10] Their parents divorced at the rate of 230 per 1,000 marriages,[11] a rate thirteen times higher than the married population at large. Almost 80 percent of those whose parents divorced said they had unhappy childhoods, although they did not always attribute their unhappiness to the divorce.

I experienced my childhood as something much heavier than mere unhappiness, and I do see the primary source as being my parents' divorce. At school, I pretended that nothing had happened. I regularly told stories about the things I did with my father, the places he took me and the toys or dresses he bought me. As the time of day for catechism would approach I began to feel anxious and tense. Then I listened in horror to the tenets that said divorce was a mortal sin.

Although Catholicism played such an influential role in my development and made my parents' divorce more difficult for me, I found no similar connection among my participants between unhappy childhoods, divorced parents, and Catholicism. One-third of the eighteen women who had both divorced parents and unhappy childhoods were Catholic. However, this ratio of childhood Catholicism corresponds closely to the level of childhood Catholicism in the study group as a whole (28 percent).[12] Since only 19 percent of the general populaton at the time were Catholic,[13] there is a higher than average prevalence of Catholicism in my group, but this may be meaningless. The Census figure of 19 percent is based upon church membership, whereas my figure of 28 percent is based upon religious beliefs held. Only further studies of the absentee mother can help resolve this issue.

It is important to stress that the high incidence of parental divorce is causatively related to absentee motherhood in several ways. First, that one is more likely to divorce if one's parents have divorced is well established, and since in most cases a woman's divorce must exist before the possibility of absentee motherhood can exist, this is the initial contribution of parental divorce to absentee motherhood. In addition, a child of divorce is more subject to emotional maladjustment even into adulthood and thereby harbors a greater risk of inability to parent well. Finally, like F. O. Keller, I believe that significant numbers of absentee mothers (especially concentrated in the father-death category and less densely visible in the mother-custody divorce group)[14] exhibit unresolved Oedipal strivings which contribute to their becoming absentee mothers.[15] As children, they wished to live with their fathers with no interference from their mothers. Obviously, in cases of parental divorce and the most common mother-custody arrangement, this wish was made all the more unattainable and exacerbated the Oedipal strivings. When divorcing their husbands, my participants gave their children what they had never been able to attain for themselves—life with their fathers with no competition from their mothers.

Parental Attitudes

Parental roles are an obvious factor to be analyzed in absentee mothers' childhoods, given the theme of imagery and imitation I have pursued. Keller reported that the noncustodial mothers in her study tended to perceive their fathers as the more nurturing parent. My pursuit of parental attitudes resulted in some unexpected findings. For instance, as many mothers of my participants as not had positive attitudes toward parenting, and the same balance of negative and positive parental attitudes existed among the fathers. Only after separating the absentee mothers into their reason-for-relinquishing categories does another picture begin to emerge.

POSITIVE AND NEGATIVE PARENTING EXTREMES

The first group I looked at for signs of a parental-attitude pattern was the group of eighteen women who had experienced serious emotional problems as mothers. In this group there was a clustering at the two extremes of parenting possibilities.[16] One-third of the women with emotional problems had been parented by both a mother and a father who disliked being parents; another third in this category had two parents who felt positively about their parenting roles. Some would suggest that this means that parental attitudes bear no relationship to emotional problems. I suggest, however, that any extreme in a child's environment can be counterproductive to that child's emotional health, even if the extreme is one of harmony. Two parents who largely reject one as a child can produce an adult who feels inadequate and unable to cope with the tasks of life. He or she may also feel unlovable, undeserving of happiness. There is a similar danger in two parents who dote on a child. The child may not be properly prepared to cope with the world. Overprotection or an unusually harmonious environment do not prepare one for independence or conflict. The all-important element of good parenting is balance. Extreme imbalance of any kind distorts the child's expectations of the adult environment and submits the child to eventual distress when reality insists upon being addressed. This distress may have occurred among the women who eventually relinquished custody due to emotional problems when they became mothers or, in some cases, when they became single custodial mothers.

UNHAPPY MOTHERS AND ATTENTIVE FATHERS

When a negative maternal imbalance did appear, it was within the two involuntary groups of absentee mothers, those who had lost their children in court and those whose children had made the custody decision. It was an overwhelming imbalance, with 72 percent of the participants indicating that they had unhappy mothers. No other category of absentee mother approaches this level of negative mothers by less than 22 percentage points.

Three-fourths of the women who had lost custody in court had mothers who exhibited varying degrees of dislike for their care-taking roles, predominantly very negative feelings. There were those who hated being mothers and avoided the responsibilities, those who hated it but forced themselves to fulfill the responsibilities; those who seemed oblivious to their children's needs but haphazardly fulfilled their physical requirements, and those whose attitudes constantly fluctuated. This same group of twelve absentee mothers had a preponderance of fathers (two-thirds) who exhibited positive attitudes toward parenting.[17]

Among the thirteen absentee mothers whose children had decided to live with their fathers, nine reported having unsatisfactory mothers and, important once again, their fathers were seen to be the opposite of their mothers. Eight of the thirteen fathers were perceived in a positive light.[18]

Of twenty-five absentee mothers who were, on the surface, forced into their noncustodial positions, eighteen had the sort of childhood parental image I believe predisposes a woman to becoming a voluntary absentee mother. The message seems clear: most of the women who lost their children due to forces outside their control may have had more to do with its happening than they realize. A woman who has had a bad enough relationship with her mother and not dealt with its effects on her own mothering may well contribute to her children leaving her or the court taking them from her. She may drive her children away by imitating her mother, or she may insure the court's decision by the same imitation. Add the childhood image of an involved and enthusiastic father. She could identify her husband with her father, and thus feel quite comfortable about her children living with him and less uncomfortable and less aware of her part in the children's decision to leave or the court's decision against her. Given the extreme social disapproval of a mother who lives apart from her children, even the unconscious belief that a father is the more nurturing parent is not enough to protect this absentee mother from socially and self-imposed guilt. So she maintains the defensive position that says, "It was not I who wanted this; it was imposed on me." There are cases where this is a genuine statement, but there may be more instances when it is not entirely so.

Absentee mothers who felt themselves victims of the custodial arrangements tended to be highly agitated at the merest suggestion that they examine whether they may have wanted or contributed to the custody decision. They were also the group most inclined to write lengthy explanations for how they had become absentee mothers, and often expressed marked disturbance at being compared to other absentee mothers, the ones "who wanted to give their children away for selfish reasons."

Here are samples of their descriptions of their parents' attitudes toward parenting.

My mother seemed to resent our imposition on her life.

My father seemed extremely happy to be a father and was very devoted.

My mother seemed to take care of us only because she had to.

My father was warm and loving.

My mother saw little pleasure and much pain in having children.

My father loved me a lot and spent time with me and my sister.

My mother wanted us to pay for her unhappiness.

My father was very loving and tried to keep harmony in the family.

My mother functioned, but there
was a tremendous lack of
affection.

My father showed more than the
average degree of pleasure in
being a father and of involvement
with his children.

PARENTS WHO ACCEPTED THEIR ROLES

Among one small group of absentee mothers in my study, three
out of four grew up with both a mother and a father who seemed to
enjoy their roles without being extreme in their parental attitudes.[19] This same group also expresses a unanimous evaluation of
their childhoods: each feels it was happy. These four women
relinquished custody primarily because they felt their husbands
were more nurturing parents, and I do not believe it is coincidental
that they are clearly among the most comfortable with their custody decisions. They were as calm and open to scrutiny as the
unwilling absentee mothers were excitable and defensive. I believe
the difference revolves around the smaller group having had
nonextreme positive parenting from their mothers as well as their
fathers. I suggest that they felt themselves to be good mothers in
their imitation of the past-generation mothers, and that they
therefore did not feel it necessary to convince themselves or
anyone else that having their children live elsewhere was not a
negative reflection on their own capabilities or morality. They had
no trouble imagining that a father could be most satisfactorily
nurturing; wrapped in the security of their positive self-
evaluations, they were aware that the differences between themselves and their husbands as parents were in degree only, not in
kind. I regret that this category is so small and therefore inconclu-
sive.

The second group of participants who had both positive mothers
and positive fathers prevailing relinquished custody in response to
intimidation from their husbands.[20] Obviously, this is a negative
outcome of having two positive parents, the opposite of that found
among the father-more-nurturing group of absentee mothers with
two positive parents. In response to this finding, one is inclined to
feel at this point that having two positive parents can mean
anything. However, the innumerable combinations of life's elements often produce seemingly contradictory results, but those
results may still be traced to a common major element and thus be
considered compatible. In the case of the absentee mothers here,

the major ingredient is having both a positive mother and a positive father; the specific variable ingredients probably have to do with the individual makeup of each participant and the subtle variations of even the supposed common ingredient—the positive parents. The results in the first group of absentee mothers with two positive parents were good, in that the individuals were well adjusted, and in the second group the results were bad, in that the individuals were unable to cope with intimidation.

Within the group of fourteen absentee mothers who were intimidated into relinquishing custody, nine had both mothers and fathers with positive attitudes toward parenting. Did the largely harmonious relationships they experienced with their parents leave them unprepared for conflict, unable to deal with the intimidation their husbands used so successfully? I am inclined to think so, although it does not seem, in some respects, that it ought to be possible for parents to be *too* good-natured in their relationships with their children. It is largely acknowledged, however, that maturity does not develop without the seasoning of adversity.

POSITIVE MOTHERS IN THE SELF-REALIZATION CATEGORY

Several years after I left my husband and gave him custody of our children, I started college, very tentatively. If there had been a scientific instrument capable of measuring human confidence, the reading on me would have indicated, "disastrously insufficient." But something wonderful happened for me: Rochelle Distelheim. She was my first and most helpful writing instructor. She did for me what her mother had done for her; she told me I could do it. Then she guided me through a process which convinced me I could. She was seeing to it that her own daughters received the same kind of essential ingredient toward self-realization. The right person recognizing your abilities and letting you know they do, especially over a protracted period, is the catalyst of personal development. It is best if this protracted period is childhood. In most cases, it seems to be best for little girls if this encouragement comes from their mothers. I was lucky to find Rochelle, even if the finding came late.

In my case, I can see in retrospect that I received a fair amount of praise from my teachers in grammar school and high school. Nevertheless, I felt inadequate as a student. My father, the few times I saw him, made it clear that he thought I was special, yet I felt inferior. The person whose approval I was constantly and unsuccessfully striving to win was my mother. I evolved from an insecure little girl into an insecure woman. The last Christmas I spent with my mother before she died in 1981 was the occasion for what seem to be her final words to me, words keenly symbolic of the message she had been giving me my entire life. She had opened her present from me, some embroidery work I had done. She looked at it in silence at first, with an expression of consternation on her face. Then she looked at me and said quickly, "*You* can't do this!" while simultaneously flinging my embroidery on the floor and picking up her next present.

The only group of absentee mothers in this study among whom positive mothers prevail is the group who relinquished custody to achieve self-realization.[21] Almost twice as many (eleven) of the participants in the self-realization category had mothers with positive attitudes toward them as had mothers with negative attitudes (six), compared to an even distribution among the study group as a whole. I believe that these women were more confident than the others, more aware of their potential and more desirous of developing it. Their reason for relinquishing custody makes that statement, and the prevalence of positive mothers in only their category of absentee mother supports the statement. In a sense, it validates the existence of genuine motivation toward self-realization within this group. It gives substance to the assertion that these women were not frivolous in their decisions to relinquish custody. Their superior employment when compared to other groups of absentee mothers and as discussed in Chapter 2 is significant proof that their mothers prepared them well.

NEGATIVE FATHERS IN THE FINANCIAL REALITIES CATEGORY

Seventy-two percent (thirteen) of the eighteen women who relinquished custody for economic reasons had fathers who were obviously not pleased with their role as fathers.[22] This is the only category of absentee mother to display this particular imbalance. The significance seems clear.

During the years my absentee mothers were growing up, the clear-cut and almost sole responsibility of a father was to provide. That narrow role has just begun to be questioned seriously. If it was clear to the participants as children that their fathers were unhappy as fathers, it seems reasonable to conclude that they might also have felt uncertain of whether their fathers would continue to fulfill that role. It would be a logical progression for them to feel insecure about whether all their physical needs were going to be met. A woman who has felt this particular insecurity as a child might well marry in an attempt to alleviate the feeling and also might well feel more marked anxiety about financial provisions than other women when divorcing. Suddenly, her fear has been realized. Her father/husband will not continue to provide. Take this same woman and add the responsibility of providing for her children as well as herself, add the real inferiority of women's earnings, and you have a mother who does not feel up to retaining custody.

Incest

Cissy told me that she cannot remember when it started, but her father molested her for years. She told her mother about it once when she was around nine years old, in a frantic effort to avoid her father, but nothing was done. Cissy's mother did not say whether she believed her little girl, but she did ignore what she had been told. Cissy's one-word description of her mother as "passive," combined with the way her mother failed to address the problem, affirms the assertion that the mother in a father/daughter incestual household contributes to the unhealthy situation.[23] On some level, she usually wants the daughter to take over for her with the father. Cissy was eventually sent to live with an aunt at age thirteen, but no reference was ever made to indicate that incest had anything to do with the move. It was years too late to save Cissy from the terrible psychological effects of the sexual abuse. Neither did sending Cissy away take into account her three younger sisters who remained under the same roof with their father. In fact, the father simply resumed his incestuous activity with the next older daughter and began the practice of masturbating in the bedroom doorway of the other two girls. Finally, two years after Cissy had been sent away, her mother forced her father to leave home, but she did so in continued silence about the incest. Cissy feels the whole experience has "permeated [her] entire life at all levels."

Julie, a second absentee mother in my study, who describes herself as having been a fat child, was also a victim of her own father's emotional imbalance. He sexually abused her for seven years, from the time she was eight until she was fifteen. In response to her being overweight, her mother "starved and medicated" her over that same seven-year period. It was a double-barreled message for Julie: she was bad for eating too much and she was bad for allowing the unspeakable with her father; she was ugly and loathsome. She did not have to endure a sister being hurt in the same way because she had no sister; she was an only child. But neither did she have a sister in whom to confide. Her position was all the more stressful for it. On one hand, she was being subjected to extraordinary tension by her father, and on the other, she had her one source of comfort—food—taken away by her mother.

The third woman in my study to have suffered incest as a child was not a sexual victim of her father; he and his religious wife confined their abuse of Grace to regular beatings. It was her two brothers, one older and one younger, who used her sexually at first. Later, when she was sent to live with her mother's parents at age twelve, her grandfather imposed himself on her.

No one really knows in any exact sense with what frequency incest occurs, because only reported incidents are there to be seen. There is increasing reason to believe, however, that the reported occurrences of incest are only a tiny fraction of the number which actually take place. A decade and more ago, it was thought that fewer than ten incestual incidents occurred per million population, but today we know that that estimate was inaccurate. People are being encouraged by social workers, medical personnel, and former victims to confront incest in their own homes. An organization like the National Center on Child Abuse and Neglect is now able to make a more realistic estimate in the matter: at least 100,000 cases of child molestation occur per year, most perpetrated by a family member (and more often than not by the father or step-father). Other authorities suggest that about 250,000 children per year may be sexually abused.[24]

Even if I use the higher estimate for comparison, the rate of sexual abuse among my absentee mothers as children is higher. But I have compared today's estimates to the 1950 population, the approximate time at which my participants were experiencing incestuous imposition. The U.S. population in 1950 stood at a rounded 150,700,000, about 76,000,000 fewer than today, and it is felt that the rate of incest then was lower than today's estimates.[25] The three cases among one hundred participants is, obviously, an occurrence rate of 3 percent. Among the population at large in

1950, less than 0.25 percent were victims of incest. Therefore, the rate of incest among my absentee mothers as children was at least twelve times higher than among their peers.

Cissy, Julie, and Grace, as happens with most victims of incest, lived with the debilitating conviction that they were inferior and undeserving. For most of their lives, they believed that however negative their circumstances might be, they deserved for things to be that way. What they did not realize in advance, however, was that there is a limit to how much self-deprecation one can tolerate. For each of them, the failure of their marriages became the point at which they could no longer bear their self-images. They had to learn to love themselves or die; they had to prove to themselves that they were worthy of respect. Their decisions to relinquish custody were anything but frivolous; they were life-or-death decisions. Cissy, Julie, and Grace relinquished custody because it was essential for them to concentrate their energies on themselves.

The Only Child

In one respect, Avery Corman, the author of *Kramer vs. Kramer*, was not out of order in portraying his absentee mother character as an only child. There are, indeed, an unusual number of "onlys" in my study group: twelve of the hundred. As 6 percent of American adults today are only children, there are twice as many only children among my absentee mothers as among the female adult population at large.[26] However, the reasoning behind the choice to portray Joanna Kramer as an only child is wrong. It is based upon two false assumptions: that an only child is typically spoiled and selfish and that an absentee mother is typically the same.

The Center for Population Research of the National Institute for Child Health and Human Development has worked in this area since 1978 and concludes, "There are no major differences between only children and others; no negative effects of being an only child can be found."[27]

And, based on a study of absentee mothers by herself and J. M. Cardea, Dr. Judith L. Fischer states, "Primarily, mothers who live apart from their children resemble women of their age who live with their children. No particular traits, dispositions or lifestyles appear to uniquely characterize women who live apart from their children."[28]

Discussing results of another study comparing noncustodial mothers to custodial mothers, M. A. Isenhart, a clinical psychologist, observes, "There was no measurable difference between the two groups on most of the dimensions examined in this study.[29]

So why are there twice as many only children among my absentee mothers as among other adult women? My response is based upon the "duplication theorem" of the German psychologist Walter Toman, which suggests that we each attempt to recreate our childhood sibling position with our marriages and that, to the extent we are successful at doing so, we are also successful at being happy in our marriages and parenting. For instance, if the oldest sister of brothers marries the youngest brother of sisters, she is most likely to have a happy marriage. If that same older sister of brothers has only sons, she is most likely to be happy with her mothering role. Obviously, when this theory, to which I ascribe, is applied to only children, one is faced with the suggestion that they are likely to be happiest if they never become parents. They are accustomed to having no brothers or sisters and will, therefore, be most comfortable having no children. Toman advises married persons not to have children with a spouse who is an only child unless one is prepared to do most of the parenting alone. This is not tantamount to saying that the only child is spoiled and selfish, just that we are all more content when we find ourselves within familiar structures.

So I believe that one may safely say that an only child who becomes a mother is more likely to be unhappy as a mother. Further, the best chance she has of enjoying parenthood if she does become a mother is to have one child. This allows her the possibility of identifying with her mother rather than with herself as a child. Unfortunately, ten of the dozen "onlys" in my study had more than one child.

The Oldest Child

Forty-four of my participants (exactly half of the eighty-eight who had siblings) are oldest children. Thirty-one of these oldests had at least three siblings and as many as eight, in spite of the fact that, on average, the group is typical of others their age in having either one or two siblings. This suggests to me that these absentee mothers were caring for children while they themselves were still children. The details of their childhoods tell me that their child-care responsibilities were often much heavier than their undeveloped emotional structures should have been expected to support.

In addition to the forty-five oldests in my group, two women, though technically middle children, are oldests in effect because of the many years separating them from their first-born sibling: in one case nine years, in the other ten. Birth-order psychologists consider five years' difference to be the significant number for deciding whether a child should be considered in one category or another.[30] At any rate, it may be that too much responsibility for brothers and sisters takes its toll on the magnitude of responsibilities one is able or willing to assume and maintain as an adult. This, on the surface, would be contrary to the duplication theorem supported in the previous section, but I suspect the theory does not apply to family constellations which have been experienced as unpleasant. Toman seems not to have addressed that possibility. It makes sense, however, to draw that conclusion, and it has been pointed out by the director of one voluntary sterilization program, for instance, that almost all of the childless women who decide to be sterilized at that clinic have been the primary caretakers of at least one younger sibling.[31]

Another factor that may add to the preponderance of oldests in my study group is that nine additional middle-sibling participants had only brothers as older siblings. In other words, they were the oldest girls in the family. Given the tendency to put female children in the caretaking capacity, these nine middle children may have been oldests in effect. They may even have had some responsibilities, such as laundry or cooking, related to their older brothers' day-to-day needs. If so, a total of fifty-five of my absentee mothers (63 percent of those with siblings) could be considered to have been in the position of oldest.

One of the fifty-five, the oldest of eight, began caring for her first younger sibling when she herself was only four. She believes her mother hated being a mother but had no escape from the endless babies because she was a traditional Catholic. The oldest daughter escaped the trap by the very door which had confined her mother: the Church. She entered the convent at seventeen. As I mentioned earlier, my own sister did the same thing at fourteen, although I know she did not see her action as an escape. She had, in fact, so thoroughly taken on the responsibility for myself and our younger sister that she felt terribly guilty about pursuing what she wanted for herself and had spent many months of anguish over whether or not she had the right to "desert" us. I believe she felt very much like an absentee mother for a long time after entering the convent.

Another oldest child in my study had her position intensified by an alcoholic mother and the absence of her father due to divorce. She was the oldest of five, two of whom had been fathered by her mother's second husband and two by a third husband; my participant was the offspring of the first husband. "I was not allowed normal childhood activities," she says, "and there was always so much screaming and yelling." Chaos, diapers, dirty dishes, the whole range of adult responsibilities, are all she can remember of her so-called childhood. And a drunken mother who had detached herself from all of it.

The position of oldest child apparently invites abuse as well as excessive responsibilities. When adult performance is not forthcoming from oldest children, troubled parents can strike out at these children as if they were the source of all their problems. In one "oldest" absentee mother's case, an unemployed alcoholic father treated her as an extension of her mother. He beat them both regularly.

My father was the town drunk, an immigrant illiterate who beat me and my mother. I was a girl, and bright, born into an Italian family that thought both were a curse and the combination a tragedy.

Two more absentee mothers who were in similarly woven families have responded to the early trauma, they believe, by "forgetting" their entire childhoods:

I'm still trying to locate and understand things from my childhood which try to reveal themselves to me, but I believe I suppress them out of fear.

I can't remember my childhood at all before about age twelve.

I recall quite vividly the fear of getting out of bed in the morning to face all of the demands which I had, invariably, failed to prepare for the night before. My little sister and I would both need dresses for school. They had to be ironed. Clean socks without holes had to be found and matched, scuffed shoes needed polishing. My sister never wanted to go to school, so I had to force her to do everything that she *could* do. Every morning, I felt overwhelmed and in a state of panic.

The childhood image and feeling that I could not cope with taking care of children had not disappeared before I became a mother. Rather, it had lain dormant until then and was reactivated by the duplication of circumstances; once again, I had a child to care for on my own. My subconscious quickly said, in a duo with my mother's voice, "Hey, wait a minute. Have you forgotten? *You* can't do *this*." And I responded just as I had as a child. I went about daily mothering enveloped in a sense of anxious desperation. How long would it be before I broke, before I would prove again to myself and to my mother that I could not really handle this? The discomfort I had felt as a surrogate mother to myself and my little sister was the same discomfort I felt as a mother to my own children. There is reason to believe, as I have shown, that a meaningful proportion of the hundred absentee mothers in my study may have shared this order of events with me.

Attempted Suicide in Childhood

I used to pray in bed, "Don't wake me in the morning." I was only seven when I started pleading for release. It was not an on-and-off thing. My prayer and my hope that it would be answered were my teddy bear of comfort every night. Unlike most children, I was always anxious to go to bed, to lose my pain for a while, to have another chance at making God understand how much I needed to be with Him. By the time I was ten, not only had my father and older sister gone, but my mother had moved us out of the apartment in my paternal grandparents' house. She said they were watching every move she made. They probably were, but for me, moving away from them was awful. They were the only ones who seemed to care; they were certainly the only ones who would hold me and listen to me and seemed to think I mattered.

My mother, free from the prying eyes of her former in-laws, began dating more than ever, and my hatred for her increased every time she went dancing; I felt my deprivation more sharply every time she brought home a man. One night I woke at the sound of voices in the living room. They belonged to my mother and a man; another stranger who was getting what was supposed to be mine, my mother's attention and caring. After what seemed a long time of straining to hear but being unable to discern anything, I got out of bed and crept on my hands and knees through the kitchen and down the hallway which led to the living room. At first, I just listened. The man said something and my mother laughed. I felt a fire of jealousy ignite in my chest. She was listening to him; she was responding to him. I wanted to kill her. I risked being caught by peering into the room. They were sitting on the love seat. My mother was twisted from the hips up toward the man, leaning on him; he had both arms around her. I imagined myself launching a fierce attack against my mother, accompanied by a shriek of rage which might kill her in itself. I wanted her to die in pain. Instead, I rushed into the bathroom and slammed the door. I started crying. Sometimes a sound would escape from behind my hands over my mouth and it would echo in the room. Then I would wait for my mother to come in. But she didn't. I wondered if a lot of aspirin would kill me. I took two at a time, but my stomach started pulling in on itself, and I retched everything into the sink. My mother must have heard; the bathroom and living room shared a wall. But she never came in. I remember thinking that if I were to kill myself in a room less necessary, my mother wouldn't even know I had died until the school called about my being absent. I just went back to bed and started doubting for the first time that God loved me.

Three of the absentee mothers in my study also attempted to kill themselves before reaching adulthood. The first has already been referred to in Chapter 2. She is the child who attempted to kill herself four times by the time she was fourteen, but she related no details of motivation or implementation. The other two who attempted suicide while minors did so as unmarried, pregnant adolescents. Three in a hundred does not seem significant at first, but like so many other elements, it is more than it initially appears to be. In 1959, the median year of mid-adolescence among my absentee mothers, the total number of suicides among females between fifteen and nineteen years old was 101.[32] Since for every suicide there are probably ten attempted suicides, there were about 1,010 attempted suicides among girls of the ages mentioned.[33] Adolescent girls intent on self-destruction during 1959 were a minuscule 0.0006 percent of the population. At 3 percent of the study group, the suicidal teenagers who became absentee mothers could represent, statistically speaking, a rampant behavior pattern in comparison. Technically, I should count the multiple attempts by the one participant as part of the attempted suicide rate. If I did so, it would bring the rate to double that already cited: 6 percent. The existence of a fourth absentee mother (myself) who attempted suicide as a child confirms the pattern even further. In a group as tiny as my study, compared to hundreds of millions in the U.S.

population, the appearance of a specific pathology even once is reason to take notice, and repetitions are likely to be significant. Given the paucity of absentee mother research, I daresay it is reasonable to suggest that suicidal behavior during childhood is a condition that appears in suspicious degree among noncustodial mothers. A person who has had difficulty sustaining her own existence is more likely to have difficulty sustaining that of another as well. This is especially so if the underlying causes for the self-directed aggression have not been addressed before the new responsibility develops, as is precisely the situation in the cases discussed.

Among the four who attempted suicide, reactions were quite different. Whereas my failure at suicide in childhood gave root to doubting God's love, one of the other absentee mothers who failed in the same way began to believe that "there is a Christ who is near, regardless" and that one is "never completely alone or unloved." Another of the suicidal children, as an adult, has no remembrance of how she felt afterward, but one of the absentee mothers with no suicidal behavior in her background, only a miserable childhood, kept God and suicide out of her life altogether for the sake of revenge. She was not about to give her mother the satisfaction she believed her death would bring. Neither did she meekly turn to God for comfort. She responded defiantly to the negative treatment she received. The six-year-old girl screamed at her mother after a beating, "You can hit me all you want, you can't *kill* me!" I find her six-year-old response to maltreatment poignant and perhaps all too representative of the anger and hurt so many absentee mothers felt in connection with their childhood.

4

Let It Change or Disappear: The Absentee Mother's Marriage

She had trouble defining herself independently of her husband, tried to talk to him about it, but he said nonsense, he had no trouble defining her at all.

—Cynthia Propper Seton, The Half-Sisters

Rigid, Authoritarian Husbands

I married a mechanical engineer who, I now believe, must have perceived me in the same way he perceived the production machinery with which he worked. My functions were clearly delineated, my maintenance and repair were expected to be minimal, and I was to endure for a lifetime. Unfortunately, I accepted his view of me, which of course had been implanted in both of us by our culture. I was available for sex, gave birth to babies, sat devotedly at his side during corporate functions, cooked meals and washed dishes, cleaned house, did laundry and ironing and mending (I even darned socks), went to confession on Saturdays to confess being tired and to Mass on Sundays to beg for the strength to persevere. Sometimes I found myself seriously wondering whether I ought to stay awake nights just in case the children might need me. When I made friends with a housewife across the street and we discovered a common interest in skating, we made enthusiastic plans to take lessons and "free" skate afterward once a week. The very mention of the word *free* polarized our husbands against it; they both refused permission. I wanted to learn to drive; my husband was against it. I could not even go grocery shopping alone. Assuming I could either get a ride or find a location within walking distance, I sometimes went to a Tupperware party (demonstrative in itself of my desperation), but I had to leave a phone number where I could be reached. And my husband would call during the course of the evening to see if I was there.

Eighty-eight of the absentee mothers in my study had husbands much like mine. Only ten of the ninety-eight women who married could say that their husbands recognized their needs as individuals apart from marriage and motherhood. One participant, when asked this question about her husband, expressed her bitterness in one loud word: "Ha!" Another short but piercing response was, "Absolutely not!" Still another, "Never!" Indeed, anger came spitting out in all directions when former husbands were the topic:

I was to be the person to help him fulfill his plan to be successful, doing as he planned in the manner he dictated.

He expected me to be at home with him unless I was earning money or had accomplished all he thought I should at home.

After fifteen years of marriage (thirteen years at home with the children), I decided to go back to school. I signed up for one summer school course. When I told him that I would be taking a course two nights a week from seven to ten, his exact words were, "What do I do about dinner those two nights?" I knew then that I would have to choose between myself and my marriage. We separated after the second meeting of the class.

Even the wives who felt their husbands had some sense of their wives' personal needs were held in strict restraint while trying to fulfill those needs:

He cooperated in my pursuing personal interests when the interests involved the home, but not when it was college or anything else away from home.

He decided which of my needs were valid for him to support.

He cooperated only when my personal needs fit into his idea of what my needs should be, like garden club and other home-related spheres.

*Outside pursuits were allowed only if I weren't gone too long; I went to
church and sang in the choir.*

The median span of my subjects' marriages was from 1963
through 1972. *The Feminine Mystique,* commonly held to have set off
the current feminist movement, was published in 1963. Naturally,
it took some time for its insights to spread. The National Organization for Women was not established until 1966. It would be
unreasonable to expect that husbands should have been ahead of
others in their social surroundings. But even among the fifty-eight
marriages in this study that existed later than the median of 1972
and as late as 1979, there is the same concentration of rigid,
authoritarian husbands. Obdurate husbands still exist and are still
at the core of many divorces. What has yet to be determined
through further comparisons is whether there are more of these
men among wives who become absentee mothers than there are
among other divorcing mothers.

Low Degree of Self-Awareness and
Self-Realization

Just as many husbands of the middle and late seventies were
insensitive to their wives' needs, more than one-third of the wives
in my study from marriages of the same years did not realize their
own personal needs. Forty-one of the ninety-eight wives in this
study were unaware, for most of the time they were married, that
they had individual needs. The others, who usually had mere
suspicions of needing something more, felt nervous about these
feelings; they were guilty secrets in almost every case. One participant likened her married condition to being unconscious, not
knowing that she had needs but feeling very unhappy in an
unspecific way. Another participant said she did not even begin to
think until 1971. A third woman said she did not realize what was
missing from her life until she began to notice that she was happier
when she was away from home. Others expressed being in an
even further reduced state:

I wasn't sure I was an individual.

*I was asleep during most of my marriage; the awakening of me was a large
cause of our divorce.*

I knew that someday I would be a person, but didn't see how or when.

Those who believed that once a woman married she could not allow herself individual needs spent enormous amounts of energy suppressing their feelings of yearning and frustration. For example, when my husband left the house on Saturdays with all three children to run the week's errands (something I had engineered), I felt as light as chiffon. I would play a Haydn symphony and dance my own dance. I was lithe and breathtakingly graceful, but full of impressive strength and control. My leaps were comparable to the best male dancers'. This was the me who came out when everyone else was gone. She wanted to be free more of the time; she was beginning to demand freedom. She frightened me, but could I kill her? No. I had to make her understand that she had no right to exist. She had promised to be a wife and mother.

To be a wife and mother is not only what everyone in the study promised to be, but it is really what they were prepared to be. The typical woman in my study married at nineteen at a time when the median age of brides was twenty-and-a-half. Their grooms were almost exactly the median age of grooms at large: twenty-two-and-a-half. Although one-third of the brides were full-time students on their wedding days, only ten pursued their educations full time until their first pregnancy, and only two continued full time beyond that.[1]

Another third of the brides were either clerical workers or salesclerks; the final third were either service workers (waitresses, nurses' aides, and so forth) or unemployed. The vast majority lived at home until they married. Once married, three-quarters worked outside their homes for at least portions of their marriages, and half attended school (see Table 8). However, they were holding the same sorts of jobs as when they were single, jobs which they felt to be only sources of extra income for the family and most of which were temporary and short-term. The school attendance was extremely limited and usually aborted after short periods.

With limited higher education, jobs that offered little beyond minimal paychecks, and no experience with independent living, most of these women, one may readily conclude, had not developed a strong sense of themselves or the various possibilities in the world around them. They have stated that this was in fact so. They seem to have assumed that marriage would be the source of their ultimate satisfaction, as they had been taught. Unfortunately, absentee-mothers-to-be were to learn along with the rest of the female population that marriage cannot be the complete source of self-fulfillment for any but a minority of women. An institution that requires the stifling of an individual's curiosity, freedom of movement, and growth must be the antithesis of personal well-being and happiness and, thereby, of a healthy social order. So Germaine Greer's ultimatum is not only a reflection of feminists' hard-learned realizations but an essential instruction to our society: "If marriage and family depend on the castration of women, let them change or disappear."

Unwanted or Unplanned Children Born Close Together

I was pregnant two weeks after marrying. Although my husband and I were Catholics (he a convert at my request) and thus using only rhythm as a means of birth control, I cannot blame the Church or rhythm for my early pregnancy. Neither can I place the blame on my husband. He did not press for intercourse at an "unsafe" time of the month, nor did he seem particularly anxious to have our first child. I did the pressing, although I had no desire for a child. What I did want, primarily, was quickly won approval and attention. Only secondarily, I also wanted to satisfy my curiosity about what it was like to be pregnant and give birth. Pregnancy was the next prescribed step in my life. Through one timely act of sexual intercourse, it seemed, I could win continuous attention and approval, two commodities that I had learned in childhood were rare and precious things. Only my pathological need for those things can explain the irresponsible way I approached the creation of a child. Although my body was pregnant, my mind was not prepared. I had planned, of course, in all the usual, apparent ways for the eventual arrival of a baby, but my psyche had not absorbed the reality of what was coming. It was merely a distant abstraction. Even labor and delivery were unsuccessful as harbingers. The flurry and care, after all, were still mine. Not until I tried to nurse the baby I had delivered did reality crash into my senses. A person was my responsibility—a live mass of demands who had no conception of my utter weariness, who would not keep still simply because I was sore and depressed.

I was filled with guilt because I did not like having the baby, because I treated her badly. I would let her cry, sometimes for hours, before going to her. I would scream at her when I did respond, shaking her and yelling that she had to leave me alone. Things got better, but they did not change enough. I had managed to stop the more overtly awful behavior, and I had begun to find pleasures and satisfactions in my baby, but I was still mostly unhappy to be a mother. I pitied my little girl with all my heart that she should have been cursed with a mother like me. I was ashamed of the way I had mistreated her in the beginning, and I would make myself sick wondering how it must have harmed her emotionally. I despised myself.

Meanwhile, my husband had decided that it would be best for our daughter if she had a brother or sister who was close to her age, and I agreed, giving the matter no real thought. Only this time I knew that I hated being a mother. But how could I say no to a second baby without confessing the way I felt to my husband, without failing in my beliefs as a Catholic, in my purpose as a woman? What better way to hide my negative maternal reactions than to continue having children? I would learn to love being a mother the way I had learned to hide that I did not. So I was expecting a second child when my first was nine months old. And a third when my second was two.

In my very early first pregnancy, I was atypical of the women in my study, who avoided pregnancy for a median of fifteen months after marrying. However, they became pregnant sooner than their average peers, among whom the median lapse between marriage and first pregnancy was twenty-one months. The absentee mothers were six months more reluctant to begin having children, although nine were already pregnant when they married.

Where the women in my study and I rejoin is in the short periods of time between our children. We had shorter intervals between births than the national median of thirty-one months; my intervals were only one month less at a median of thirty months, but the study group had intervals that were the median of seven months shorter than that of other married mothers. Two of the study participants had twins, and the twins were not their only children. When it comes to looking after infants and toddlers, who acquire abilities at an impressive rate, seven months one way or the other can make a great deal of difference in how difficult it is to care for them simultaneously. Even in later childhood, children who are closer in age usually present greater problems for the parents. Although there is the potential for close sibling relations when they are near in age, there is also usually increased competition and fighting as well as financial pressure.

The hundred absentee mothers and I part again in the number of children we had. Whereas I had three children, one more than the national average among women who had children at all, the hundred absentee mothers averaged two children each. They are exactly typical of mothers at large, although not typical of the divorcing woman, who averages only one child.

Perhaps the most significant similarity between the absentee mothers in my study and me is the common nature of the way we allowed ourselves to become mothers—not just the first time but over and over again in the cases involving more than one child. Only one-fifth of the 212 children born to my participants were born because their mothers had a personal desire for a child. Unless this is typical of the way most infants are conceived, it must be relevant to absentee motherhood. Whatever the rewards of parenting, it is unarguably difficult. Single parenting involves a still greater leap into difficulty, so it would seem that only those with substantial commitment, stamina, and preparation would be able to sustain its responsibilities. To what extent can commitment develop from careless procreation? To what extent can unsuitable or unwilling mothers be happy in maternity and therefore strongly committed to their children?

Two-fifths of the children in this study were never intended to happen; they were accidents, failures in contraception. Another fifth came in their mothers' attempts to please others, such as husbands and in-laws, or to fulfill their perceived religious and social duties. The remainder of children born without being particularly wanted, another fifth, were simply allowed to happen either because it seemed the natural thing to do or because there was no preception of choice. (Sixty-three percent of the mothers felt they had no real choice in the matter of having children.) No one asked herself if she wanted a child, or why she wanted a child, or whether her reasons were good ones. No one asked if she were capable of nurturing a child. The unanswered question of nurturing capacity may mean lifetimes of pain for many people.

Maternal Love and Unwanted or Unplanned Children

To what extent can careless procreation and unsuitable or unwilling mothers result in loving commitment to the children born? Based on the hundred mothers in this study, women of all kinds who become mothers for all sorts of "wrong" reasons can become loving and committed mothers.

The reader should be reminded that the mothers who found serious difficulty with nurturing make up less than one-fifth (18) of the absentee mothers in this study. Therefore, I am not representative of the study group in this respect. However, even among mothers who have had emotional difficulties, it is important to point out that our problematic psychological makeup has not meant that we do not love and enjoy our children. It *has* meant that we had personality disorders that needed medical treatment. We were ill; our illness produced destructive behavior in response to the *situation* of motherhood, not in response to the *individuals* our children were or are. The sad necessity for divorce and separate living from our children must not be equated with callous lack of interest, hedonism, or the inability to love.

Only four absentee mothers in my study did not enjoy their children at all while living with them (I do not, by the way, place myself in this category). Forty-two have only good memories of living with their children, and fifty-three speak of both the positive and negative aspects of mothering their children.[2] The latter group strikes me as being perfectly normal. They have a healthy grasp on the reality of nurturing: pleasures and irritations, joy and weariness, satisfaction and deprivation. They are no different than healthy custodial mothers. Perhaps the forty-two who speak only of the positive aspects of living with their children are not yet fully adjusted to their noncustodial status. They may be protecting themselves from further condemnation, from within and without. A woman who is condemned by those around her as a bad mother, who may believe the charge herself, is in no position to refer to the negative aspects of nurturing. She must keep trying to convince herself and others that she was and is a "good" mother. Selective memories result. Nevertheless, such mothers' positive experiences with their children are not fantasies. They enjoy their children in the same way other mothers do:

They were thoroughly enjoyable little people who gave me a sense of fulfillment. Mothering was the one thing I felt I did reasonably well.

It was wonderful seeing her discover and learn about the world, always having someone I could love freely, without reserve, who loved me back.

I found them challenging. We played and talked. Little minds are fantastic.

I enjoyed taking her places, going for walks with her, and just sitting while holding her and reading stories.

Statements like these, full of love and enthusiasm, abound in my study. It is impossible to differentiate between my absentee mothers' feelings toward their children and those of custodial mothers. This supports the assertion that absentee mothers most often relinquish custody for reasons that have nothing whatever to do with how they feel about their children per se. Their reasons, outlined below, almost always contain elements of what is in the "best interests" of their children.

Emotional problems (18 members of the group):
Children are removed from mother who was incapacitated by illness; protected from possible physical and emotional damage resulting from mother's emotional imbalance.

Financial realities (18 members of the group):
Children are spared the deprivation associated with drastically reduced income and are assured the fulfillment of their material needs.

Self-realization (17 members of the group):
Children are spared the guilt of being the "obstacle" to mother's fulfillment and the unhappiness of living with a seriously frustrated adult.

Intimidation (14 members of the group):
Children are more effectively prepared to deal with the world around them by the more assertive parent.

Problems in second marriage (4 members of the group):
Children are removed from the trauma of living within a troubled marriage and/or with a stepfather who treats them badly.

Father more nurturing (4 members of the group):
Children are placed with the more suited parent, which should lead to a healthier and happier unbringing.

Children's decision (13 members of the group):
Children's maturation process is encouraged by the freedom to choose
and to learn about themselves and life from the results of their choice.

Lost custody (12 members of the group):
Rather than a continual attempt at reversing the court's decision and the
ongoing turmoil that would create for her children, the mother goes
along with the court's view and hopes that her children are, indeed, in
the "best" place for them.

Returning to the discussion of the extent to which absentee
mothers enjoyed their children while still married, I would like to
examine the four absentee mothers who speak of only negative
memories of living with their children. One had earlier placed
herself in the category of having relinquished custody because she
had emotional problems and another had placed herself in the self-
realization category. These two motivational categories, it seems to
me, are quite compatible with the fact that these mothers did not
enjoy their children. Not enjoying their children could readily
contribute directly to the creation of emotional problems and to a
pronounced need to seek self-realization elsewhere. Thus, it seems
likely that these two participants have been honest, or at least
consistent, in stating their reasons for relinquishing custody.

The remaining two absentee mothers are another matter. They
had earlier placed themselves in the category of having relinquished custody because of financial realities. It is my feeling that
this is not consistent with the fact that they did not enjoy their
children at all. Would they really have retained custody if they had
been financially well off? Not enjoying one's children does not
reasonably lead to relinquishing custody for primarily financial
reasons. My impression in these two cases is that they have not
been truthful, even to themselves, about the motivation behind
relinquishing custody. They have been unable to say, straight out,
that they gave up custody because they did not enjoy being
mothers. In our culture, a statement like that makes a woman an
instant heretic. So they grasped at a readily available and partially
real (finances are an element of virtually all noncustodial decisions)
explanation for their absentee motherhood.

Speaking of mistakes and returning to the larger body of absentee mothers, it is enlightening to learn that, among the entire one
hundred women, only a dozen are personally sorry that they had

any children, that is, sorry because of the impact it had on them personally:

I was too young, knew nothing about myself and was very insecure. I became selfish and crazy, still not knowing where to turn.

It wasn't all the joy and excitement I had been led to believe it would be. My life became one big drudge, and I looked old and haggard at twenty-five.

I was very depressed after the divorce because of all the responsibility, but I felt guilty saying, "I wish I didn't have a child."

The latter statement was made by an absentee mother who later remarried, had two more children, and whose first child then chose to live with his biological father. She goes on to say:

I no longer feel guilty when I'm tired of parenting, but I feel very restricted, that perhaps I could have achieved great things in life if I had remained childless. Maybe I still can, but I also frequently regret having kids because they interfere with the husband/wife relationship and activities.

It is important that absentee mothers be honest with themselves about the reasons they relinquish custody. Otherwise, the chance that they may have additional children when perhaps they should not lurks as a definite possibility. In most cases, however, it appears not to be a problem, in large measure because the mistake is so clear:

I was only seventeen years old when I got pregnant and had to get married. I was a junior in high school, very active, popular and an honor student. I was looking forward to my senior year because I was going to receive special honors and positions. I was also getting excited about college, planning to go to medical school and study psychiatry and was fully confident of my ability to do so. I felt as if the future was mine, but then my periods stopped.

I was such a child. I had never heard of abortion or adoption clinics, so I had no idea of what to do. I didn't want to get married—I had all those plans, and I knew they would come to a grinding halt if I got married. So I just "forgot" about it, completely put the pregnancy out of my mind until the day when I was six months along and my boyfriend guessed. I was married three days later, sent to live with him at his parents' house where we stayed until my daughter was three months old. Then I got a job doing clerical work so we could move away. My husband was working only part time so that he could finish his education which was so much more important than mine (nine years later and I'm still seething!) according to him, his parents, and my parents. I was outnumbered.

So yes, I am sorry I had my child. I can never recover those lost years. I can never get into medical school; they tell me I'm too old now, and I no longer have that confidence to try anyway. I am back in school, studying psychology (my prime motivation for giving up custody), but psychology is a second choice, a poor substitute for psychiatry in my eyes.

In addition to the dozen absentee mothers who are personally sorry they had children, eight regret having had children because of what the children have suffered. One of these women recognized the link between her own childhood and the mother she was. She said that her childhood had been miserable and that she had thought that everyone's must be the same. She was really still a child herself when she became pregnant at seventeen and now feels strongly that all she did by becoming a mother was to pass on her legacy of pain. The rest of these eight women identify their children's suffering with the divorces that occurred and with the aftereffects of living in a single-parent home and being used by the parents to hurt one another, "which, in turn, hurts them." These mothers believe that their children's suffering has been so great that never to have experienced life would have been better.

So a total of twenty absentee mothers (one-fifth) would rather that their children had never been born. There is also a subgroup of nine regretful mothers who are sorry that they had more than one, two, or three children. All nine tied their regrets to the effects that having too many children had on themselves: half were forced to postpone their plans for divorce because of the additional pregnancies, for instance. The other half simply felt unable to function well as mothers past a certain point—a point which varies with the individual, obviously, but which seems to be described in essence by one mother's sense of being overwhelmed:

I had three Caesarean deliveries in thirty months and a hysterectomy ten months later. I felt totally depleted and couldn't cope with the children physically or emotionally, and they were so unrewarding in so many ways.

The fact that each of us has a different tolerance level for children is highlighted by the fact that, although the majority of the twenty mothers who were sorry they had any children felt their children were "too much," they averaged only one child each. This is one less than the average both in the study group as a whole and among peer-mothers at large. On the other hand, the nine mothers who are sorry about having only some of their children had twenty-eight children among them, an average of three each. Perhaps it should also be noted, however, that the twenty mothers who are sorry they had children were, when divorcing, the mothers of the youngest children. The median age of the children was five-and-a-half. In addition, six of these women (30 percent) were those who had relinquished custody due to emotional problems, even though the "emotional problems" group is only 18 percent of the study group. The rest of the categories from the study are more evenly represented among the twenty regretful mothers. I see this as a good sign that many of the participants who should not have become mothers now recognize that and are unlikely to repeat their mistake.

The remainder of the study group (seventy-one mothers), in spite of having twice as many children as those who are sorry they had any, and in spite of many of the same negative experiences with parenting and divorce, are happy that they had their children. As a matter of fact, nineteen of the seventy-one actually wish they had had more children. One of them has taken in numerous children over the years and has helped raise three stepchildren. Several others, who average four children each, describe their feelings in the matter:

I love children and give a lot of myself to them, not as a dragged-out, overworked mother, but in enjoyment.

I gave whether or not to have children a lot of thought and have found my children to be enriching to my life.

I love family. I was the baby.

Thus, almost three-fourths of the absentee mothers in this study have done anything but reject their children in relinquishing custody. They love their children, appreciate the quality they bring to adult life, and enjoy whatever involvement is possible as noncustodial parents. Even among the participants who are sorry, to some extent, that they had children, the prevalent attitude is simply one of children having come at the wrong time or with the wrong man, or of regret at not having been prepared for motherhood. Very few absentee mothers actually dislike children in general, and none feels she has rejected her own.

Young Male Problem Children in Longer-than-Average Marriages

There is little, if any, dispute regarding the fact that infants and preschool children demand the most care; their needs are fundamental and their vulnerability great. During the early years, as well, it is essential for the child to be fondled, spoken to, taken step by step through new experiences in order to develop well emotionally, physically, and intellectually. Early school years relieve this situation, but the hours spent at home following the school day are ones in which the child bombards the parents with every detail of his or her day. The child needs to be listened to, responded to, reinforced, all of which can become tedious for an adult, especially if there is more than one small child and if the primary caretaker (almost always the mother) has limited contact with other adults and activities.

It appears that the hundred absentee mothers in this study were in a more trying set of circumstances, if one applies some conventional beliefs, when compared to other divorcing mothers. At the point of marital separation, their typical oldest child was six-and-a-half and their younger child four-and-a-half years old.[3] Since 60 percent of my participants' children were boys, the children were more likely to be both boys than one boy and a girl. In comparison, 51 percent of children at large were boys. A mother, then, relinquishes custody of a son more often than a daughter. More than a statistical fact of birth rates is apparent here. In the cases where mothers retain custody of some of their children while relinquishing custody of others, the children retained are almost always girls. Boys seem to be more difficult for a mother to raise; it is often felt that boys have a greater need to live with their role model fathers. The matter is open to speculation, but the single mother of a boy is probably more uncomfortable than the single mother of a girl. I believe the more influential reasons cluster around the gender-model suggestion, given many Americans' exaggerated fear of (especially) male homosexuality. In addition to single mothers worrying about the effects of living in a matriarchal household on their sons' masculine identities, they may sense that a male child will offer more resistance at the onset of his mother's socializing with men other than his father. The boy feels that *he* should be the one to take his father's place. A daughter is more likely to respond positively to a new man on the scene, since it is clear that he is not meant to replace *her*.

The average absentee mother in my study approached divorce with two children aged about four and six; her counterpart, the average custodial mother who divorced in 1970 or so, was more likely to have one than two children but did share the situation of having a four-year-old. The difference in number of children is due, for the most part, to the fact that the absentee mothers' marriages were of longer duration and their children were born more closely together. Their marriages were a median length of eight-and-a-half years, while their peers' marriages lasted for only a median of six-and-a-half years. Given the previously suggested Oedipal strivings among my participants, I suspect that the decision to divorce was more labored for them because they were, subconsciously, married to their fathers. To walk away from what had been such a powerful desire for most of their lives required much more than the usual effort in divorce decisions. Thus, it seems the decision also took more time.

Beyond the factors of younger, more numerous, and more male children, a significant number of my participants' children were born with or developed a handicap or special problem: one-quarter of my mothers had at least one handicapped or "problem" child. The range is wide but includes many serious conditions. Two of these children died as a result of their disabilities: one was mentally retarded and did not die until he was fourteen, the other was born an encephalic and died after one month. There were a half-dozen other cases of serious illnesses or malfunctions involving the children as infants only, such as premature birth with many of its attendant complications. There were fairly common conditions, like allergies, croup, and eczema that were described as severe cases that extended over unusually long periods. There were two cleft lips, one child with drooping eyelids, and another with an abnormal formation of "extra" skin behind her ears. The group of children also included one with a bleeding ulcer, a child with only one functioning eye, and one who required open-heart surgery for a major heart defect when he was five years old. The most highly represented problems, though, are hyperactivity, speech and learning disabilities (including one case of severe dyslexia), and emotional disturbances. I have one child who required speech therapy as a toddler and another who has been diagnosed as hyperactive. Several of my participants had two such children, and one had three (of her four) children who fell into this category.

Whether the level of handicapped and problem children here is comparable to the general child population or to the children of custodial mothers, I do not know. Even if it is average, however, it is relevant in combination with the other factors that combine to make my participants' roles as mothers perhaps more difficult than the norm. Only if the level of physical and emotional problems is below average would it cease to have meaning. Obtaining a comparison would require a study unto itself, however, primarily because there are so many different ailments involved. Thus I cannot put a great deal of emphasis on the element of handicapped or problem children in the absentee mother's experience before relinquishing custody. Neither have I been able to find anything in my data that would indicate that the emotional problems among these absentee mothers' children were connected causatively to their mothers' attitudes; these children were spread among mothers from every relinquishing category.

In summary, I see my absentee mothers as having been in high-pressure situations: suffocating marriages, and intense child-raising circumstances created by things additional to those just addressed. For instance, almost half of the women in my study never spent more than an evening away from their children during their entire marriages. Only one-quarter of the mothers in my study had ready access to someone who would look after the children for more than a day at a time. And their feelings reflected it:

I felt so confined, as if I were trapped for the rest of my life, even though that isn't reasonable. I was very angry about the burden of mothering.

It was the constant responsibility of motherhood that got to me.

The children had unrelenting needs. It was always, always something.

The fighting, screaming, whining, and crying would hang on me like additional children. They were all too much with me.

I was so tired and did so need just a little freedom and quiet, some time to be alone, to take a leisurely shower.

The extremely negative version of motherhood experienced by so many absentee mothers can do nothing but create outrage among those who are accused of selfishness, irresponsibility, or narcissism in relinquishing custody. Most made the mistake of attempting to be selfless, not of being self-centered; of attempting to fulfill all the responsibilities of parenting all of the time, not of avoiding them; the mistake was being able to accept only others' needs, not of focusing solely on their own.

Spouses Who Were Involved Fathers

Seventy percent of my participants' husbands took part, to significant degrees, in the care of their children, an involvement which made them anything but typical of their contemporaries. In the Chicago suburban neighborhood where my husband and I lived during the final years of our marriage, he was the only father who had anything at all to do with fulfilling his children's needs beyond "bringing home the bacon." He was viewed rather cautiously by the men, but the women thought he was wonderful. So did I in that respect, although he really did not do so much by today's standards, and the degree to which he helped did not change when I held outside jobs. His involvement with the children was notable only relative to what other fathers were doing in the 1960s.

Most of my participants were also married to men who wanted to be involved with their children. This is especially interesting in light of the fact that 75 percent of these men had no previous experience or instruction in child care. (My husband's casual ability to take care of the children came from having cared for an infant brother and having earned money as an adolescent by babysitting.)

In conjunction with looking at these involved but unprepared fathers, it is pertinent to consider the women they married from the same preparedness perspective, since they were parenting together. In Chapter 3, I showed that about half the women in my study were the oldest children in their families and had, therefore, a good deal of experience with child care and early responsibilities. The other half of my participants are the opposite: they had no child-care experience or instruction before they produced their own children. None of my participants displays a *moderate* degree of preparation for motherhood. They either feel they were overburdened in childhood or were completely ignorant until their own babies were born and they were forced to learn under the pressure of the moment. Only nine women in the study who were unprepared for infant care were fortunate enough to marry someone who *was* prepared, as I did. But absentee mothers have many good things to say about their former husbands as fathers:

He was a very devoted father; the children were his whole life.

He had a lot of energy. He took time to explain things to our daughter. She loves him very much.

He was very proud of being a father and tried to be a good one.

He spent most of his time with the kids, took them and their friends everywhere and stayed home when they were sick.

He would almost always tend to the children when we were at a restaurant, and when we were at our own table, he'd feed one for me.

It was obvious that he loved his child.

He was very patient and willing to do anything for our son, down to cooking for and feeding him. He didn't feel the child was in the way at all, like I did.

He was involved in their rearing and showed them love.

He was a super father!

Neither my husband nor my participants' husbands, for the most part, would do housework, however. Only one-third of them helped with housework, and even those who did were not usually gracious about it. Says one woman, "He would help only if I were very ill." Another husband, according to his wife, "would help if we were having company, but only if the people coming were *his* friends."

Extended Households

It was shortly before Christmas in 1963. My daughter was eighteen months old, I was seven months pregnant and trying to rally some lost esteem for my husband. His latest drinking incident had involved a tavern argument; he was beaten and robbed in an alley and given a police escort to our front door. The night it happened I had been lying in bed, awake, waiting, almost afraid to breathe in fear of what the night might bring. A flashing red light appeared from nowhere, reflecting off the bedroom ceiling. Then a terrible banging on the front door. The pain in my side when I jumped up made me think I had begun premature labor. When I opened the door, I saw a uniformed policeman supporting my husband by the arm. Bill's glasses were missing and there was dried blood around his mouth and a huge stain of it on the front of his shirt. My husband, reeking of vomit, had a smirk on his face. The policeman asked, "Mrs. Paskowicz?"

"Yes," I said. I hated having to admit it.

"We had to bring your husband home. He isn't fit to drive."

"Where's our car?" I asked.

"We really don't know. We found your husband in an alley, and he can't remember where he parked it. Hell, Ma'am, he can't even talk right now."

"Well, thank you anyway," I said, feeling mortified.

The next day, as always, it was Bill who was mortified, and he refused to discuss what had happened or what he was going to do about his drinking. I was in despair, sitting there with the big belly that made me powerless, with my toddler playing by me, seemingly so secure in her environment. Then the phone rang and Bill gladly left the room and the pall over it to answer the call. The news on the phone was that his mother had died—from cirrhosis of the liver at forty-five. He had never been able to love her because of her drinking.

The police found the car; it had been impounded. As soon as we got it back, Bill left for Michigan and his mother's funeral. I stayed behind to prepare for the two new family members he would be bringing back with him. Since Bill's mother had been widowed by her second husband, her fourteen-year-old son from that marriage was now an orphan with nowhere to go except to his older married half-brother, my husband. Bill's adult younger sister also had a problem. She was single and pregnant, and the father of the child denied having any responsibility for the situation.She lived in a small town where such things were still a scandal, so she was coming to our place for the duration of her pregnancy and the process of giving her baby up for adoption. She lived with us for about six months. Bill's half-brother lived with us for four years while he attended high school.

Shortly after my sister-in-law finished the adoption process and went home, she was replaced by one of *my* sisters. She was eighteen and had married too quickly. When her new husband was sent to Vietnam, she stayed with us for a few months while gaining momentum toward self-reliance.

After my younger sister left to live on her own and Bill's half-brother had graduated and left for military service, my *older* sister became part of our household for a while. She had been a nun for fifteen years and had recently made the decision to leave the convent. Her predicament had one thing in common with what my younger sister had faced—she had never before been responsible for herself. The Order had provided for her physical and spiritual needs and had determined everything for her: what occupation she would take up (nursing), where she would live and work, what she would eat, and how much time she would spend in recreation. Since she had begun her dedication to the religious life as a high school freshman, she had never even been on a date. After an anxiety-ridden attempt in another city to enter "the world" without assistance, she realized that she needed some support through her transition and accepted the offer that she stay with us until she could ease into total independence. She lived with us for four months before getting her own apartment nearby.

Since I had given birth to my third child prior to my older sister moving in with us, the number of persons in our household had been consistently at six for almost four emotionally charged years. During these years, there was always at least one member of our extended family living with us.

Forty-eight of the married women in my study also had extended households while married. During a period when only 12 percent of the country's households consisted of six or more persons,[4] half of the wives in my study lived in homes that averaged six persons, either because they had taken in relatives or friends or because they themselves had been taken in. This group includes six participants who had households of six or more even before they took someone in. Only a half-dozen of the forty-eight fall into the category of having, themselves, moved in with another family. Few of the women liked it.

The average amount of time my participants maintained or lived in these extended households is one year and three months, a significant length of time to have persons outside the nuclear family living in one's home. In two cases, the extended household arrangements existed for the entirety of the marriages. In one of these cases, divorce came after three years, in the other after five. Both of the marriages included two stepchildren each, and both wives feel the stepchildren were strong contributing factors to their divorces.[5] One of them describes the impact of the living arrangement on her marriage: "It was devastating."

In another instance, my participant and her husband took in both her father and his mother for eight years. Additionally, her brother lived with them for one year after returning from Vietnam. Says the wife, "I disapproved of our parents living with us, but my husband wanted the extra financial help—they both paid rent. I felt I had no privacy."

The majority of women felt that the extended family situation had a largely negative effect on their marriages and, in a few cases, on their parenting. However, not all of them felt that way (see Table 9).

I, for example, experienced the four-year stay of my husband's teen-aged brother as negative because he was another child on top of my own, whom I already felt as burdens. He was really a very nice boy, but I was no more prepared to nurture this orphan than I was to nurture my three children, and I resented the extra work his being there involved. When my sister-in-law lived with us for six months, however, it was a positive experience. We liked one another and were both pregnant for the first two months of her stay, which lent a feeling of common predicament. Pregnant women share an increased vulnerability and the sense of being "centered." She helped me with everything in running the house, and when I came home from the hospital with the new baby, she took care of him during the night until I recuperated.

When my younger sister stayed with us for several months I was pleased, too, although there were disappointments. We had always been compatible and felt close, but she was out more than she was in and seemed to be avoiding any substantive contact with me. Not until after my divorce did she confide that my husband had made advances toward her whenever he had been drinking and I was not around. My older sister's residing with us had the most profound effect on me. I felt that her leaving the convent showed me the possibility of independence, of doing what one had to do for one's own well-being even in the face of powerful opposing forces. My sister had to confront, if only in writing, the Pope himself to be released from her marriage. And once released,

she had to cope with a world for which she had not been prepared—family and friends who had known her in adult life only as
a nun and, in many cases, who were against her being anything
else. I was in awe of her monumental courage and, subconsciously, identified very strongly with her action.

I do not believe that any of my participants with extended
households were as strongly affected by their residents as I had
been except for the two cases involving stepchildren already mentioned and for a case in which the residents were an unrelated
married couple with their two children. In that instance, my
participant's husband fell in love with the other woman in the
house; two divorces were the result.

Only thirteen of the forty-eight extended households were made
up of resident friends, however. Three-fourths of the additional
household members were either siblings, parents, or other relatives—one-fourth each. The "other" relatives included grandparents, nieces, nephews, and cousins. The remaining fifteen
residents consisted of six stepchildren and nine unrelated children,
such as an exchange student and foster children.

Within my extended household the temporarily resident relatives were half my husband's and half mine, but I do not believe
there was any correlation between my negative reaction to my
husband's brother and the fact that he was not *my* relative. It was
more a matter of adult versus minor. Neither does there appear to
be such a correlation among my participants. Their negative reactions, where they existed, were almost evenly divided between the
husband's and wife's relatives or friends.

I believe that the most important element of the extended
household issue is that four-fifths of the participants involved felt
an impact on their marriages as a result of the residents.

Depression, Suicidal Feelings, and Attempted Suicides

Some of the women in this study stayed too long in their longer-
than-average marriages. In their effort to remain with their father-
husbands in spite of all the destruction to their adult spirits, they
found themselves in an agonizing dilemma. For six women, this
meant the onset of serious depression and anxiety. Six others had
feelings that were more vague but equally disturbing: a sense of

being trapped in a small enclosure, of confusion in their mental processes, or simply of being "unable to enjoy anything." Those in the latter category, the ones who did not identify what they were feeling as depression, were the ones who entered therapy.

Seven felt they wanted to die. While driving, they might feel the impulse to pull in front of a truck. A gun might be taken out of its storage place and inserted into a mouth. Pills were an easier option. Six women followed through on their suicidal thoughts. Most of them would not talk about it; they were still afraid of themselves. But Mary told me how it happened with her. She tried to kill herself twice during her twenty-one-year marriage:

I don't remember all the details of the first attempt. I do remember that the precipitating factor was papering the bathroom ceiling. I had been quite depressed for a while, and in the process of working on the bathroom with my husband, I had to take the blame for all the difficulties involved in the job. It was always my stupidity that was the problem, the fact that I was supposedly so smart but had no common sense. I remember that it was just before Easter. I took some pills, but not enough to kill me. It was a cry for help, help I never got, although my husband did seem solicitous for a time and gentler for a while. But from then on I slipped further into depression.

Over a period of about two years, I really became withdrawn. Eventually, I was going out only to church and market, with an occasional substitute-teaching job. My husband started drinking more heavily, sex became almost nonexistent, and I cleaned house less than ever, yet I have no idea what I did during days at home.

Finally, there was a long evening of my husband berating me with my not contributing financially and asking, "Why don't you go live with your parents?" and "Why don't you take pills again?" All this was a regular litany while he was drinking. He told me he was still in love with the woman he'd been engaged to at twenty-one and that he had, in fact, slept with her. Then he said that he wasn't sure we were legally married (after nearly twenty years!) as he'd never gotten final divorce papers from his first wife.

I threatened to take pills. In fact, I said that he should force them down my throat since he was the one doing all this to me. He wouldn't. I went upstairs and found it very easy to take a heavy group of his sleeping pills and tranquilizers. He knew I had taken them but merely said he was going to bed and then did just that. Later, he called down to remind me that our eldest was leaving to compete in a national track meet the next day, and this would be so upsetting for her.

I remained alone in the kitchen until I started getting very woozy. Then I went up and stuck a toothbrush down my throat to cause vomiting, but it didn't work. I took mustard in water, which was also unsuccessful. Eventually, I told my husband that I wanted to go to the hospital, but not because of him, only because of our daughter. He took me there, though I don't remember much of the ride. I was out pretty deeply, but I remember the tubes down my throat; I thought someone was trying to choke me. I was in intensive care for a couple of days, and had come very close to dying.

After Mary had spent four or five days on the medical floor, her family doctor suggested that she spend some time in the psychiatric unit, and as she phrases her response, "I *jumped* at it." It was a very important four weeks for her, the beginning of her journey toward mental health, which included divorcing her husband two years later.

The six wives who actually attempted to kill themselves indicate that my sample, when compared to the female population at large, has a much higher incidence of suicidal behavior: 176 times higher than among other women in 1970.[6] If it were conceivable to enlarge the population to the extent that would be theoretically necessary, this would mean that for every thirty-four women at large who attempted suicide at that time, six thousand women in marriages like those of my participants would attempt it.

5

The Tragic Equation

It is in the nature of guilt that it demands punishment.

—*Froma Sand,* The Life Wish

Some months ago I received a rather sinister anonymous phone call. The caller was a divorced woman whose husband had simply disappeared after their divorce. She had never remarried and so had raised her two, now grown, children alone. She had seen one of my advertisements for absentee mothers and called, evidently, to point out the differences between herself and an absentee mother. She wound up doing a lot more than that.

"I'm very maternal," she said at one point. "I love my children . . . Self-sacrifice is the only way to live." Much later, in a low confidential tone of voice: "A friend of mine has an adopted daughter who wants nothing more than to find her real mother— so she can kill her! That's what *you* have to look forward to!"

I cannot say I found the notion of matricide terribly threatening; it seems hardly likely that the children of absentee mothers are waiting out there with anything more than, at worst, fantasized murder on their minds. But I did find the anonymous caller herself disconcerting in her smugness and hostility.

The anger and aggression exhibited by this woman are typical of one of the ways in which society at large responds to the absentee mother. Friends are shocked and withdraw. Mothers, sisters, and grandparents are horrified and may refuse any further contact.

Children are hurt and often condemnatory. At every turn in her attempt to function in her changed circumstances, the absentee mother receives another blow to her feeling of self-worth. She frequently has no source of desperately needed emotional support. The power of this judgment and rejection is almost impossible to overestimate. When it combines with the absentee mother's own doubts and anxiety, the result is the tragic equation: guilt reinforced by society's rejection leads to destructive behavior.

Self-Directed Aggression

The significance of an individual's isolation is well established in the field of mental health and starkly described by one psychologist: "There is no greater fear in the human heart than the fear of abandonment by others, the terrifying sense of standing alone in an empty universe devoid of those who demonstrate love and concern and compassion."[1]

Neither is the relationship betwen guilt and violence questioned by professionals. They have repeatedly stated that the guilt-ridden person either wreaks havoc on herself or on those around her in the form of hostility.

SUICIDE

The degree of suicidal behavior among the absentee mothers in my study reflects the magnitude of the social rejection and guilt they experience in response to having relinquished custody of their children. Whereas approximately seven out of every one hundred thousand American women commit suicide each year,[2] if I were to extrapolate the findings among my one hundred absentee mothers to the same base of one hundred thousand, I would be faced with the staggering suggestion that for every seven other women who commit suicide, one thousand absentee mothers bring about an end to their lives.[3] Of course, the large number of existent absentee mothers this would tacitly imply probably do not, in fact, exist. (There are no reliable statistics, only educated guesses, as to how many absentee mothers actually exist.)[4] My sampling of one hundred is probably too small to justify such an extrapolation, in any case; nevertheless, the contrast involved is so stunning that narrowing the difference, even substantially, by a large enough study would still be likely to leave a dramatically higher rate of suicide among absentee mothers than among women in general.

Another point of interest which further supports the proposition that absentee mothers are much more likely to commit suicide than other women is the fact that Margaret, the woman in my study who killed herself during the year I spent researching, was black. Black females display the lowest rate of suicide (at 3.5 per 100,000) of all the population classifications, and black females were underrepresented in my study, at 4 percent as opposed to 12 percent black females in the general female population.[5] In other words, with every statistical reason to expect otherwise, a suicide occurred among an extremely small sampling of women during a very short period of time, and it was carried out by a member of the least likely segment of the group to exhibit suicidal behavior. I believe the explanation for this phenomenon is closer to the exceptional stresses to which the absentee mother is subjected than to chance. A black absentee mother may be considered less deviant than a white absentee mother, due to differing community attitudes toward maternal situations.[6] Thus the stress concomitant with the status of absentee mother would be less severe for the black mother. This makes the suicide an even more powerful indicator of the emotional stress that is part of being an absentee mother.

I remember distinctly my first contact with Margaret because of her obvious emotional distress. She was another phone respondent. When she had heard my explanation of the project and was giving me her address (which included a street name along the line of, say, Sweet Life Road), she hesitated for a second and then said bitterly, "It *sounds* so pleasant, doesn't it? But it's just a warped joke." Margaret was forty-seven, the mother of four, and had been married for twenty-six years to a man who indulged himself in constant infidelities, persistently "put her on trial" for her shortcomings, and "heaped constant blame" on her for every household detail that was not just right.

At the time she left her marriage (three years prior to completing my questionnaire), the reactions around her had been formidable, and since then had become a permanent part of her life. Her two grown sons chose simply to ignore her existence. One of her brothers refused to speak to her, in spite of the fact that he had never even liked her husband, and her friends "couldn't understand how she could give up her children for *any* reason." At work, where she was a secretary, she evaded all discussion of her children out of fear that someone would learn that her nine- and sixteen-year-old daughters did not live with her. This made Margaret feel like a criminal. Margaret's daughters were also bewildered by their mother leaving them, but how could she have told them that her despondency allowed her only two choices—death or "running away?" Children cannot perceive a parent's depression as something unrelated to their own worth or behavior, nor can they fathom its powerful depths. Margaret told me about her daughters' response in two sentences:

The girls couldn't understand. One cried and told me she could see me leaving their father, but "what about us?"

That question melded with the pain of all the surrounding disapproval and became for Margaret a weight to be carried each day. Like Sisyphus, she resolutely struggled up the incline many times over, but unlike Sisyphus, there came a day when she could not do it again. On New Year's Eve of 1980, Margaret dropped her burden forever with the help of alcohol and pills.

Two months had elapsed since she completed my questionnaire, one month since I had sent her a set of clarification questions. She was not found for several days, which seemed a sad indicator of her isolation. The unanswered clarification questions lay on her dresser, but they had been answered nevertheless. Margaret's action was a shattering response. A person does not kill herself unless she feels it is wished by others.[7] Margaret had simply carried out the sentence that society had indicated to her was called for.

ATTEMPTED SUICIDE

Six weeks after Margaret's death, I received a half-completed questionnaire from Gwendolyn, an absentee mother in the Midwest. The return address was the psychiatric ward of a hospital; Gwendolyn was recovering from a suicide attempt. When her husband of eleven years had left her and their two daughters, aged nine and ten, in 1979, Gwendolyn found a full-time job as a dental assistant and started attending freshman classes at a local college, but she soon began to feel overwhelmed. Five months after assuming full care of her girls, she relinquished custody to her husband. It took only three months thereafter for the impact of her "weakness" to take the form of an attempt at self-destruction.

I do not mean to say that a low level of self-worth is the only factor at work in any given suicide attempt. Suicidal behavior has a number of complex facets, regardless of the initiator, but I will concentrate here primarily on the aspects of attempted suicide that I feel are particularly pronounced for the absentee mother. Therefore, only in passing do I observe that, in Gwendolyn's case, it is likely that at least two types of suicidal motivation were operative in addition to her diminished self-esteem. Her husband had withdrawn his love, which she could not accept, and she must also have been feeling much anger toward him. Suicide may be felt as a means to regaining love and as an indirect act of murder against the person with whom one is angry.[8]

It is estimated that anywhere from six to ten times the number of people who commit suicide each year try to do so.[9] This translates into a mere one-sixth of 1 percent of the female population. Compare this to the attempted suicide rate of 7 percent among my absentee mothers (since becoming absentee mothers). If I include the multiple attempts at suicide made by three of the seven suicidal women in my study, the truer attempted suicide rate among my hundred absentee mothers is 10 percent.[10] In addition, six women had nervous breakdowns that did not involve attempts at suicide. Six had suicidal plans at some point. Thirty-five have received psychiatric care, and eleven currently feel the need for psychiatric help but have been unable to obtain or are fearful of seeking that help. This brings the portion of the group that may be considered psychologically troubled in conjunction with their being absentee mothers to an astronomic 60 percent, and a number of these women can probably be regarded as seriously troubled.

I tried to kill myself about eighteen months after I had left my husband and children. I was on my third job, experiencing increasingly intense anxiety at the onset of each workday, and involved with a married man named Ron. I had been working late. My employer of six months had made his first advances toward me. He told me that one of his reasons for hiring me as his secretary had been that I was divorced and did not have my children living with me. That meant that I would be free to work after hours as often as he would like and thereby make it possible for him to have an ongoing affair with me. (This was the third boss in succession who had assumed that I would be amenable to a liaison.) When I made it clear that I did not want an intimate relationship with him, he became angry and spat out that he did not see why I should draw the line with him when I was already involved with another married man and had left my own children. After all, how much lower could I get?

I ran out to my car crying. I was so overwhelmed with self-loathing that over and over I begged God to kill me. I started driving, but I could not see anything clearly. I imagined letting the wheel go and obliterating myself against a concrete wall. I found myself stopped in the parking lot at home where I cried over the wheel for a long time. When I at last went up to my apartment, the only thing I could find in the medicine chest was a brand-new bottle of aspirin. I started taking them with water. I kept gagging, but I think I took the whole bottle. Then, fully clothed, including my high-heeled shoes, I crawled into bed and pulled the sheet and blanket over my head.

But the phone rang. It kept ringing. Finally, I forced myself to reenter the real world, leapt from the bed, pulled the phone jack out of the wall, and immediately returned to the protective womb I had created. Then another sound stopped my heart. Someone was opening the door with a key. It had to be Ron. He was the only one who had a key. I could not imagine how he knew to come over, but I knew that now I would have to face the humiliation of discovery.

At that point, I shared something with the 11 percent of the absentee mothers in my study to whom I have referred, the ones who feel the need for psychiatric care but either do not recognize it, avoid it, or do not find it accessible. I felt terrible. A day never passed when I did not have headaches; my back muscles refused to relax unless they were kneaded before I went to bed; I started feeling sharp pains in my mid-section. An internist had suggested I see a psychiatrist.

In spite of the fact that I had attempted suicide and that I had so many physical manifestations of emotional conflict, I did not see these things for what they were. My immediate response to the internist's suggestion was the conviction that he was "all wet," but I made the mistake of telling Ron about it. I think he had been wanting to suggest the same thing, because he seemed to leap on the idea (after all, he was the one who had forced the aspirin up and out and the one who was now kneading my knotted back every night). From then on, he virtually crusaded for the purpose of my making an appointment at some local mental health clinic.

I went to the clinic merely to get Ron off my back. I had no intention of seriously pursuing analysis or therapy. At that time, I did not even know the difference between the two. I felt there was nothing wrong with me. I was simply responding with tension and anguish to a world replete with tension and anguish.

Within five minutes of the therapist closing the door, I had erupted into uncontrolled weeping. I was so utterly unprepared for and horrified by the occurrence that I never went back, but I did pretend to go back. Once a week for months Ron believed me to be at the mental health center. I did not know it, but I was insuring what was to come. There is a critical period of about four years following any attempted suicide. If the person who has tried to kill herself is not helped within this period, she will almost certainly attempt suicide again. Most second attempts are successful.[11] Some of the women in my study are in that phase now.

Gretchen, for instance, is one of the four in the hundred who never married or lived with the father of her child. She became pregnant at eighteen while still in high school; the father of the baby was only sixteen. After her son was born, six months following graduation, Gretchen started college while still living with her parents, who cared for the boy when she was gone. When her son was eighteen months old, she quit school, moved out of her parents' home, and started sharing an apartment with another single mother. Her son was with her.

The two of them lived an insecure, chaotic life, supported much of the time by the welfare system, although there were periods when Gretchen was able to work as a go-go dancer or a waitress. The fact that she was responsible for both herself and the child caused a great deal of anxiety for her. She started drinking and using drugs. She had a nervous breakdown and was unable to take care of her then four-year-old son. He went to live with his father's parents with their assumption that Gretchen would use the time to recover and become strong enough to reassume her parenting.

Gretchen never recovered in anything more than a superficial way and made no contact with a mental health professional. If anything, her condition could probably have been considered worse, since her use of alcohol and drugs increased. At any rate, based on the misguided belief that Gretchen had gotten well, her son's paternal grandparents returned their grandson to his mother's care about a year after they had accepted that charge.

By this time, Gretchen was no longer living with the other single mother. She had begun living with a man who was also involved with drugs and alcohol. Once her son had returned, I believe it became more and more difficult for Gretchen to accept or justify her erratic and irresponsible way of life. She felt extremely guilty for subjecting her boy to what she knew was an unsuitable environment, yet she was equally unable to impose the necessary changes on herself. The gross emotional conflict this situation caused raged within Gretchen for five months before she reached for a razor blade.

Gretchen's slashed wrist neutralized the war of polarities she had been waging; her son, this time, went to live with her parents. The living arrangement for Gretchen's son this time was permanent, and seven years have passed, but Gretchen continues to avoid the confrontation absentee mothers must endure if they are ever to find peace. They must recognize their guilt; dig up the sources of their original feelings of inadequacy (which invariably are there with suicidal absentee mothers); release the stored avalanche of hurt and self-loathing; and, finally, forgive themselves. Sadly, Gretchen does not appear to be gaining ground in this respect, but rather continues to show signs of internal turmoil. As late as the summer of 1979, she was hospitalized after a prolonged period of insomnia and inability to eat. She has lapsed from Alcoholics Anonymous and feels "unable to appreciate the fine, kind man" with whom she now lives. Even after seven years of persistent emotional combat, Gretchen is not, apparently, ready to put an end to her avoidance.

There are degrees of avoidance, however, and Gretchen has, in fact, proven an admirable bravery by taking part in the study and by the quality of her participation. Not everyone was able to do that. Fifteen percent of the absentee mothers who committed themselves to taking part in the study were unable to follow through on that commitment, most of them clearly because they were not prepared to face the emotions they realized later would be engendered.

Marlene, whom I called after many personal notes had failed to produce a completed questionnaire, told me in one defiant sentence that she had thrown the questionnaire out. That was all she said. Then she just stopped, and there was determined silence. When I said I was sorry that that had been her decision and asked if she could tell me her reasons for it, the same absolute silence set in. So, awkwardly, I fulfilled the amenities and she hung up. Something dramatic was happening in that exchange, and I believe it had to do with Marlene having glimpsed something she did not want to see.

Others were able to tell me that they could not withstand the emotions that the questionnaire was evoking; and still others had gotten through the questionnaire by way of quick, superficial, and probably misleading responses, but abruptly terminated their participation upon receiving a set of clarification questions, the completion of which would have required more substantive consideration. Twelve of the participating absentee mothers withdrew at this juncture. I feel they were evading the cataclysm that awaits most absentee mothers.

When that cataclysm insists on happening in the unconscious and imposes suicidal behavior on us, there are those who are wise enough and courageous enough to recognize the destructive action as something more than a frightening occurrence to be forgotten as quickly as possible. Judy is one such absentee mother.

At seventeen, she entered a semicloistered convent and spent four "very content" years in an order where prayer was the first priority; her studies progressed well. When the liberal changes occurring throughout American religious orders broke upon her particular community, Judy became troubled. The traditional habit was replaced by more practical clothing, prayer was given lower priority, and the community life became "full of strife." Judy describes one more new problem at that point in her life:

In the new "worldly" atmosphere, I found the vow of chastity suddenly very difficult. I wanted close one-to-one relationships, and now could not justify sublimating it.

A friend of Judy's arranged a blind date for her one week after she had left the convent:

We dated on and off for two years. Then I found out I was pregnant with his child. He had wanted to marry me anyway, so I said yes even though I had many misgivings. My mother organized a huge wedding with three hundred guests. One week before the wedding date, I quietly miscarried. I did not have the courage to back out and was married as scheduled.

Judy was not in love with her husband, so when their differences became apparent and their arguments persistent, it did not seem right any longer to remain in the marriage, in spite of the fact that it was four years old and had produced two sons.

I finally admitted how unsuited we were to each other. There were differences in our goals and values. He was letting things happen, I wanted to act. He wanted to stay home and drink beer in front of the TV, I wanted to go out. He was a very poor lover and had a very low sex drive. He was very strict with the two boys, I was not. I did not want the children raised in a household of fighting and no love.

Since Judy's husband was "broke and unemployed" at the time of their separation and divorce, Judy agreed that he be given their house in the property settlement. Judy, herself, was working full time as a programmer. These two factors were the primary reasons for the divorce decree stipulating joint custody. The children would remain in their familiar household and Judy would be able to work without full-time child-care problems.

The boys slept at the house weeknights. I picked them up and had them every evening from four to eight and weekends. But my work then began to include a lot of travel, so my ex-husband had the children more and more of the time.

Two years passed in this fashion before Judy found herself in love with a Canadian. She decided to move to Canada to be with him and tells us how the changes unfolded:

My ex-husband got a court order keeping me from taking the boys out of the state. I did not have any money to engage a lawyer and fight it . . . I was then unemployed. Then my ex-husband went to court again and said I was unwilling and unable to have custody. That was totally untrue, but he got full custody anyway. The boys were very settled in their schools and neighborhood. I didn't know then if my new life was going to work out. So I left.

Judy's sons were three and six when she left. Judy felt a "profound sense of loss" and "extreme depression."

In time, though, with the emotional support of a fulfilling second marriage, Judy's initial reaction to relinquishing custody of her sons eased. (She tried to ignore the headaches, stomachaches and bowel problems which replaced it.) Once a year, she would travel twenty-three hundred miles to spend two weeks visiting her sons. Each summer, they would make the trip to their mother and stay for the entire three months. But simmering somewhere in a sensitive part of Judy's psyche was the conviction that she had "run away" in the beginning when she agreed to joint custody because she did not feel she could cope with a full-time job and two toddlers. She had wanted to be—felt compelled to be—a perfect mother, but had failed. Indeed, before marrying she had also sought perfection of her soul in the convent of a strict order. A six-month period of unemployment and depression and a hysterectomy complicated by pneumonia, followed by four weeks at home in bed, added to Judy's psychological disarray.

The boys had to be sent home before the summer was over. Judy had, once again, failed to be a perfect mother. One week after her sons had gone back to their father, she swallowed "a handful of Dalmane" while her husband was at work. She needed to escape her imperfection. She slipped into a place Virginia Woolf dwelled upon in *Orlando*:

Are [sleeps such as these] remedial measures, trances in which the most galling memories, events that seem likely to cripple life for ever, are brushed with a dark wing which rubs their harshness off and gilds them, even the ugliest and the basest, with a lustre, an incandescence? Has the finger of death to be laid on the tumult of life from time to time lest it rend us asunder? Are we so made that we have to take death in small doses daily or we could not go on with the business of living?[12]

Judy, then, had her sleep "such as this" and woke from it; her husband had come home early. She also heeded the appeal her subconscious had made; she began visiting a psychiatrist once a week and has been "on the upswing" in the two years since.

For those who may be inclined to think that Judy's attempted suicide had nothing to do with the social judgment to which I have been referring, that it had to do only with the view she held of herself, some things should be made clear. Although suicide appears to be the most personal action an individual can take and its sole purpose seems to be self-destruction, other people play an important part in its causation and are as much the intended victims as is the more obvious victim. The individual is too entwined with the social matrix to be considered apart from it.[13]

Directing Aggression Outward

If Judy's attempted suicide was in part an act of aggression against others, I would suggest that, in addition to her former husband, her aggression was directed toward the friends she told me withdrew from her; the employers whom she said displayed such total lack of comprehension of her position that she began explaining it with the misleading statement, "The boys attend a private school in the States"; the people at parties she described to me, representatives of society-at-large certainly, to whom she learned "never to mention it, to usually just say that [she] had no kids," because of the disapproval exhibited and expressed when she told the truth. Any mother who is shamed into denying the existence of her own children is likely to be justifiably full of hatred for those who impose such pressures.

Until now, we have been dwelling on the awful equation as it is enacted by an absentee mother who chooses to direct her destructive behavior toward herself. But in other absentee mothers the crisis-stage aggression may take the form of outward-directed destructive behavior. Before the crisis stage, the absentee mother's guilt, when so directed, most often simply takes the form of hostility toward others in her daily social interaction. But if and when a crisis level of aggression develops, the point at which so many of my absentee mothers have attempted suicide, it is also quite possible that a choice might be made to unleash that aggression through physical violence against others. When I use the phrase "a choice might be made," I do not mean to imply that this is a calculated, conscious choice, but rather an unconscious, irresistible choice.[14]

MURDER

One can see evidence of this phenomenon. On January 7, 1980, for instance, Darlin June Cromer was arrested for the murder of a five-year-old boy whom she had kidnapped two days earlier. The little boy had been strangled and buried on a beach. Darlin June Cromer is an absentee mother.

Also in early 1980, I learned from an acquaintance that she has a cousin who is currently charged with the murder of her former husband. This cousin is an absentee mother.

One night in late 1973, I stood over the sleeping man in my bed. I was gripping a hammer with both my hands, and the hammer was raised over my head. I was going to murder Ron. It could have happened. I might have been a murderer, as might any other perfectly sane, usually harmless absentee mother. Murderers are not people set apart; they are us. They are people whose chronic frustration becomes unendurable.[15]

In the case of an absentee mother, that frustration lies in the inability either to obtain "forgiveness" from her own society or to obtain forgiveness from herself. As Froma Sand points out, our relationship to ourselves becomes our relationship to the world; the world as it stands has withdrawn from us the emotional nutrients that are necessary for what she calls *inspired survival.*[16] This inability to forgive exists in part as an outgrowth of something we witnessed in the story of Judy, the former nun, something also addressed in Chapter 1, but which bears repeating. We all continue to be slaves to the ingrown notion of the perfection of womanhood and, in particular, the perfection of motherhood.

PERFECTIONISM'S INFLUENCE IN AGGRESSION

The feminist force itself has fallen into the same trap, having simply approached it from a different direction. Whereas the initial myth was one of pure goddess/eternally persevering and self-denying mother, it has accidentally begun metamorphosing into the myth of superwoman, capable of all things at all times. We are more wonderful and perfect than ever. An excerpt from a 1978 speech by Ellen Goodman at the Association of National Advertisers highlights this:

Superwoman gets up in the morning and wakes her 2.6 children. She then goes downstairs and feeds them a grade A nutritional breakfast, and . . . then goes upstairs and gets dressed in her Anne Klein suit, and goes off to her $25,000-a-year job doing work which is creative and socially useful. Then she comes home after work and spends a real meaningful hour with her children, because after all, it's not the quantity of time, it's the quality of time. Following that, she goes into the kitchen and creates a Julia Child 60-minute gourmet recipe, having a wonderful family dinner discussing the checks and balances of the United States government system. The children go upstairs to bed and she and her husband spend another hour in their own meaningful relationship, at which point they go upstairs and she is multiorgasmic until midnight.

What has been passing for liberation so far is mostly just more responsibility and more pressure to be more than ever.

I see in my own behavior some of the same attempts at perfection that appear in Judy's history and the histories of many of the other absentee mothers in my study. I too, for instance, first sought perfection through the religious life. I spent one year as an aspirant in a Franciscan order of nuns. While I lived with my husband and children, I was driven by the need to be a perfect mother and a perfect housewife. My right to live seemed totally dependent on my ability to be perfect in the execution of my duties, and this same mania has been present among many of the hundred women in my study.

After I had become an absentee mother, this same perfection syndrome took the form of a preoccupation with my supposed physical deficiencies. I went so far as to schedule numerous cosmetic surgical procedures for myself, although I did not follow through on these in the end. As it happens, however, at least one of the women in my study did follow through with two such operations for herself. There could be more of this sort of misplaced concern among my study group, but it was not something I thought to pursue in time to include such a line of questioning in my research.

Whatever the origins of these expectations of perfection in women as objects and in women as mothers, it should be emphasized repeatedly that they are cruelly destructive, because they doom women to failure. It also needs to be recognized more fully that, in spite of what we like to think about ourselves, far too many of us still cleave to these expectations of perfection.

STIFLING AGGRESSION: THE BOOMERANG EFFECT

My own conviction that I was unforgivably inadequate, continually reaffirmed by the society around me, reasserted itself one week after I had been able to stifle my urge to murder Ron. The volcanic aggression within could not be permanently subdued after all, only redirected. It was the first day of the new year, 1974, and I felt, once again, that I could no longer bear the horrible consequences of my dual role as an absentee mother and an "other woman." The secrecy required by my illicit relationship with Ron compounded the isolation I felt already as a result of my absentee motherhood. My life energy was utterly depleted.

The beginning of a new year can mean new hope, replenished strength, possibilities, even joy. Or it can mean the prospect of twelve more debilitating months, the fortification of the wall which separates you from others, and a sense of crushing desolation.

Ron was at his summer home with his wife and children. My children were also far away, with their father and stepmother. Both my sisters were at home with their husbands, my mother at home with her husband. I was alone in my one-room apartment.

I wandered back and forth in the tiny apartment for hours, crying and touching things. It was as if the walls, the clothing, and the furniture were to be my last companions, and I was saying goodbye to them.

When my wandering and weeping tapered into sitting and staring, I began to see where I was going. The bottle of Valium tablets was in back of a drawer, under pajamas and nightgowns. My conscious self had hidden them from Ron; he was such a prude in some ways, thinking I should not use tranquilizers. My subconscious had saved them for now; I knew, somehow, the time would come. I felt calm and in control, warm and comfortable. Somehow I did not feel mortal. I felt as if something awaited me—perhaps the unconditional love that I had always craved. Some psychoanalysts believe that the human mind is incapable of conceiving death, that man does not wish for extinction but for Nirvana. Looked at in this way, they say, suicide is intended as an act of self-perpetuation, a denial of the barrier separating life and death.[17]

I took the pills easily. They were much smaller than the aspirin had been, and much more potent. I knew there were more than enough to do it right this time. But I answered the phone when it rang, and my door was not locked when my sister got there. Do the absence of precautions against survival mean that the person attempting suicide expects to be rescued? Erwin Stengel says not. In his view, the absence of precautions simply illustrates that suicide is not as a rule a rational, carefully planned and executed act.[18]

Most people who commit suicidal acts do not either want to die or to live; they want to do both at the same time, usually the one more, or much more, than the other. It is quite unpsychological to expect people in states of stress, and especially vulnerable and emotionally unstable individuals who form the large majority of those prone to acts of self-damage, to know exactly what they want and to live up to St. James's exhortation: "Let your yea be yea and your nay, nay."[19]

I remember a nurse holding me up, with something being held at my mouth. I was supposed to drink it all down and I did, but I could not feel or taste anything. No sooner had I swallowed the substance than the stomach I did not seem to have started convulsing and heaving the poison lava. Then everything ceased to exist again.

The Stages and Effects of Suicidal Behavior

I do not know how long I slept, but when I woke I was first aware of my bladder. Then I was conscious of my arms and legs, and they were a tremendous weight I could not lift. I could see I was in a small cubicle of a room, not much bigger than the bed I was in. Absolutely everything was white—it seemed a part of Space Odyssey. A couple of feet from the foot of the bed was a white door. It was closed, but had some kind of wire-enmeshed window in it.

It was urgent that I find a toilet. With the sort of effort that must be required to do the final mile of a marathon, I got out of bed. My feet were bare and the floor was concrete-cold. I looked out the door-window. Beyond a square hallway with a door off to the left, I saw a large room with patients seated here and there on sofas, and a glass-enclosed nurses' station to the right of the large room. My door was not locked, so I started toward the door on the left in the square hallway, using the walls for support. It was a bathroom.

When I woke again, I knew it must have been another day. I was hungry, but there was something else too, something incredibly good. I felt light, unburdened, refreshed as never before, as if my blood had been mentholated. I wondered why I had wanted to kill myself, and I was glad I had been found out in time. I felt I must have deserved to live after all. I have since learned that many suicidal attempts can be compared with an ordeal—that is, an ordeal in its ancient ritual meaning of a trial in which a person submitted himself (or was subjected) to a dangerous test the outcome of which was accepted as the judgment of the deity. I have also gained some insight into the sense of well-being I felt that day:

The release of aggressive impulses directed against the self in an emotional outburst may have a beneficial cathartic effect on a person's mental state . . . it may relieve pent-up tension and thus restore emotional equilibrium, at least temporarily. This is possibly one of the reasons why some people feel much improved following a suicidal attempt and why they do not contemplate repeating it [at that point] . . . In those rare instances, the method employed caused the patient to be deeply unconscious for several hours or days. It would be difficult to attribute the recovery in these cases to purely psychological processes. It is more likely due to an effect on the brain . . . [which comes out of] short periods of unconsciousness.[20]

Within a week, I was released from the psychiatric hospital. Ron picked me up and drove me home. As soon as I saw him and during the drive to my apartment, I knew he was no longer essential to me. The welcome-home gift he gave me seemed oddly inappropriate: a ten-speed food blender. Not too many months passed before I made the final break with him, which was my first move toward what Froma Sand would call my life wish.

After Ron brought me home from the hospital and left, I started sorting through the mail that had piled up while I was in the hospital. There was a letter that must have been there before I tried to kill myself, probably unopened because of the distracted depression that had preceded the attempt. The letter was from my cousin Peter. Peter and I had both been raised in Chicago, where I had remained while he had moved to California. On one of his home visits, at a time when each of us was despairing of our romantic situations, we found ourselves attracted to one another in a new way and had become lovers. After that, we were also regular correspondents. Looking at his unopened letter, I remembered having written to him before Christmas, and I opened the envelope:

Oh dearest dearest Trish,
You are ever in my thoughts and heart, my beloved cousin and unhappy lover. The tone of your note tears my heart and fills me with anxiety for you. How I wish I could somehow send you some sort of happiness or even a bit of solace.

I must have been giving a warning in that letter before Christmas, but I had not been aware of it as such. Some warning of suicidal intention is almost invariably given, in that those who attempt suicide tend to move toward other people in the process leading to the event. Peter went on in his letter:

I tried to call you just now when I got your card and will try again. Please, won't you do the same? Couldn't a friend, a cousin, a lover—someone who wants to care in whatever way he can—help? For God's sake, call me—collect—anything—if you really feel badly. Please!

Your devoted and anxious,
Peter

I had no sooner read Peter's letter than the phone rang, and his comforting voice was on the line. He had called to wish me a happy 1974. Somewhere during the phone conversation, I made some obscure reference to what I had done on New Year's Day, but the meaning of what I said had not been clear to Peter and we just concluded the phone call in a casual way. But a few days later there was another letter from him. Lightning had struck:

God damn it Patricia! You can't do things like that! You have a responsibility to people who care for you and you really put them in a terrible position with such acts. I'm just full of feelings of guilt and frustration and, more than anything else, a feeling of impotence. I still can't really take it all in. I didn't understand when I talked to you on the phone; it took some reflection before I could appreciate what you'd told me . . . Please write.

In retrospect, I can see this exchange between my cousin and me in the light of the psychodynamics of attempted suicide. I sounded an alarm with my letter to him and he responded to my appeal for help, each of these things occurring although neither of us was aware that an appeal, as such, had been made. Peter's expressed feelings of guilt were not unusual under the circumstances either. I understand that it is natural for relatives and friends to respond to the appeal effect of the attempted suicide with feelings of guilt. In fact, people close to the person who attempted suicide, and society, try to behave as they feel they would have behaved had the outcome been fatal.

Something else in Peter's letter, it turns out, was significant. Peter said:

I'm sure there ought to be something I could do or should do, but I just can't find it.

The people around an attempted suicide often wonder what a suicidal act is an appeal for. The answer is, it is not usually for anything specific, just for help. Stengel says the attempted suicide states no more and no less than "I want to die—or *do* something for me," even though everything possible may have been done. The doctor also points out that the emphasis in this double message varies.

It was not too long after Peter's letter that he sent me a little gift.

It was a record, one that was popular then, called "Lean on Me," by Bill Withers. Our relationship grew and intensified. Very often, the appeal of the attempted suicide, made and answered, results in a change for the better. This may be one of the reasons that a repeated attempt at suicide rarely takes place immediately after the first. In this case, a very big change in my life occurred: Peter and I got married.

It is not my intention to suggest that my second suicide attempt and the major change in my life to which it contributed meant that my psychological problems were over. They have meant, however, a recognition on my part of my emotional conflicts. But best of all, I know now that, critical or not, I am capable of facing those problems and that, with the proper help, they are not invincible. I know, too, that I want to live and that being an absentee mother does not mean that I deserve to die.

I feel myself fortunate that my attempts at suicide did not result in permanent physical damage. Until recently, I took that fact for granted, but I have since come to know Gloria. And I will never again be able to recall my attempts without feeling a shudder of fear for what could have happened to me somewhere between complete recovery and death.

Gloria's suicidal behavior differs from the other absentee mothers, although one aspect of Gretchen's story is comparable. The difference in Gloria's case from the other absentee mothers discussed here lies in the fact that both her suicide attempts occurred while she was attempting to function as a single parent following separation from her husband. So the special stresses of absentee motherhood were not part of Gloria's suicidal causation. Nevertheless, Gloria's story makes another point within the context of absentee motherhood.

Gloria married at sixteen. She had completed the first year of high school and three-fourths of the second. Her husband was eighteen and worked in a gas station. It would not be difficult to take these simple facts and develop them into dozens of possible succeeding events (all of them negative), but those that actually developed are too staggering to encourage looking elsewhere. Gloria's letters and questionnaire responses held my eyes and my spirit from beginning to end:

I had a baby at seventeen, another baby boy at eighteen. I was so overwhelmed by all this that I separated from my husband and began seeing my younger brother's friends. I was renting a duplex with a girlfriend my age and her two-year-old boy. Some friends of ours, also the same age and who had managed to stay married, lived in the other side of the duplex.

We had wild beer parties and the police knew we had minors there. So we were always being harassed by the police. And my roommate's mother-in-law was always on me; she thought I'd broken up my roommate's marriage, and in a way I probably did. Our friends on the other side of the duplex kept telling me to go back to my husband, he loved me, the kids needed him, and so on. The times I'd get too drunk or uncaring about my kids, my friend on the other side of the duplex would take care of them. I even had pressure about settling down from this friend's mother. And the church people. I began to think I really must be a monster for not wanting to live like normal people.

After a while, when I did decide I should do that, I could not stop the crowd of teenagers who had gotten used to partying at my place from coming over. I remember I tried for awhile, but being sixteen and seventeen, they had nowhere else to go, and I or my roommate would make an exception here or there, like letting at least each of our boyfriends come over. Then their friends would come by and see their cars there and stop. I would try to turn them away, but everyone would say, "We'll come in and have just one beer and then leave." With that, they'd push their way in and, of course, never left. And it would mushroom from then until it was out of my control. I was really bummed that I could not get my own home back under control, it was just a party house.

There was one particular policeman who would come to the house. I'd come out and sit in his car and talk to him about why I let this go on, about why didn't I go back to my loving husband, but I didn't want to stop what was going on that way, and why didn't I think about what I was doing to my two boys and my roommate's boy. (My roommate had a weaker personality than I, so everything that happened to her was thought to be my responsibility.)

I was so tired of the way things had gotten out of control. I made a stepped-up effort to stop it all, but it didn't work. After that, I began thinking of suicide.

I thought about it for a month. My kids would be better off. I'd quit influencing my roommate. And I wouldn't be there for my brother's friends to use anymore. That was the only way out I could see. I told my roommate I might do it if I got enough courage, so she hid the gun that used to belong to my husband in one place and the clip in another. It was a twenty-five caliber with a hair trigger.

Then a bad weekend came. All week my husband had pleaded with me to come back. We'd been together for our second son's first birthday. I wanted to be alone to think, but people kept coming over. It was the Fourth of July holiday weekend, and everyone felt like partying, except me. My roommate started letting everyone in, and I saw it was no use fighting it. So I joined it. I got more drunk than I'd ever been, but I didn't get happy. I got violently angry that these people had taken over my home again. They burned holes in everything, broke glasses, blared music even if the kids were trying to sleep. They just took over.

I don't remember a rational decision like "Tonight I'll kill myself." I just remember tearing about the linen closet and drawers looking for the gun. The house was such a shambles anyway, no one realized what I was doing. I found the gun and clip and ran outside into the back yard of our friends next door. I remember sitting there thinking, "Should I do it? Where will it hurt the least? I don't want to look ugly at the funeral." So I decided I'd shoot myself in the stomach. I didn't know that you could shoot yourself and live, under any circumstances. Too many cowboy shows I guess. I figured you get shot, you die—period. So I did it.

After a while, people noticed I wasn't at the party, so my roommate went next door to our friends, Emmett and Marie, to see if I was there. They said no, but they thought they'd heard something outside their children's room. Emmet went outside and found me.

I wasn't bleeding externally, and the gun had fallen in the bushes. It was around midnight and dark, so no one knew for sure what had happened, although Emmett was aware of my suicide threats. He carried me into my bedroom, and the whole party followed him. He noticed I was turning all black on my back, so he looked for a bullet hole and found it.

Then I became conscious. Emmett was screaming for everyone to get out and for his wife to call an ambulance. I looked around but couldn't remember what had happened. I just knew I felt sick and started throwing up blood. Then the ambulance was there. I could hear Emmett instructing his wife to take my kids and my roommate's to their side of the duplex. Amazingly enough, all three kids were asleep in their room.

The bullet had entered the right side of my stomach, but it didn't exit or shatter; it lodged in my sacral canal and was pressing on my spinal cord. When I was conscious, I'd be swearing at the doctors for saving me. They operated that night, but when they discovered where the bullet was, they decided to wait until they could call a specialist in. I almost died that night; I was in intensive care for about two weeks. My pain was tremendous. If someone even jarred the striker frame I was on, it felt like I'd had electric current sent through me. Doctors and nurses thought that was strange since most paraplegics have no feeling. I was a terrible patient. When I was finally moved out of intensive care, I developed pneumonia; I begged them to let me die.

After some months, I was moved to a teaching hospital (I was on welfare) so they could get the bullet out. The operation took about seven hours. I was told later they did not get the bullet and that I had almost died again. Two weeks later, they tried again to remove the bullet. This time they succeeded. If the bullet had slipped upward while still implanted, I would have been a quadraplegic. As it turned out, my spinal cord was not severed, but it was damaged far enough to leave me paralyzed from the waist down. I was put into the rehabilitation ward to see if they could teach my atrophied muscles to work. My bladder didn't work at that point either, but after a time it began to function again and my right leg function returned partially too. My husband and I had reconciled while I was in the hospital, so I went home with him one weekend on a hospital leave. That's when I found I could still have sex with feeling and partial movement of my hips.

My children would sometimes come to see me in the hospital, but I frightened them. My mother had been taking care of them, but this was a strain on her. That's when my cousin Marion first said she'd like to help, and the boys were sometimes with her.

After my ten-month hospital stay, I moved back in with my husband, but I was terribly bitter and complaining. I couldn't take care of my house and kids from a wheelchair, and that frustrated me no end. The kids learned they could get away with a lot because of my condition and really took advantage of it. I was sure my husband figured he'd gotten a rotten deal, and I constantly hurled insults at him. We tried for about a year, but he finally left.

I was bitter that I was now in a much worse situation than I'd started with and that there was nothing I could do about it. How could I ever learn to cope with it? I was seeing psychiatrists all the time, and I did a lot of plea bargaining with God, but nothing helped. In spite of the lesson I thought I'd learned, I started drinking again and eventually became quite promiscuous, to prove I could still be attractive I guess.

At this point I was nineteen years old. The only reason I had somewhere to live was that I lived rent-free in a house my parents owned. I was back on welfare. For two years, I lived like this. I still hadn't accepted my condition, so I tried to kill myself again.

I'd been saving sleeping pills, thinking of doing it in a less violent and painful way. Whenever I sounded suicidal to my psychiatrist, he'd say, "But what about your children?" I always thought, "Damn it, what about me?" One evening when I was alone, I put the kids to bed and took fifteen Seconal. A friend called, though, and I answered the phone. When my speech started slurring, my friend called my parents, and I was once again in the hospital—this time in a psychiatric ward.

My kids were alone again, so my cousin Marion helped me out by taking the boys in. I was in trouble with welfare now for not having considered the fact that, had my attempted suicide succeeded, my children would have been the ones to find me dead in the morning. They were about three and four years old. Finally, in a desperate move to gain security for myself and my sons, I married a guy in the Marines just so I'd have allotment money to live on. My new husband was based in another state, and I lied my way out of moving there with him; so I was in my own apartment with my boys, and the oldest began kindergarten.

School was hard for me with my kids. They were embarrassed by my condition (by now, braces and crutches), and so was I. When my husband returned from the service in three years, I felt I should live with him and give my boys at least one normal parent. It was okay for a while. The boys liked "policing up their room" and all the disciplining my husband did, because he made it seem they were playing army. And they would listen to him but not me. But I couldn't fake it very well as a wife to him. I didn't love him. One day, my youngest son said, "Mom, why do you always laugh with your friends and never with Chris [his stepfather]?" It was then that I realized I wasn't doing my kids any favor. I felt I was teaching them all the wrong things about marriage. I got a divorce.

My boys were then seven and eight and getting into trouble in school. One was hyperactive and began lighting fires and breaking windows and would not mind me at all. I was afraid that if my kids didn't get a normal family life soon, it would be too late for them.

My cousin Marion had moved to another state, and she suggested that, as a seventh birthday gift for my youngest, I send him to her house for the summer. It would help him and me. She was married and a good Mormon and had five kids of her own. I thought she was very generous, so, on his seventh birthday, my son got on an airplane and went to my cousin's.

Things kept getting worse with me. My oldest son wanted to know why I couldn't be like other mothers. Then my cousin suggested I let the older boy come up too—for a school year. The youngest seemed to be doing well up there, so I decided to do it. I sold my washer and anything I could get my hands on to get enough money to drive my son and his belongings up to my cousin's. A girlfriend of mine did the driving. On the drive, my son kept saying, "You're not going to leave me there forever, are you?" I told him, "Of course not!"

When we got there, my younger boy seemed wonderfully adjusted. He played the piano, was doing well in school, and he was giving a talk in church he wanted me to come and hear. He proudly introduced me around. He was totally changed. It seemed like a miracle! My cousin Marion suggested we go to a lawyer's office. It now seems a blur. The lawyer talked forever and kept shoving papers at me. All I know is the last paper said adoption. I said, "No way." But my cousin said, "Gloria, if you don't let me adopt them, I won't take them at all." She said she loved them too much to let them go again. That sounded like a good reason, and I had no future to go home to. I argued, but they, of course, had good points to make. So my children were adopted by my cousin Marion.[21]

Society's Role in Aggression

That is the end of Gloria's story, for the most part, but there are many mothers who are unsuited for the role in which they find themselves, for a multitude of reasons. They are not only doing a poor job of nurturing their children; they are also hating their positions and brewing their own versions of the tragic equation. In one sense at least, troubled mothers who remain with their children and absentee mothers have the same problem: society's insistence that a mother remain with her children, no matter what. The following incidents represent, I believe, the kind of horror this societal intransigence creates.

In late 1979 in Oakland, California, a woman barricaded herself and her little girl inside their apartment. She had a gun and was threatening to kill her daughter and herself. She was talked out of the apartment without incident.[22]

Also in California, as 1980 began, a twenty-five-year-old mother put her eighteen-month-old baby boy into the oven "to drive the devil out of him." He was hospitalized with severe burns.[23]

A woman was stopped from jumping off the San Francisco Bay Bridge on October 15, 1979. Found in the trunk of her car was a little boy, her son, who had been beaten to death. He had a rope around his neck.[24]

In Syracuse, New York, late in 1981, a mother was arrested for scalding her two children to death, once again, "to get the devil out of them." They had been tied up during the scalding.[25]

On June 11, 1974, "the first hot day of summer," Joanne Michulski, thirty-eight, the mother of eight children ranging from eighteen years to two months of age, took a butcher knife and decapitated and chopped up the bodies of her two youngest on the neatly kept lawn of her suburban house outside Chicago.[26]

These horrible cases are extreme, but they ought to make it impossible for us to continue overlooking the magnitude of the problems, even in less dramatic circumstances, which come about as a direct result of mothers continuing to bear the entire burden of caring for and nurturing their children. As Adrienne Rich points out, "The physical and psychic weight of responsibility on the woman with children is by far the heaviest of social burdens."[27] When this heaviest of weights descends upon a woman who is emotionally troubled, simply immature, or overburdened, neither mother nor child can be all they need to be to one another. And we all pay for this. There is something wrong with a system of child rearing that not only creates desperate mothers but offers these desperate mothers (and the vilified absentee mothers who have dared to break the rules) no options outside of debilitating behavior, murder, and suicide.

6

Afterlife

Becoming

But the ashes dance. Each ashfleck leaps at the sun.

—Marge Piercy, "Noon of the sunbather"

INDEPENDENCE AND REMARRIAGE

It was eight years after my divorce before I even considered remarriage. They were eight of the most significant years in my life. At the age of twenty-nine, for the first time, I became responsible for myself in every way. In the beginning, I was scared witless. I had no car, no place to live, no furniture, and a total of one hundred dollars in my purse, the final paycheck from a part-time job I had held before leaving home. I borrowed a car from a friend, searched all day and into the evening for an apartment, and borrowed the first month's rent and security deposit from my mother.

That all sounds fairly smooth, but there were problems. I was supposed to return my friend's car before her husband returned from work; I did not make the deadline, and my friend's husband was not at all pleased. A friend of mine since high school, he turned his face away from me when I spoke and left the room without a word. I was no longer an androgynous friend to him but a threatening and uncontrollable female, a mother committing the unthinkable crime of desertion. My husband's plea that I leave the children with him was irrelevant.

My mother was also a problem. "What will people say?" (She had herself, her entire life, enjoyed making people's tongues wag.) Maybe I would be forced to stay with Bill and the kids if she would not help me. I was crazy for throwing away a good husband. (It dawned on me how self-destructive it had been to hide Bill's drinking problem and how much worse it made me seem to everyone now.) The money she finally lent me was the first and last help she gave me for years. Afterward, she put herself in my husband's trench, phoning him almost daily to commiserate. It did not surprise me. It brought to mind the evening the wife of a past boyfriend was a guest in my home, along with a number of others. My mother spent the entire night in the kitchen with my former rival, telling her in great detail what an inept wife, mother, and homemaker I was and praising every project my guest described which had been accomplished in her kitchen or at her sewing machine. My mother did not like me even before I was an absentee mother, so, for a long time after, her feelings reinforced the terrible reduction in self-esteem and the intense guilt that followed me inexorably.

The landlords with vacant apartments were a problem too. I had no job and no credit history, and where would they be if I decided to reconcile with my husband? I failed completely to convince any of them to rent to me.[1] The apartment I finally managed to get was a sublet from a woman tenant also in the process of divorcing, but even she did not readily identify with me; she was not the spouse initiating divorce.

I found an employment agency a long walk away from my apartment and then a job where one of the other employees was willing to give me a ride temporarily. When I received "my share" of the proceeds from selling the marital house, I used it as a down payment on a car. My share turned out to be a minuscule $750; with my overwhelming sense of guilt, I had allowed my husband to use the formula shown on page 171.

If I were to consider the monetary value of my eight years as a wife and mother in this light, it would mean I had been worth $93.75 per year. In the same length of time, my husband had been deemed worth approximately $108,000 and was paid accordingly.

Gross proceeds from sale of house	*$26,500*
Balance of mortgage paid	*(18,500)*
Net proceeds from sale of house	*$ 8,000*
Balance of street & storm sewer assessment	*(2,200)*
Balance of outstanding household debts	*(950)*
Balance on husband's car	*(617)*
Fee for husband's attorney	*(500)*
To neighbor for showing house	*(50)*
Balance of net proceeds	*3,683*
Rounded balance of net proceeds (a $17 "generosity")	*3,700*
My share of net proceeds (determined by dividing five ways among husband, three children and wife)	*740*
My share of net proceeds rounded (still another "generosity")	*750*

I had no attorney, I waived my right to alimony and I never appeared in court—all outgrowths of blind guilt. I deserved nothing; I received little. But I had my apartment if I could meet the rent, and I had three pieces of furniture borrowed from someone's basement, my very own car if I could make the payments, and my minimal-wage clerical job. In the years that followed, I was able to upgrade my employment, housing, and education; I discovered my desire to write, pursued my lifetime wish to dance, and my eight-year wish to take long, hot baths. All relative accomplishments, but they were important developments for me. In addition, I owed my body to no one; neither man nor church nor state could any longer demand that I use the full capacity of my womb. I became involved in the civil rights movement, and I worked in the political campaigns of liberal Democrats. I was in love with a man who shared my interests and who never went near a bottle of Scotch, a can of beer, or a televised sports event. By the time I remarried eight years later, I knew who I was, what I wanted, and had begun to suspect what I could do.

The great majority of the absentee mothers in this study also gave themselves time on their own. Only nine women of the ninety-eight who had been married remarried in less than a year. As one can see in Table 10, the fifty women in my study who have remarried waited four months longer than their divorced counterparts. Perhaps the stunting marriages from which they had extricated themselves contributed to the slightly longer hesitation.

The fact which gives much more support to the suggestion that absentee mothers value and maintain single life longer than other divorced women, however, is that they remarry at a rate more than one-and-one-half times lower (62.5 per thousand per year) than their peers (104). Forty-eight of my participants remain unmarried after a median of four years—more than twice the length of time by which other divorced women would already be married. And none of these women is currently considering remarriage. In addition, only six of the forty-eight say they would like to remarry. Fifteen definitely do not want to remarry, and the remaining twenty-six are highly dubious about remarriage.[2]

In contrast (see Table 11), the majority of former husbands of my participants have been anxious to reestablish themselves within a marriage, and they have done so at a rate that outstrips their former wives by almost 20 percent. Again, I believe that the child custody arrangement has had much to do with it. Custodial fathers, if their former wives' evaluations are correct, are usually in a hurry to find a second wife to care for their children—unless they have mothers who are able and willing. This tends to discredit the apparently flourishing myth that the custodial father is a hero or patron saint of dads who enjoy childrearing. In reality, he may experience child custody as something of a hot potato to be tossed into the lap of the first willing woman (see Table 11).

Twenty former husbands of my participants remarried before a year had elapsed, more than double the number of absentee mothers who remarried in such a short time. Furthermore, as one can see by comparing the Tables 10 and 11, the thirty-seven former husbands who have not yet remarried have been divorced for a shorter time than the former wives who have not remarried.[3] By the time the thirty-seven unmarried men have progressed to the same lapsed time as the forty-eight unmarried absentee mothers, their ranks will have diminished even further. If their rate of remarriage were slowed to that of the women (twenty-five per year), thirteen more would be remarried by then. If their own quicker rate of remarriage continued (twenty-eight per year), fourteen of the thirty-seven would be remarried by the time another half year elapsed and brought them up to the four years elapsed for the unmarried women. This would mean a forty-eight to twenty-three (two to one) ratio of unmarried absentee mothers to unmarried former husbands.

These figures contribute to the suggestion that custodial fathers do, indeed, consciously rush toward remarriage, compared to their ex-wives, but the higher rate at which they remarry could merely be a reflection of the fact that divorced men in general marry at a higher rate than divorced women in general. (Single men have proven to be the unhappiest segment of society.) It has been suggested by some absentee mothers that these hurried remarriages are meant, in part, as punishment for them; quick replacement as wife (and perhaps more so as mother) can be quite hurtful. Such bitterness-related motives for remarriage aside, however, being a custodial parent must be a major reason for remarrying sooner. Both custodial fathers and custodial mothers remarry sooner at a much higher rate than absentee mothers. Single parenting is agonizingly difficult, and marriage is, I believe, the most common way to reduce that difficulty to a more tolerable level. It is interesting to note, however, that divorced fathers with custody may well have a more difficult time finding women who are willing to take on the responsibility of stepchildren than do divorced mothers with custody finding men who are willing to do so. I base this conjecture on two facts: first, although custodial mothers who remarry remain single for a median of two months longer than custodial fathers who remarry, they remarry at a rate 25 percent higher. Second, noncustodial fathers find it possible to remarry at a rate more than double that of fathers raising children. The single life is best enjoyed by the child-free. As a matter of fact, even married life is best enjoyed by the child-free; studies indicate that the most content people are married couples with no children.[4] (This supports my assertion that a portion of the anger displayed toward absentee mothers results from repressed resentment among custodial parents that they must bear the burdens of childrearing while absentee mothers go free.)

LIVING WITHOUT CHILDREN

> When I am alone I am happy.
> The air is cool. The sky is
> flecked and splashed and wound
> with color. The crimson phalloi
> of the sassafras leaves
> hang crowded before me
> in shoals on the heavy branches.
> When I reach my doorstep
> I am greeted by
> the happy shrieks of my children
> and my heart sinks.
> I am crushed . . .
>
> —William Carlos Williams, "Waiting"

I have been living in an adult-oriented environment for twelve years now. I think about my children, I write and call them, I care about them and their lives. We visit when finances allow for the travel involved. My nineteen-year-old daughter has married and given birth to a little boy; we spend a good deal of time talking to one another over eight hundred miles of telephone wire. She has an extraordinary, and completely intuitive, understanding of herself already and has real insight into human relations. I look forward to the day I get my first chance to babysit. Mother, father and baby have even considered moving to Grandma's state so we might all be more a part of one another's lives. I would like that.

My oldest son is eighteen; in the fall of this year, he will enter college. He has a special intellect but is in a sensitive transition wherein he seems to be asking those around him to love him apart from his "gift." (He deplores the term *gifted*.) I hope to help him feel more comfortable with it, and being far away from his critical, demanding, and competitive father and unaffectionate stepmother will be a large step in that direction. As soon as my daughter left home to marry and was free of her father's and stepmother's scrutiny and rigid rules, she began reaching out to me more and responding to me more readily. I believe the same may occur with both my sons.

My youngest son is fourteen. His most outstanding characteristic is an outgoing personality. Within a few hours or so of arriving anywhere for a visit, he will have introduced himself to neighborhood teenagers. He is a doer: skateboarding, roller skating, cooking, and karate are merely a sampling of his interests. Curiosity is his driving force. Friction in his "reconstituted" family has become his unpleasant companion. I have let him know that he will always have the alternative of coming to me; his father has agreed to let him go if he decides he would like to, but he has decided to stay in his father's home. I think it would be terribly difficult for him to leave his half-brother and sisters, his friends, and his father during this passing into manhood. It is probably best.

In spite of the pleasure my children bring me now, I have never regretted relinquishing custody. It has remained clear to me that I simply could not have supported three children emotionally over the years. Recently, however, I began to feel that perhaps I had finally become capable of nurturing, especially if it were only one child. I began feeling aware of a missing element in my life and contemplating the intimate pleasure of pregnancy and the delight in the phenomenal discoveries toddlers make. I had married a previously unmarried man with no children, the only male in his generation of family. He and I seriously considered having a child, but we are both forty, so we could not afford to dawdle over the decision. In the process, I learned a number of things about both myself and my husband.

I realized that in all my longings toward becoming a mother again, I consistently dwelled upon the infancy and toddler stages of having *a baby;* I never thought beyond to having *a child.* If this sounds familiar, it is because I have already related noticing in retrospect the same mental block in myself prior to having my first child almost twenty years ago. I realize now that what I really want is impossible, a baby who would never become older than five or six. I had been choosing to remember primarily the pleasant aspects of being with my babies, probably as a defense against guilt about the things I found unpleasant. Since my oldest was seven when I relinquished custody, my live-in mothering experience did not reach beyond, leaving my subconscious with the dangerous impression that the task of raising a child really was completed in seven years.

In spite of the improvement in my emotional health, the thought of raising a school-age child is still unpleasant. It feels to my imagination like an unceasing demand inflicted on sensitized nerves and depleted stamina, with very little reciprocation or reward. Endless details about school. Lots of incomprehensible drawings that look alike but have to be admired. Whining, noise, chaos.

Another reason I was leaning toward becoming a mother again, in spite of my earlier negative experience, I realized, had to do with uncertainties related to personal achievement. Having a baby would be an acceptable way to avoid this. Having a baby, for me, would require all my energies. I proclaimed over and over again when discussing it with my husband that I was not one of the superwomen who raise families *and* pursue careers. I believe that part of me began to reach for a baby as an "out" from expectations (my own as well as others') that I succeed at writing and from the intimidating challenge that represented.

I still feel answerable on some level to society for having become an absentee mother; I believe I felt that having another child and "seeing it through" this time would release me at last from censure (which, indeed, it tends to do for absentee mothers). I also felt an obligation to my childless husband to provide him with a child regardless of all other factors. I had assumed that he must want to experience fatherhood and to continue the family name. However, after extensive discussions I learned that he really was not overly anxious to become a father. His interest in parenting, I learned, lies in the later years of development. This might seem the ideal balance for my early-years preference, but I doubt that reality would accommodate "serial parenting." (Now that you're seven, dear, you must pretend I am not here and go to your father for everything.) My husband, at any rate, is an only child and fits, I now believe, the prototype of which Walter Toman warns: only children tend to make rather uninterested parents. We have decided not to have a child.

Eighty-five of the hundred women in my study have similarly refrained from having additional children.[5] In general, they feel that having children is a phase of their lives which has passed, that it is time to go on to other things. There are, however, exceptions.

Seven of the eighty-five who have not yet had additional children plan to do so, and seven more say maybe to the possibility. Seventy-one of the eighty-five are definitely planning never to have more children, although it should be pointed out that there are seven among these seventy-one who feel that whether to have children is a moot point due to their median age of forty-five. Fifteen of the seventy-one are no longer physically capable of producing children; thirteen of them simply state that they "can't," almost as though they feel the need to defend their not having more children and welcome the unassailable alibi. They do not expand on whether they find their physical limitation a curse or a blessing, but the remaining two of the fifteen do comment further. One says, "I would like to, but I can't." The other says, "I am unable to have additional children and am happier for it."

Only forty-nine of the eighty-five could be defined, in the purest sense, as having *made decisions* to have no additional children. Since I am a firm believer in the meaning of allowing time and circumstance to make decisions for you, I therefore believe that the bulk of the eighty-five women have, in effect, decided against having further children. However, the ambiguity of a minority of cases is embodied in one woman's response:

I have such a negative view of having children now; my daughter's birth and childhood were so traumatic for me. But I do acknowledge that I might eventually have another child if I ever fall in love again with a man who really wants kids. I doubt this will happen, but it is a possibility. I think that if I really felt as strongly as I say I do about not having more kids, I would have had a tubal ligation a long time ago. I haven't had one, so there must be some doubts there.

What might really be there I believe, is the fear that one might fall in love with a man but be rejected by him if one is not willing or able to have children "for" him. Having children *for* someone does not work; I am encouraged when there is an absentee mother who decides *not* to have additional children *for everyone*, especially herself and the potential child. The words of two women represent what I see as better decisions for most absentee mothers:

I feel I have lost two children already. In a way, I blame myself for ruining their lives. I couldn't do it to any more children.

At the age of thirty-two, I am going to college and trying to get ahead in my career. I have already messed up one try at motherhood and don't wish to do it again.

When in strong doubt of one's parenting capacity, saying no seems the only conscionable response. But too many continue to ignore this and to promote the production of human life as an immutable good. At the same time, they ask, "Why is there so much child abuse?"

KEEPING CHILDREN IN THE PICTURE

The passionate belief in the superior worthwhileness of our children . . . is stored up in us as a great battery charged by the accumulated instincts of uncounted generations.

—Ruth Benedict, quoted by Margaret Mead in
An Anthropologist at Work

Retaining Custody of Some

It should be pointed out that thirteen absentee mothers in this study never lived child-free until some of their children became adults. These women retained custody of one or some of their children; they are the mothers of thirty-five children, and retained custody of fifteen (43 percent). Eight of the children kept by their mothers were girls who were the median age of twelve, the other seven were boys of the same median age. Offhand, one might conclude from this that a mother is no more likely to retain a girl than a boy, but that is not so. In the eight cases where a mother had only one child of each sex, she always retained custody of the girl; and of the mothers who kept custody of boys, in all but one case, they had no daughters. In addition, they left behind twice as many boys (23) as girls (12). The median age of the children left behind was ten. It is pertinent to note, however, that fourteen of the thirty-five children left behind were left at their own request, and two more were ordered to stay with their fathers by the court. The nine mothers (69 percent of all the mothers who retained custody) of these sixteen children (46 percent of all the children left behind) would gladly have retained custody of all their children if they had been given the option.

Resuming Custody

The first of two groups of participants who do not any longer live child-free numbers seventeen: these women have resumed custody of some or all of their children. They waited an average of almost four years before doing so—enough time to establish themselves and know more surely what they wanted and would be able to sustain. Most absentee mothers reassuming full-time childrearing did so at a reduced level from that carried during their marriages. That is, they resumed custody of only some of their children, usually only one; and those who resumed custody of all their children had, on average, no more than two children.

Fifteen of the children who returned to their mothers were girls and fifteen were boys; their median age was fourteen at the time of resumption. Among the children *not* taken back, ten were boys and eight were girls, a fairly even distribution. On the basis of this sample, when it comes to resumption of custody, as opposed to retention of custody, there is no indication that a mother will resume custody of a girl more often than she will resume custody of a boy.

I have found, however, that the mothers who have resumed custody share some pertinent childhood characteristics that set them apart from the rest of the study group. More of them lived with both parents for their entire childhoods,[6] they are more likely to have had mothers with positive attitudes toward parenting and fathers with negative attitudes,[7] and they include more women who were middle siblings.[8] In addition to a preponderance of positive mothers, these seventeen women had more than the rate of positive relationships with their sisters closest in age than the rest of the study group.[9] Also to be noted here is the high representation of women who were raised as Catholics: eight of the seventeen (47 percent) as compared to a rate of only 20 percent among the rest of the hundred. Of further interest, the mother resuming custody is almost twice as likely to be unmarried as married, and her former husband tends to be atypical of the other custodial fathers in that he also has not yet remarried. Another noteworthy fact is that the mother resuming custody is a mother who has maintained a residence two and a half times closer to her children than the median distance between the other mothers and children.

Most interesting, almost half the women resuming custody are from two relinquishing groups: those who sought self-realization and those whose children had made the decision to live with their fathers. In the first group, the mothers accomplished their major goals and resumed custody. In the second, the children changed their minds, and their mothers resumed custody. (The most highly criticized group of absentee mothers, those seeking self-realization, resume custody more often than any of the other voluntary absentee mothers.)

Having More Children

Fourteen absentee mothers in the study have had additional children since relinquishing those from their first marriages. Among them, they have had a total of twenty additional children, fourteen of whom were planned. (There is still a small degree of careless reproduction occurring, but it is minuscule compared to that prevalent in the first marriages.) In one of the cases involving unintended births, where two unplanned children were born, the mother seems to have gained some insight, however, from taking part in the study. She says, "Looking through this survey makes me stop and think about questions that should have been answered a long time ago." But even a planned child can result in regrets. Another second-family mother, who has had one additional child after losing two daughters to her former husband, is bitter in her renewal of motherhood: "Nothing has changed. I still have to do most of the work and work outside besides to supplement my husband's income."

Nine of the fourteen women had only one additional child, four of them had two more, and one had three more. Half of these fourteen second-family mothers are *involuntary* absentee mothers (those whose children left them and those who lost custody in court) in spite of the fact that involuntary absentee mothers make up only one-quarter of the whole study group. But even these women have a revised perception of motherhood the second time around, as two of them describe:

My first experience with mothering was somewhat negative because I felt so totally responsible and alone. This time, I feel relaxed and comfortable and enjoy sharing the responsibilities and pleasures. . . . In addition, I don't think I could be hurt by them in the same way I was by the first. I'll never let kids be the sole focus of my life again. My son figured in everything I did and I tried to "make up" for being a single parent. I now feel I went too far in being apologetic.

I'm older now, more experienced, wiser, and I know how I want my children raised. I finally learned to love myself and in so doing I also learned how to love others more fully. I feel that makes my mothering this time more "real" somehow.

The second most likely absentee mother to have additional children, at one-fifth of the fourteen who have had more children, is the "self-realization" mother. This is further evidence that these women merely needed time to "find themselves" before they could fully enjoy and meet the demands of custodial motherhood. Combined with the fact that self-realization mothers most often resume custody as well, it is also strong refutation of Joanna Kramer as being anywhere near representative of the real absentee mother who seeks self-realization. Three of the women describe their experiences with motherhood the second time around.

I am not overburdened with the responsibility this time. . . . My mother was not an adequate parent, and I feel I suffered from this, but I have learned to parent in therapy these past years and still see a therapist at times for further help with parenting my daughter.

I see mothering more realistically now. I'm not sure that I was "meant" to be a parent, but I love my son and am seeing just how much a child needs you, how much he trusts you, and I want to work hard this time at not betraying that trust. Now I am able to do that. Something I didn't see when I was younger was that responsibility is part of life. But, of course, you have to be ready for responsibility.

This time, mothering has been mostly a joyful, satisfying experience. I have been amazingly pleased at my own maturity and ability to aid in my children's development and my degree of patience and sensitivity to them. I was thirty-four and thirty-eight when each was born. I lost one child when he was thirteen weeks old from sudden infant death syndrome, and it was a crushing blow. A year later I had my last child, as planned, and it was such a joy to have him—a real gift!

Thus, it would be a mistake to generalize that absentee mothers are child haters when, in a group of one hundred, thirty-eight absentee mothers are (or have been until their children became adults) also live-in mothers. Most of these mothers retained or eventually resumed custody of some children from their first marriage or had more children during a second marriage. The vast majority of these absentee mothers have kept or reintroduced children into their lives because they value a life that includes children and because they believe that close relationships with their children are worth the hardships of single parenting, the difficulties of a reconstituted family, or the limitations of a child-oriented lifestyle.

EDUCATIONAL DEVELOPMENT

Only seventeen women in this study relinquished custody primarily to pursue self-realization, yet it is apparent from the striving for education and accomplishment among all one hundred participants that what I perceive to be self-realization is being sought by almost 60 percent of the absentee mothers. This figure strongly supports the impression that many of the women in this study left their marriages, if not their children, for the sake of personal fulfillment. Most of them, however, felt they were running from their marital confinement and not necessarily *toward* fulfillment. In large measure, pursuit of fulfillment has followed instinctively once the participants were free of their restrictive husbands and, sometimes, their children. For many, this pursuit has taken the form of seeking further formal education.

Since their divorces and/or relinquishing custody, ten women have earned their high school diplomas. At this level of adult accomplishment, the "emotional problems" group is most highly represented. Three times as many women from that group as from any other voluntary group are among the postdivorce high school graduates. This is another indication that lack of education contributes to emotional problems and the inability to address them.

Nineteen absentee mothers in the study have earned bachelor's degrees since divorcing an average of ten years ago. None of the ten who gained their high school diplomas is among these college graduates, but seven of the ten late high school graduates have begun attending college and have completed an average of two years. Similarly, two of the nineteen who have earned their bachelor's degrees have begun work on master's degrees. Among the nineteen who have graduated from college, there are a substantial number from the self-realization category—one-fifth of the total. The only other group with an equal number of representatives among the postdivorce college graduates is the group who relinquished custody in response to intimidation. Evidently, once without children, they made good use of their new situation. Going to school can act as an excellent distraction from pain, of course, but one must also wonder whether or not the suppressed desire to be child-free played a part in the success of their husbands' intimidation.

There have been nine postdivorce master's degrees and one Ph.D. Among the women who have gained advanced degrees, there are more participants from the group whose children made the custody decision than any other relinquishing group, probably because the women with the most advanced educations at the point of divorce or relinquishing were also the mothers of the oldest children. They are some of the women who had the opportunity and ability to pursue their educations, to a greater extent than most, during their first marriages, single parenting, and/or during second marriages (see Table 12).

Twenty-two of the twenty-five women who have earned college credit toward degrees, like myself, were high school graduates when they divorced or relinquished custody, and their credits are for undergraduate work. The other three participants were college graduates who have earned credits toward master's degrees. Only seven of the participants, however, are currently full-time students (two of the seven are graduate students). The rest have either put aside formal educations temporarily or have ceased planning to resume studies. It is my impression, although I do not have precise information on the matter, that the majority of the twenty-two with undergraduate credits do not intend to earn their degrees. Others continue to attend classes part time, more for the immediate satisfaction than for the fulfillment of long-term goals, and perhaps as means to locate opportunities and reinforce self-esteem. Opportunities glimpsed and confidence in place, these women have gone off to pursue the former and build on the latter in their own ways. But there is also a minority who cling to the hope of "someday" returning to school. Either way, formal education has played an important role for the absentee mother who is "becoming."

PROFESSIONAL DEVELOPMENT

When I married, I was a secretary. When I divorced and relinquished custody, I returned to secretarial work. With experience at nothing else, only a high school diploma, and no sense at all that I could do anything else, it was a reasonable course of action. Twenty-four (80 percent) of the thirty women in this study who were clerical workers when they married returned to clerical work when they divorced, and they have remained in that line of employment. More than half the women in this group (fourteen of the twenty-four) have not indicated that they hold higher ambitions and have not furthered their education since marrying. Their average educational level is high school graduate, two years lower than the study group as a whole. However, the remaining ten have advanced their educations by an average of two years, very gradually; one of them has earned her bachelor's degree and another is within a year of doing so. Most of these ten have ambitions to improve their level of employment, but they seem rather vague about the nature of their hopes.

More encouraging, the participants in this study who were either unemployed or full-time students when they married have blossomed since divorcing and relinquishing custody. These women had never established an image of themselves as part of the labor force, so they were free to imagine that they could be any number of things. They had not yet been classified as workers. They were free to believe that the hopes and plans they had held before marrying, or had developed since, were still possible. So they picked up where they had left off, as did the clerical workers, but their point of departure was one of possibilities, whereas that of the secretaries was one already established and limited. From the ranks of the twenty-nine former students and the fourteen formerly unemployed have come, for the most part, the forty-five professionals, executives, and entrepreneurs among the hundred absentee mothers in this study. The women in this study have done extremely well compared to the general population both male and female (see Table 13), although the professionals are largely in areas that have been long acceptable for women. In that sense, the participants in management positions represent the greater difference societally.

Two more absentee mothers managed to break through traditional barriers to better pay for women by going in a less glamorous direction, that of blue-collar work. One, who had never worked as anything but a housewife, is now a painter and general laborer. The other woman once worked as a waitress but now earns much more money as a salt miner. She stopped seeing her therapist when she "began to notice some weird shit about not being a 'real woman' coming from him. Maybe he suspected a case of Lesbianosis coming on," she says. But in light of the fact that she was being paid well for the first time in her life, "Who cares?" Among the general population in 1970, 36 percent of the economically active were blue-collar workers, but only 19 percent of blue-collar workers were women.[10] The two participants here who broke into this realm were (and still are) true pioneers. They have company among the five women who own their own businesses, two of whom are in traditionally male fields: locksmithing and commercial fishing.

In contrast, the clerical workers in this study and the service workers, who followed the same pattern of returning to the work they left at marriage, are almost in keeping with the numbers of general population similarly employed (see Table 14).

Nineteen absentee mothers who are not part of the labor force are made up of the seven full-time students discussed earlier, one retiree, four unemployed, and seven housewives (19 percent). At large, 23 percent of the adult population fall into this category (which includes students, housewives, the unemployed and the retired). More meaningful, however, almost half of all married women are full-time housewives. Although half of my absentee mothers have remarried, only seven are housewives, and it is clear that economic necessity has less to do with this than personal fulfillment. Four times as many participants (thirty-seven) cite their jobs as one of their most valued personal interests today than did so when referring to their interests during their first marriages (nine), and based on other information from them, I believe there are many more for whom their employment is very satisfying and important. Because my question was formed around the phrase "personal interests," I am sure many women excluded employment from consideration, feeling that I was asking, in essence, for their hobbies. Their words from other sections of the questionnaire, however, leave no doubt that expansion of employment has been vital to their good feelings.

According to my in-laws' standards, I used to feel that my babies would die if they were not immaculate at all times. . . . I never saw anyone but the family. My time was spent entirely on caring for my babies and housework. . . . But now I enjoy so many things, one of which is my interest in business. I work full time and am gone from home about eleven hours a day. . . . I live a full life.

I'm intensely interested in becoming financially independent.

I love my career.

One of my most valued personal interests is pursuing a career in the legal profession.

Professional growth and fulfillment are very important to me.

I value being a whole person who can be respected by her children, being successful in my work.

It is evident that, to a very high degree, the one hundred absentee mothers in this study have not fallen back into what had been suffocating situations for them. Paid labor, of almost any type or status, has made them happier than they were before becoming absentee mothers. Says one sociologist, "Work, even low-status work, plays an important part in a person's self-image. . . . People who are unemployed, retired or incapacitated by illness feel considerable strain and anguish because they begin to see themselves as useless. Aside from the fact of working itself, a key cause of job satisfaction is social contact. For human beings, isolation is a devastating punishment, and the workplace is a clearinghouse of friendships and camaraderie. . . . wives [in my study] who held [unglamorous] jobs were happier and more satisfied with their lives than the women who were full-time housewives."[11]

Development of Bisexual and Homosexual Preferences

I became an aspirant in a Franciscan nursing Order at fifteen, as a high school freshman. It was the same convent in which my older sister lived, but we were rarely allowed to see one another. She was in the strictest period of training, the novitiate years. The only people with whom aspirants were allowed to associate were other aspirants; postulants, those in the second stage of training who were usually high school graduates, associated with other postulants, and so on. This meant that one's classmates, with whom one studied, ate meals, accomplished chores, prayed, "recreated" (in convent terms) and shared rooms, became one's world. The year I was an aspirant, there were about thirty of us, so our world was a fairly small one.

The only men in that world were well removed. There were the priests at the altar behind a rail guard or in the confessional behind a partition; there were the brothers who sang in the choir loft, isolated above the chapel, or there were boys from the trade school which the brothers operated. We glimpsed these boys occasionally but they were hardly part of our lives.

The nuns in charge tried to forestall our redirecting repressed sexual interest in the alternate direction. One of the first things I noticed in the aspirant school was the emphasis our head nun kept putting on our not making "special" friends, the way this was watched for and interfered with, condemned as counter-productive to community spirit. Then I noticed a type of gravitation toward one of the senior aspirants by almost every one of the younger girls. Dolores was the best athlete among us and would often engage in "hands-on" instruction with the rest of us. She had attractive, well-chiseled features, short wavy hair which was worn combed back, and an assertive personality. She cultivated all the traits which, in those times, were considered to be "masculine." She made a point of playing the role of ever-solicitous friend. Soon I noticed that I was just as attracted to Dolores as almost everyone else was. I found myself admiring her from a distance, then seeking her attention, daydreaming about her and, finally, having explicitly sexual dreams about her. When I began to sense that Dolores was particularly interested in my best friend (yes, I had one, in spite of the rules, as did everyone—secretly), I was filled with jealousy that it was not I. But the night I accidently found them fondling and kissing in the bathroom ended all my interest and attraction. It frightened me into retreat.

Five women in my study experienced what was, in effect, accidental homosexuality which included physical involvement; that is, they chose love-objects of the same sex in an environment lacking the opposite sex. They were adolescents when their sexual experience with other girls took place. This is a common time for such developments, given the struggle to establish one's identity and the surge in libidinal energy that takes place during puberty. The isolation of individuals who are not deemed desirable by the opposite sex or who are too timid to jump into the mainstream also encourages sexual intimacy between same-sex friends. Five participants in this study related their early homosexual involvement. For three of the five, strictly heterosexual interaction endured only for the length of their marriage.

Among the hundred absentee mothers in my study, fourteen are currently involved with other women. Ten of the fourteen consider themselves bisexual (although I recently learned that one of the fourteen has had sex-change surgery and is now a male); four are exclusively homosexual. Combined with the two participants who had homosexual involvement only before marrying, a total of sixteen absentee mothers have had overt homosexual experiences. This is a somewhat higher incidence than Kinsey found within his female sample (13 percent who had "overt contact to the point of orgasm"), but hardly a strikingly higher rate. The incidences are, indeed, close enough to suggest that the existence of homosexual activity among my absentee mothers is merely reflective of the same activity among women at large and, given changing opinions in the psychiatric community regarding homosexuality, my participants need not be considered pathologic any more than, in some circles, other homosexual and bisexual persons are. Each of us, after all, has a bisexual nature, two elements of sexuality, and Jung suggests that homosexuality may be no more than a woman choosing to live the masculine in herself and a man the feminine. The question is still being debated, but it is interesting to note that Kinsey's study revealed that 28 percent of the women and 50 percent of the men had experienced homosexual responses. Can we call that large a portion of our population "sick" without the word losing all meaning?

On the other hand, for the purpose of delineating what goes into the making of an absentee mother, I cannot ignore what F. O.

Keller found among sixteen heterosexual participants and whether there is a connection to be made between it and the development of bisexuality and homosexuality among my participants. Keller found:

a strong measure of mixed identification. Although the primary identification was with the maternal figure, paternal identification was strong and compelling. There was evidence that this mixed identification was the source of much of the nonconforming behavior evinced by these women. It was postulated that many nonconforming individuals may be products of mixed identifications, and that they thereby find themselves in conflict with societal injunctions to conform to the prescribed roles of their own sex.[12]

Is there a link between the bisexuality/homosexuality among my absentee mothers and the fact that they are absentee mothers? Do noncustodial mothers harbor a high level of mixed identifications and, if so, is their mixed identification expressed in and beyond their absentee motherhood into the choice of same-sex love-objects? Are they subconsciously confused about their roles because they have internalized both their fathers' and their mothers' perceived thoughts, feelings, and actions as their own? Or are they merely exploring, expanding, flexible human beings who pursue their individual inclinations regardless of societal demands to ignore them? Or are they both? If a particular sexual preference is not "sick," does it matter how it came to exist? "Perhaps" is all I can answer to any of these questions; I simply do not have the knowledge of my sample necessary to form a definitive opinion, and the larger issues continue to unfold in the professional literature.

On a personal level, however, I wonder about the efficacy of building our psyches and our society on a foundation of inflexible sex roles and single-minded codes of morality. I also find it almost impossible to consider those of us who vary from those biologically assigned roles and codes as anything but forerunners of the androgynous society that I believe will someday be in place. Plurality in matters of love-object and occupational choices must inevitably become the norm among both males and females if we follow our faculties of reason.

Emotional Readjustment

Long is the way
And hard, that out of Hell leads up to light.

—John Milton, "Paradise Lost"

Chapter 5 dealt with the absentee mothers whose extreme feelings of guilt were catalyzed by injurious social responses into suicide, attempted suicide, and, among women outside this study, even murder. And the 10 percent incidence of suicidal behavior among my hundred absentee mothers is shockingly high. But what of the other 90 percent? Most of them are also haunted by guilt; they, too, experience hurtful social attitudes. How have *they* responded to these formidable forces?

MECHANISMS OF DENIAL

Our subconscious is clever when it comes to preventing our demise. The walls it builds can prevent our conscious minds from "seeing" the events (or certain aspects of events) that harbor the most potential for injuring our self-esteem and protect us from facts we are not ready to confront. Sometimes the subconscious finds it more practical to protect the conscious by merely placing a sheet of colored glass between awareness and the dangerous information. Thus, information is not totally denied but merely muted to suit one's capacity for dealing with emotional dilemma. Either way, the process, in effect, denies the reality of certain "facts" that are perceived (often accurately) as life-threatening.

In my opinion, scores of my participants use denial, with some success, to defend themselves against both their own guilt and the reprobation they encounter. If you deny being what it is you feel guilty for being and what persons condemn you for being, then you are not deserving of, nor are you required to accept, the guilt and abuse. My absentee mothers frequently avoided troublesome questions in their questionnaires by dashing off a clearly defensive, inappropriate response. They tried to explain that the question was not relevant to their particular situation, or to rationalize the negative reactions from others rather than describe the reactions. For instance, in response to the question of how an absentee mother's friends had responded to her custody arrangement, she might say, "They also had problems" or "I have different friends now than I did then." To the question of how the strangers the absentee mother met responded to her custody arrangement, she might say, "Those people were not involved." From another absentee mother, when asked about reactions in her workplace, "It was none of my employer's business."

These, it seems to me, are obvious evasions of the issue, and I believe they are evidence of denial in action. Friends and strangers responded in negative ways the participants did not want to remember, so they refused to remember. I found my feeling in this respect confirmed by one of the participants, who later had the same insight into her earlier defenses:

It occurs to me that, in fact, there may have been more criticism than I remembered when replying initially. It was too painful to hear, so I may have avoided "attending" to it as much as possible.

Aside from evasive responses to questions, withdrawing from the study altogether, or "overlooking" particular questions in the questionnaire, the roads my participants used to reach the safety of denial take any of five basic directions.

"I'm not like other absentee mothers."

When I first learned that a certain woman in my apartment complex was an absentee mother, I had every intention of avoiding her because I was sure I would not like her. Upon reflection, I was horrified by my response. How could I complain about being persecuted as an absentee mother when I had instantly judged and rejected the first noncustodial mother who crossed my path without even meeting her? Years later, a friend of mine who teaches at a women's college asked for a copy of an article I had written about how I had come to be an absentee mother. She had a student, a divorced mother of two children, who was agonizing over whether she could or should relinquish custody to her former husband so that she could more readily pursue her education. My friend gave her student the article, and a few months later the student wrote to me:

[I have] recently let my children go to live with their father and his wife for an indefinite length of time. . . . What I liked most about your story is the understanding you have reached about your decision and your action. I

haven't gotten my understanding yet, and that is why I haven't written (until now). . . . I was too righteous to write to you at first. I was even feeling toward you as you felt toward that other "bad mother" at the complex. I was surprised to feel that way.

I was fascinated that this seemingly inexplicable reaction had occurred again, but I did not attempt to investigate it further until I began this study and started noticing versions of the same phenomenon in the questionnaires I was receiving. By the time I had studied all hundred questionnaires for signs of "rejecting one's own," almost one-fifth (nineteen) of the absentee mothers indicated, sometimes only subtly, that they did not identify themselves with other absentee mothers.[13] For those who voiced such feelings, it seemed quite important to declare distinctions between themselves and other women who did not live with their children, but often the distinction they were claiming was unclear. All the following quotes are from "voluntary" absentee mothers. Technically, they all had alternatives to relinquishing custody, but it is obvious that they consider themselves different from others in the same category.

I would fight being classified with women who have purposely given up their kids, deserted them, even though I have some of their advantages.

How can a mother ever have anything negative to say about mothering? [In effect, setting herself apart from the absentee mothers she knows do have negative things to say about mothering.]

I now have a few women friends who have given up custody, and they think their decisions very wise, but I would not give up my children regardless. [She has had two additional children since relinquishing custody of those from her first marriage.]

I feel if a mother gives custody it should be more for what is good for the children than for her own egocentric reasons. [A criticism of mothers who relinquish custody to pursue self-realization.]

The one main thing that I would like to put across is that . . . my case is an economic one. When I became an absentee mother, nothing was for nothing. Today, there are more agencies helping than in my time.

I want to emphasize that I relinquished custody for a limited period of time for economic reasons.

Rarely, if ever, should a mother relinquish custody.

Relinquishing was difficult for me, anyway.

Two "involuntary" absentee mothers made the same point: they do not approve of other absentee mothers:

I am for liberation, ERA, women's rights, people's rights, etc., but do not think these should come at the expense of the family. I know many young couples today who are choosing not to have children, people who will not help to continue the species. This also seems wrong.

[Referring to her former husband's second wife]: *She has one child who lives with them only off and on; she can't decide whether she wants her own child or not.*

So some absentee mothers claim they could not or would not or have not done things or said things which they have said or done. Others reach to make significant distinctions between their situations and those of other absentee mothers when the situations are not terribly different.

The reasons for these reactions seem obvious now, but I never saw them on my own. Ray Mitchell, a friend and advisor in the public health field, led me to the explanation. An absentee mother is a deviant member of society; deviants are "bad" and deserve to be punished, rejected, and isolated from "good" people. A given absentee mother may be convinced (as most people are) that *she* is not a bad person, so she must, logically, be different from other absentee mothers. She accepts society's premise, finds a contradiction to the premise in her own person, and resolves the contradiction by asserting that she is different from the others. Her case involves extenuating circumstances, but the others are inexcusable. The social sin becomes more precisely defined as not merely being an absentee mother, but being an absentee mother by choice or for certain detestable reasons. It seems to me an "every woman for herself" reaction in a socially dangerous situation, and the repetitious insistence with which many participants stressed their point emphasizes mine:

All your questions say, "if it was your wish." I feel that does not apply in my case. I knew I couldn't win in court—in my town! And I knew I'd probably leave eventually to build any decent life, so I couldn't guarantee the stability their father valued above all else. That doesn't add up to a wish to relinquish custody!

This participant is an example of the absentee mothers who are almost desperate to distance themselves from the "real" offenders.

They do not want to be pulled under with those who are struggling in the treacherous currents of social and personal condemnation. By saying, *"I'm* not like *them,"* they simultaneously (in theory) maintain a place in the mainstream and their ability to see themselves as good. But their disclaimers do not win them much acceptance in the mainstream, many have secret doubts (with good reason) about just how different they really are from the rest, and their positions make them something like the "Uncle Toms" among blacks or the Phyllis Schlafleys among women, instruments of negative impact against "their own." How much better it would be if they were to use their energies, instead, toward identification with and support of other absentee mothers.

"I'll have my children back as soon as . . ."

The second form of denial my participants use to offset the extreme discomfort of being an absentee mother is that of refusing to accept or admit that living apart from their children is a permanent arrangement. For some, this is a genuine and realistic position; they have specific plans, resources to fulfill their plans, and viable reasons to believe that they will indeed resume custody. But among the thirty-eight absentee mothers who say they want their custody arrangement to be only temporary and the twenty-two who are not sure what they want in this regard, concrete plans, wherewithal, and likelihood are relatively scarce.[14] For the most part, I believe that the women who say that they will have, or hope to have, their children return to live with them are fantasizing or saying what they hope will alleviate some of the guilt and social disapproval.

The group of absentee mothers who display the highest rate of denial in this way are those who relinquished custody because of intimidation. Only two women of the thirteen say that they want their custody arrangement to remain as it is.[15] Five refuse, verbally if not actually, to accept as permanent what are quite obviously final custody arrangements; their actions and plans, however, do not include or seem to allow for the return of their children. Three others feel unsure about whether they want things to change but do harbor feelings that they will, someday, resume custody. When asked for specifics of how they planned to resume custody, two of the eight under consideration were mute. Another avoided thinking about the problem by restating the way she came to be an absentee mother. Another, who is most representative of the thirty-eight women overall who have not accepted or admitted the permanence of their custodial arrangements, describes her "plan" like this:

I'll have my children back as soon as I find a way to live and work and keep them independently and when my ex-husband gives up fighting me for them.

It has been four years since this participant's marriage ended, she supports herself by taking temporary office jobs through an agency (which means lower pay than a permanent office job), and she has not attended school since leaving her marriage (she has had two years of college). She has no plans to return to school or to change her occupation. She feels a serious need for psychiatric help but is "scared" to seek it out and "was really upset" during an initial eight months when she retained custody of her two children. About her emotional upset while single parenting, she says, "I don't think I realized at the time that the responsibility of the children was contributing to it." About needing psychiatric help, she says:

I'm unsure about getting help from professionals. Part of my problem is always feeling judged by peope, and so I have ended up trying to handle this alone. I am having a difficult time asking for help. I've been upset so long that everyone treats me like I'm a "space case" or something.

In addition to these basic elements of this participant's postdivorce life, it is relevant to note that her former husband is aware of the fact that she lived for a time with a drug addict who, after she left him, was sent to prison for robbery, and that she is currently seeing him again. It seems apparent that this participant's all-encompassing generalities and her unlikely preconditions are pure evasive fantasy. But what option does she have to denial of her absentee motherhood when she feels unable to ask for help and feels

that mothering is instinctive or something, and you'd have to be messed up to try and leave it behind.

Tragically, this woman cannot yet believe that being an absentee mother is anything but sick, and she does not seek help to the extent that she, indeed, feels "sick," because that would be a form of admitting the very thing she is trying to avoid admitting: she *is* an absentee mother.

There are some participants whose "plans" for resuming custody tend to lose authenticity because they revolve around amorphous future time. They have an almost magic quality. They are vague dreams requiring no action on the part of the mother toward becoming real and, in the cases of women who never see their children, sometimes equate merely seeing their children someday with resumption of custody, as if one would certainly follow the other. The following quote was one participant's explanation of how she believed resumption of custody would occur.

I hope my children will one day want to see their mother.

Other responses turn on phrases like *one day, someday,* or *eventually.* And others attempt to be specific about the time element but seem to lose the entire meaning of the passage of that time:

As the children get older and my ex-husband needs them less, he will let them live with me—I hope. Maybe five more years . . .

It has already been seven years since this participant relinquished custody, and her oldest child was six at the time.

The absentee mothers who relinquished custody because of emotional problems display the second highest rate of denial: only four of the seventeen say that they want or expect their children to remain with their fathers permanently.[16] Three of the remaining thirteen were silent when asked for specific explanations of how they might resume custody. An absentee mother who relinquished custody seven years ago evoked pity when she stated that she will have her child back as soon as she "gets back on [her] feet." She seems to be in a time warp that keeps her eternally in the period immediately following her divorce. Another mother in this group ignored reality when she said that her daughter will continue to live apart from her only "for however long she wants it." The daughter does not live with her father; she has been adopted by another family and has no knowledge of her mother and certainly no option of returning to her. Still another woman in this group, who has nervous breakdowns once a year "like clockwork," said, "I'm hoping my husband and I can come to an agreement about custody—maybe in six months or so." No expected occurrence makes her think she will have a chance of succeeding in six months or so; six months is nothing more than a dreamlike length of time that allows her to continue denying her situation.

One absentee mother in this category, however, seems to be nearing the end of her denial, although she still holds a thread of it as it unravels:

I thought I'd have my son rejoin me once I got established in [another country]; I came here in 1974. But as time went on, I never really settled down. Perhaps when he's much older he could come up and see how he likes it. . . .

Perhaps, maybe, if, as soon as—all are vital to the vocabulary of the absentee mother protecting herself while trying to come to terms with who she is and the situation in which she finds herself. To borrow some of that vocabulary: if social attitudes toward absentee mothers change enough, perhaps my participants and many others will be able, someday, to give up denial and live at peace.

"I pay no attention to people's negative reactions."

Another means of denial used by some absentee mothers might be called "dismissal." The women, in effect, admit to hearing and remembering unpleasant remarks or occurrences, but they attempt to neutralize the pain experienced; they assert that there is no pain involved. They dismiss the negative events as meaningless or impotent. About her relatives, one woman says:

Their responses were all gossip; hence, I do not attach any importance to them.

Yet the same participant has moved far away from all her relatives and has had no contact with them at all for many years, and she has changed her first and last names "because I didn't like the name I had." Although she says that her absentee motherhood "is pretty much accepted," she has kept it a secret at work. When asked to describe the reactions she usually encounters from strangers, she says, "I do not pay any attention to strangers." When I pointed out that she had not really answered my question and requested that she do so, she replied:

Sorry that I cannot respond to this one, as I am completely immune.

By her choice of the word *immune,* one knows there have been negative encounters with strangers; stating that she cannot relate them because she is immune makes no sense. Indeed, what she is really saying, probably without realizing it, is that she cannot relate them because she is *not* immune. She cannot relate them because to dwell on them at all is too painful.

The second of only four participants who appear to be using this form of denial almost echoes the first but introduces a new element:

I've never concerned myself with people's responses because it's none of their business anyway.

One might suggest that two levels of denial coexist in this statement, and in the statements like it by the study group as a whole which express the thought that the women's actions are nobody's business. Aside from denying that people's responses have an effect on them, many absentee mothers are also apparently attempting to deny that what they are doing is anyone's business but their own. But, of course, any actions taken outside the norm are inevitably the business of a society, whose major concern is to survive. And to survive, whether an individual or a group of individuals who attempt to live with one another, it is essential to note occurrences in the environment. Where society almost always makes its mistake is by responding to deviations from the norm with instant condemnation, moral judgment without due consideration of all the elements involved and the possibility that perhaps *it* rather than the "deviant" should be the one to change. And on the heels of social judgment comes social punishment which, for the absentee mother, has taken the form of rejection and isolation, a well-established and effective method. As far away as Poland, for instance, the words that American society seems to use against the absentee mother were recently heard:

Do not meet, do not shake hands, do not talk with [them]. Let them feel emptiness all around them.[17]

"I don't tell everyone."

In the middle of what was to prove a premature flight from the married man I loved, I did what seemed a repetition of Judas's betrayal of Christ. In order to hide that I was an absentee mother, I lied about being a mother at all. On the rebound, to help ensure that I would not return to the triangle, I took up with someone else too quickly. He wanted to introduce me to his family. We embarked on a trip from Chicago to Pittsburgh, and during the long drive Paul instructed me on what I must not say while visiting his parents and married brother. At first, he merely asked that I lie about my age; he was six years younger than I, and that would disturb everyone. I believe the truth of it was that he would have felt embarrassed because he had "settled" for an "older" woman. But then he asked another favor. His family already knew I was a divorcée, but he had not told them I had children; in fact, he had led them to believe, without actually saying as much, that I did not. Would I go along with that and say that I had no children? They would never understand the children living with their father and would surely be unable to accept me if they knew.

I was hurt, angry, and disappointed in Paul. I wanted to turn back and drop this man from my life immediately (I did so once we returned to Chicago). But in the end I did what he wanted me to do. I denied my children; in effect, I validated society's insistence that, as a noncustodial mother, I ought to be ashamed. I still feel angry at myself for doing it.

Twenty-eight of the hundred absentee mothers in this study use or have used secrecy as a defense mechanism. Although I have heard of a case in which an absentee mother was able to keep her custody arrangement secret from even her relatives, the women in my study have kept their circumstances secret primarily from employers and people they meet in short-term situations. In one case, the secrecy created an awkward situation when someone who had initially been considered a casual acquaintance developed into a close friend; the absentee mother found it so difficult to reveal her true situation that years passed before she did so. The friend was understanding, but one can nevertheless see that secrecy as a protective device is rife with possibilities for anxiety and exposure. It requires constant alertness and is therefore extraordinarily draining. It also brings suffering, because one of the major inclinations of parents is to talk about their children. To suppress reference to one's children, who are fundamental pieces in the puzzle of oneself, is more than a lie, especially for the absentee mother, who must struggle desperately to hold on to even a fraction of her former relationship with her children. As much as she may be many other things, she is still also a mother, and, whether custodial or not, that remains a part of her identity. Motherhood has been an intense and intimate part of her life which is continuing in a different form; an attempt to keep it buried is very much like being partially dead.

Thus, it may be reasonable to conclude that the absentee mothers who use secrecy as a screen are those feeling the most guilt or who most fear judgment. Those who are the most desperate would employ the most extreme form of defense. Within this study, a total of twenty-eight women representing nearly every relinquishing category have used secrecy to deny their absentee motherhood. But the group of absentee mothers with the highest rate of secrecy is the group that lost custody in court. Evidently, all else being equal, a formal decision that denies a mother her children is the most injurious form of absentee motherhood. An official declaration that the children will be better placed with the father effectively amplifies the wrongful message that the mother is unworthy of human respect and consideration. Legal proclamation carries a great deal of power to convince, and highlights one's powerlessness. The group of absentee mothers who display the second-highest rate of secrecy are those who were intimidated into relinquishing custody. "Weakness," as well as absentee motherhood, creates shame. Nearly as many mothers who used secrecy are in the group who relinquished custody because of financial pressures (which were, in some instances, a form of intimidation used by the husband to pressure the wife to give up her children).

Even the absentee mothers who do not keep their custodial status a secret tend to evade referring to it when they can:

I believe that I am honest, but I generally prefer changing the subject.

Strangers question me about it. To some I explain; to others I refuse.

Everyone looks blank when they first hear, so I don't usually tell people upon first meeting. They can and have been cruel. I try to avoid it.

I am pretty close-mouthed about it. When it does come up, the reaction is generally negative, especially from women.

If I make any comment whatsoever, the usual response is first silence and then on to another topic. I've always felt ostracized and judged. Normally, I keep my mouth shut!

Nevertheless, a majority of the absentee mothers (66 percent) feel that things are changing for the better, especially among employers, although many wonder how much adjustment to being absentee mothers has affected the way responses are experienced. I believe the mothers' attitudes *are* an operative factor in others' responses to them, but I do not believe it is the factor that exerts the most power. Although about one-fourth in this study see no improvement, no one feels that reactions have become more negative, and a few have never felt public reactions to be difficult in the first place.

I hope that social attitudes toward absentee mothers will continue to improve and thus reduce the pressures that lead so many to resort to secrecy. The use of this type of denial can already be seen to be decreasing among my participants: 33 percent (sixteen) of the forty-eight women who became absentee mothers before 1975 employed secrecy in one way or another, whereas 23 percent (twelve) of the fifty-two who did so after 1975 used secrecy. If the figures indicate a trend, it is an improvement, but in a matter as essential as this, involving one's self-esteem and social acceptance and bearing so directly upon whether one lives or dies, we must not settle for anything less than complete eradication of the need for absentee mothers to hide behind secrecy or any other form of denial.

"I Wish I Hadn't Done It."

I don't like . . . being an absentee mother . . . I wish I could go back in time, knowing and feeling what I do now, for then I could have held on and fought back . . . When I gave up on my son, I gave up on myself too. There was so much pressure, I just gave in. And I wish I hadn't because I feel so guilty now. And I still haven't accomplished the one goal I need to, which is gaining complete control over my life. So I feel nothing was really accomplished by giving up my child. He really wasn't the one stopping me from my goal. It was and is me.

This absentee mother, her unrealistic and symptomatic goal of "complete control" aside, embodies the spirit of regret expressed without reserve by twenty-two of the mothers in this study. Eleven more mothers are partially regretful about deciding to relinquish custody, allowing custody to be taken from them, or allowing it to slip away from them. Another eighteen continuously fluctuate between regretting the custody arrangement and being satisfied with it. This means that a total of fifty-one of the hundred absentee mothers wish, to one extent or another, that they had not become absentee mothers.

However, I believe that a significant portion of those who express regret do so as a means of denial, to soften the sharpness of guilt and social disapproval. If one cannot deny being an absentee mother, the next best thing may be to deny that one is satisfied with it. The expressions of what these participants would do differently now are almost always based upon the abilities and insights of the persons they have become. They do not, in most cases, seem to realize that what they now wish they had done then would probably have been impossible at the time, which is exactly why it all happened the way it did in the first place. Nevertheless, the expressions of what these mothers would do differently if given a second chance are full of genuine pain, regret, and anger, and some no doubt really could have done things differently. From two mothers in the "financial realities" relinquishing group:

I'd fight to keep them, go on welfare, leave the state.

I'd find a way to keep my kids with me.*

From two mothers in the "emotional problems" relinquishing group:

I should have done anything to keep my child.*

I wonder if I would not have been able to learn to like myself within marriage. The burden of mothering would have gotten less as the children grew older.

From one mother in the "second marriage" group:

I never would've given up custody if I'd known it wouldn't make my second marriage work.

From one mother in the "lost custody" group:

I would have tried to establish myself in a manner that was above reproach from any quarter.

---

*These are the most likely candidates for evidence of denial, because they are so vague. The assertion that one would find "a way" or should have done "anything" that one had not been able to find the first time without having any idea what that way or thing might be is very dramatic, but it is also somewhat metaphysical.

From one mother in the "intimidation" group:

Fight!

Another factor that makes me suspect a good deal of denial among the women who regret not having custody is that thirty-two of the fifty-one do not specify *why* they regret it. I suspect many in this group must assume that the reasons are so evident that they do not require stating. Nevertheless, it creates something of a problem in determining to what extent the need for denial, rather than "genuine" regret (the conviction that the wrong thing was done and that a change in custody would be welcome) is present in the statements of "I wish I hadn't done it."

More than half the nineteen absentee mothers who gave reasons said that they missed their children and missed being more involved in their lives. Others stated that they were influenced by the negative treatment they were experiencing; felt that the arrangement was emotionally bad for the children or that the former husband was not a good father; or were troubled by guilt. There is no reason to suppose that these women do not genuinely regret having relinquished custody.

Interestingly, not one absentee mother of the thirteen whose children decided to live with their fathers regrets it having happened, although three feel ambivalent. There are some hurt feelings among them:

I don't think mothers are automatically the best parents or should always have custody, yet I feel rejected that my children have not chosen me.

And some perplexity:

I try to get the kids to tell me why they would not live with me (other than convenience, which is their handy excuse), but they still will not do so.

But 77 percent (ten) of these thirteen involuntary absentee mothers are satisfied with their custody arrangements. The only other relinquishing group with as marked a degree of satisfaction is the "father-more-nurturing" group of four, three of whom are perfectly satisfied and one of whom is no more than ambivalent.

In absolute correlation with the absentee mothers most likely to be secretive, the group who feels the most regret at not having their children with them are the mothers who lost custody legally, those who buckled under to intimidation, and those who felt financial realities were too much against them. The first two groups feel victimized and painfully embittered; the latter group sees single custodial mothers all around them somehow getting by, which seems to invalidate their motivation for relinquishing their children.

One of these regretful mothers is more specific about why she regrets having relinquished custody:

I regret letting my husband have the kids. Since his remarriage, he has tried to push me out of the picture. He is trying to teach the children that they are a family and I am an outsider. He tells them it would be better if I stopped seeing them and let them start a new life without me. He also tells them that it is embarrassing when I come to the kids' activities. In truth, he would like people to think I abandoned the kids and he was a hero to take care of them. When I constantly show interest in my children, it ruins the image of me he wants people to have. At the time of our divorce, I believed his main concern was the kids, but now I think he was thinking of his image as the poor, wonderful guy married to a bitch!

Among the fifty-one absentee mothers who feel to any degree that they wish they had not relinquished custody or cooperated with those who took it from them, many experience this kind of "pressure from traditionalists, which makes some days or circumstances unbearable," as one of them put it. So they withdraw, if only periodically, to a world called "I wish I hadn't done it." It offers the comfort of vocalizing their "mistake," which, in turn, helps reduce their feelings of guilt regardless of whether they actually wish to change the custody arrangement. At the same time, it denies, in effect, that one is any longer responsible for the arrangement. They feel at a certain level that if they no longer agree with their original decision or inaction, it is tantamount to having made the "right" decision or having taken the "right" action; it has merely been somewhat delayed. Once again, the failure of the subconscious to deal in terms of time lapse is involved. Thus, a seemingly simple statement makes it possible for an absentee mother to live more readily in her social environment. She needs to state for all to hear that she wishes she had not let her children go. If people believe she is sorry, they will think better of her.

PSYCHOTHERAPY

It *is* possible for a woman to relinquish custody of her children, have them taken from her or to have them leave her of their own accord and yet escape any serious emotional aftereffects. She *can* lead a happy, well-adjusted life right from the start. Forty of my hundred absentee mothers have done so. Not that they have not experienced sadness or have had no trouble at all adjusting, but they felt no need for professional support after becoming absentee mothers. They coped quite comfortably on their own within whatever "natural" support structure existed for them, or even without support in some cases.

Sixty of the absentee mothers, however, are currently in therapy or are feeling the need for help since relinquishing custody. What makes the difference between those forty who have done well in spite of guilt and negative social responses and the sixty who have had much more trouble living with their unorthodox situation?

Is it childhood background? Are those who had happy childhoods more numerous among the happy absentee mothers? No, absentee mothers with happy childhoods are quite evenly distributed between the happy and the unhappy absentee mothers.

Does previous emotional instability make the difference? Only to a limited degree. Seventeen (28 percent) of the unhappy absentee mothers had emotional problems before becoming absentee mothers, but eight (20 percent) of the happy absentee mothers also experienced emotional instability prior to giving up their children. Thus, it would be perfectly accurate to say that if a woman has had psychological problems before absentee motherhood, she is more likely to have similar problems afterward as well, but not remarkably more likely—not in the face of the fact that the vast majority (forty-three, or 72 percent) of the women who have required psychological help as absentee mothers have never before felt that need. And not in the face of the fact that one-fifth of the absentee mothers who are well adjusted have achieved that balance in spite of previous emotional problems.

Is there a connection between whether an absentee mother remarries and her emotional well-being? Perhaps to a small extent, but depending upon the individual's bias regarding lifestyles, it may not be in the direction expected (see Table 15).

On the basis of my sample an absentee mother would have a

better chance of emotional stability if she remained unmarried for at least five years. A generous period of independence for healing and growth appears to be an important link in the chain of life events for the noncustodial mother. Further, it seems that it is better for an absentee mother's emotional health if she relinquishes all her children and refrains from having additional children, but advantageous if she is eventually able to resume custody of some of her children. The absentee mother who resumes custody would best serve her emotional health by resuming custody of only one or some of her children after waiting for more than three years.

The suggestion that a woman has a better chance for mental health if she remains child-free for a period is somewhat alien to a society that idealizes the mother-child relationship. Nevertheless, additional data from this study tends to support the suggestion. The sixty absentee mothers exhibiting pathological symptoms see their children more often than the emotionally healthier mothers. On the average, all visiting days accumulated, the troubled mothers spend about three months of any given year with their children—a month more than the symptom-free absentee mothers. In addition (and considered separately from the others), a slightly higher percentage of the happy mothers *never* see their children. Six women in the group of forty (17 percent) have no contact with their children; only seven (13 percent) of the sixty unhappy mothers never see their children. This difference may not be very great, and both the differences may be only coincidental, but they do add some fuel to the other bits of suggestive information.[18]

One more element found among the "happy" absentee mothers contributes more than any other to the likelihood of establishing and maintaining emotional health as an absentee mother. It is positive input from others. Emotional support or at least acceptance from relatives, friends, employers, coworkers, and even strangers is vital.

Both the stable and the less stable women have encountered the same levels of negative responses from people around them. In other words, intense or not, negative social responses can be defanged by a high enough level of positive social responses. The happy absentee mothers have received enough positive social response to offset the potentially dangerous negative responses also received. One or two cubes of sugar may not be enough to neutralize the bitterness of absentee motherhood, but three may do the trick, it appears (see Table 16).

That an absentee mother needs more supportive social responses than most receive is important, but does it make any difference from where the supportive responses come? Yes, not surprisingly, it does matter (see Table 17).

On the basis of my sample, it seems clear that an absentee mother's relatives are the most important contributors to her emotional well-being; yet relatives also offer more censure than any other group. Friends, evidently, cannot replace family at a deep level, although friends give the most support to the absentee mother. The emotionally troubled absentee mothers received much more support from friends than relatives, and even strangers were more sympathetic than their kin. The emotionally stable group also experienced a slightly higher rate of acceptance from their employers than did the other group, whereas they received less help than the other women from friends and less support among casual acquaintances (strangers). This makes the employer and the workplace the second most important environment in the absentee mother's adjustment. That is reasonable, really, since a person spends far more time at work than with friends or acquaintances.

Only one more question needs to be asked in order to complete the picture of the "happy" versus the "unhappy" absentee mother. Is there any connection between the *reasons* for which a woman has become a noncustodial mother and her emotional health thereafter? Only to a slight extent (see Table 18).

There are representatives of all eight categories of relinquishment in the ranks of both the happy and the unhappy participants, and no relinquishing group is any more than seven percentage points more highly represented than the next most highly represented within the "unhappy" group. The largest spread at any juncture in the "happy" group is only five percentage points.

One of the correlations that approaches a marked level, however, shows that an absentee mother who gives up her children under the pressure of intimidation has the best chance of enjoying good emotional health afterward. This suggests, once again, that some of the absentee mothers who allowed themselves to be bullied into relinquishing custody may have, perhaps subconsciously, used their overbearing husbands to obfuscate their own wishes to leave behind their children as well as their husbands. Otherwise, it seems, they would be harboring much anger and frustration, as well as guilt for being unassertive, and would register as much need for psychological assistance as the rest of the study. Another explanation, of course, is that these women were so genuinely convinced that they had no options at the point of relinquishing that their level of guilt is minor, mitigates the anger, and allows for smooth psychological functioning. All things considered, however, I believe the first possibility is more likely.

The second significant correlation between relinquishing category and emotional well-being is significant in the negative sense. It appears that the absentee mothers most likely to suffer emotional problems following separation from their children are those whose children have made the decision to leave *them*. Adult or not, it is more painful to be "rejected" than to be the one who decides that separation is for the best.

For all absentee mothers who suffer, and the one who does not is certainly not present in this study, I hope for the time when society will offer her the empathy and kindness which my sister Joyce once gave to me in an hour of despair:

I know it's not ever the same for any two people, but I've known those desolate feelings that knock a person down. I'm sorry anyone else, especially someone I love, has to feel them. But there is comfort— someone cares . . .

EMPTINESS AND PAIN

There is a great yearning and emptiness. A void. And, oh, the pain on his birthday . . .

—*An absentee mother*

There need not be pathology where there is suffering. Even though forty participants in this study have felt no need for psychiatric care, only thirteen express primarily positive reactions to being absentee mothers. Beside the feelings of guilt involved, which we have already discussed thoroughly, the most prevalent form of suffering is the sense of profound loss (of something that cannot be replaced), and of grief as a companion to that loss. These feelings exist in spite of whatever positive things an absentee mother is experiencing in her child-free circumstances. It seems to reflect Camus's observation that "there is no love of life without despair of life."[19] Only the women who have lived with the two approach adequate expression of what that means.

I have been so torn! At times I am grateful for having the first chance in my entire life to be on my own. When I got divorced, I got an apartment and furnished it the way I wanted; I took a vacation, bought a car and came and went as I pleased. I didn't have to ask anyone or make excuses for my actions. Because I lived alone, I could date whenever I wanted, stay out all night if I wanted, and bring someone home if I wanted. For the sake of tasting freedom, I liked living alone. But I missed my kids terribly when I wasn't on the go. Every time I had to take them home my heart would ache, and after I'd leave them I would cry. I worked one full-time and two part-time jobs so every minute I wasn't with them I was busy . . . I was afraid to go to bed unless I was so exhausted that I'd fall right asleep. If I had to lay there and think, my mind would always go directly to my kids and it was torture to me.

It has been a very lonely seven years with much heartbreak not having my child to raise. I miss him terribly. Maybe that's why I feel empty now.

I have only one good feeling living apart from my son; he has a secure, loving home. The rest is pain, remorse and a sense of worthlessness.

The emotional adjustment has taken years . . . , but my son's place has never been filled. I have a generous visitation arrangement; this helps, but it does not fill the void.

In the beginning it was a relief. But now I'm more mature, and I can see my younger boy needs me and my current husband and I have no children, so it has turned into a large ache!

I have become a hardened person trying to fill that gap which will forever remain void.

I have built a good life that I am quite happy in; however, I also agonize over my children. What can I do for them? How can I help them? Sometimes I just miss them like crazy.

Although I've adjusted fairly well, sometimes I wish my son had never been born because I'm missing everything he does . . . and I know I might never be in a position to make any real contributions to his life . . .

The freedom is nice, but I miss the emotional closeness.

I miss them terribly. There is not one day that goes by that I don't feel the pain of separation from them.

I find it heartwrenching not to be able to share in their lives as I once did. Holidays are especially difficult if they're not with me. I enjoy my single life, but I miss my children.

I can't think of anything in my life that tears me apart more than being an absentee mother.

One participant learned a valuable lesson from having to let her son go to his father at the son's request:

It's the hardest thing I've ever done, much harder than the divorce. I worry a lot about him and miss seeing him grow up, but I've learned that I can't make anyone do anything.

A handful of participants have been able to begin filling the space which was left by their children:

At first, I was very disoriented and didn't care about myself. I found it difficult to be with other children. But after five years I remarried and took care of my stepson, which helped, and the birth of my daughter helped even more to fill the gap in my life.

I became increasingly comfortable with my absentee motherhood because my mothering is directed toward others' children. On the other hand, these same children are also a constant reminder of my own.

I have adapted partially by making time for young students and counseling them.

But many more are simply left with the wounding dichotomy expressed by one mother in a rather futile attempt to give advice to other mothers:

I do not recommend single parenthood to young women. It can be very fulfilling, but it's hard. You miss your youth, and the responsibility is vast. Yet the decision to give up your child is also hard—and painful! You feel like a failure, and it's horribly lonely.

One woman who tried to avoid these disturbing counterforces by relinquishing custody of only one child of three has not found that to be a solution:

I just wish that when I was growing up I had known there were possibilities other than motherhood. One cannot incorporate mothering and creativity in an art form very easily. So I sit and try to be patient until my children grow, trying not to let myself be buried, staying alive for the day I can really open. I admire women who could let go fully, to become themselves.

In the end, of course, there is no pure "winning." There is only making the best decision one can and learning to cope with that decision. Those who surround the absentee mother help or diminish her chances of successful coping. One of the participants expresses her own realization of this fact and her desire to offer emotional balm to other women in her position:

I can't really explain the pain and heartache, but God! if you can help someone with your book, everything I've tried to say will be worthwhile. Please help someone.

The Primary Questions: Have My Children Been Harmed? Will They Ever Understand?

> Mom, why do you have to
> go so far away?
> Why can't you
> just stay?
>
> You know I love you so,
> so why do you have to go?
> You mean so much to me,
> and so I plea
>
> Just stay with me!
>
> —[My daughter]

My daughter's poem, given to me when she learned that I was moving two thousand miles away, scraped my heart into bloody shreds. I wished that I could do what I had to without hurting her, but I could not. Neither could I ever again live the life of total self-sacrifice that had been imposed upon me in the role of woman, wife, and mother. I suffered a great deal in sympathy with my daughter's pain, and I was full of anxiety about what her two brothers were not revealing. What right had I to act contrary to their strongest feelings? Would they ever be able to understand why I had done so? What long-term harm was I doing to them? In spite of the unanswered and at the time unanswerable questions, I believed I had to live my life wherever it took me. I believed (and still do) that to make significant life decisions based solely upon the conflicting desires of one's children is a serious mistake. Living *for* one's children is a mistake, as much for them as for the parent. It results in undeveloped, frustrated "adults" waiting for their children to live the lives they themselves have relinquished, or in successful parents who wish to relive their triumphs through their children. If the children are healthy, they will walk away from their parents at the right time to pursue their own visions. I believe that a divorced mother, as things exist today, can be in very much the same position as the postadolescent in this respect. Because she is female, she may be stalled in development at the stage where she left her parents in pursuit of her fulfillment. Because she is female, she may have gone automatically into marriage and parenthood to seek that fulfillment. Because she is a unique human being as well as a female, she may not have found it there. And so she is thrown into the awareness that her time to pursue her vision is at hand. She may need to leave her children behind (although usually only in a sense), as once she left her parents behind, but they will be with their father who is a male and has been pursuing his vision all along, in whatever direction it might have taken him and at the same time as being a father. I see no blame in this.

My own philosophy aside, the questions still remain for many absentee mothers (not to mention society at large). But we may begin to look for answers within the absentee mother's experience and perception. How have her children reacted to having an absentee mother as far as *she* can tell? This topic fully pursued would require a study of its own, and so I can approach the subject only summarily in an effort to complete the picture of the residuals with which an absentee mother lives.

I wonder often if my son will someday understand that I did what I thought I had to do. Will he grow up and reject me for not "being there" when he was young? Or will he respect me merely because I am his natural mother? He calls me Mom, but sometimes I feel he should call me Mrs. So-and-so, just like a stranger. I just hope more than anything that one day he understands and can forgive me.

I hate being an absentee mother. I'm lonesome and I must live with my son's complete hatred for me.

When I decided to give up my son I felt that I was doing it in my own and my son's interests. For my son, I would give everything of myself. I have not tried to see him because I am afraid he would hate me for leaving him. I cannot bring myself to get in touch. The longer the time passes the harder it is. It's been almost nine years now. I am frightened.

Perhaps such fears can be diminished by the knowledge that the children of sixty-three of the hundred absentee mothers in this study have made their mothers feel that they are loved, appreciated, and even, in some cases, understood. Perhaps it would also help to know that only fourteen participants are uncertain about how their children feel toward them, and that none of them has any palpable reason to believe her children's feelings are strongly negative, if negative at all. Even among the twenty-two absentee mothers whose children have expressed, or seem to have, some negative feelings about their mothers, the negativity is not severe. Some conservatively reared children feel their mothers to be odd; others may feel that their mothers were at fault for the divorces; but few have expressed very high levels of anger. Only one mother has felt hatred from her child. *Dissatisfaction* might most accurately sum up the general attitude among the children of the twenty-two who have experienced negativity from them. And, somehow, the word *dissatisfaction* associated with the word *son,* for instance, does not elicit fear of a lurking Jocasta complex. Imagination is more horrific than reality, and I suspect that the façade of indifference often enacted by an alienated child may be a more real threat to the absentee mother than the expression of hostility. At any rate, the frightened absentee mother's salvation lies in resolution. And resolution lies within her own ability to diminish or eliminate her feelings of guilt, to forgive herself. Once that takes place, she will no longer fear her children's feelings to the same degree. A second important element involved in resolution is the firm placement within the absentee mother's mind that her children are not infallible saints whose feelings should automatically be considered just. As a matter of fact, their immature emotional development is much more likely to produce unjustified, totally narcissistic feelings than her own emotional apparatus. She has every right to dismiss them the same way she may dismiss criticism from other quarters when she reasons that they are wrong.

In the process of analyzing my participants' children's reactions to living apart from their mothers, one soon realizes that there is a major problem in the way of clear determinations. In 45 percent of the cases, divorce and custody arrangements occur simultaneously. How does one determine, without talking to the children especially, how much of their negative emotional responses are due to the divorce and how much to the custody arrangements? Within this study, there is no option but to use the mothers' evaluation of their children's behavior. Less than one-quarter feel that the custody arrangement was the major reason for whatever emotional upset their children suffered; a few more held divorce itself to be responsible.

I believe my participants have been quite right in their perception that their children's negative postdivorce/relinquishment emotions cannot very readily be attributed to having absentee mothers. The clinical information about their children's emotional states since divorce and custody arrangements, compared to similar information about children of divorce in general,[20] indicates that the children of my absentee mothers are actually less emotionally upset than children of divorce who live with their mothers. Even *assuming* that all the children of all the mothers who do not know their children's emotional reactions *have* required psychiatric care, the rate of emotional distress among the children of absentee mothers is almost identical to the rate among children living with their divorced mothers. Either way, the conclusion one must reach is that absentee mothers are not harming their children in any way beyond the usual problems caused by divorcing parents and that, quite possibly, the children of absentee mothers are less affected by divorce than others (see Table 19).

Epilogue

No More Masks! No More Mythologies!

Breaking a commandment is a sin. Breaking the law is a crime. Breaking a rule is only an infraction, and acting counter to a norm is merely an unusual action. The absentee mother is guilty of no more than the unusual, but because she has done the unusual (or simply finds herself placed in an unusual position) in an area of life our society treats as sacred, society responds to her as though she has committed a mortal sin or a capital crime. Because she is a product of a system that perceives her maternal status in this way, she herself believes to varying degrees that she is guilty of a wrong. The result in untenable, in my mind: terrible hostility from both quarters, frighteningly prevalent suicidal behavior, murder, and pernicious emotional tension among absentee mothers. This does no good for anyone, and I want to believe that society (especially individuals, but our institutions as well), learning of the damage being done, will want to help rectify the situation. I say *help* rectify because the absentee mother herself must be the first

The title of this chapter comes from Muriel Rukeyser, "The Poem as Mask," *No More Masks! An Anthology of Poems by Women,* ed. Florence Howe and Ellen Bass (Garden City, N.J: Doubleday, Anchor, 1973).

contributor toward acceptance of the noncustodial mother. She must accept herself; she must accept others like herself; society will then be more inclined to do the same. But how do we begin?

We begin by recognizing that some absentee mothers are such because their environments failed to prepare them for nurturing; that others, although capable of full-time parenting, have chosen for what they see as good reasons to share child rearing; and that still others have had absentee motherhood imposed on them. We begin by seeing that there is a common thread running through these different types of absentee motherhood: a rapidly changing society. For the first group of women, it has meant encountering a vacuum where there should have been a role model when they attempted to nurture. For the second group, it has meant expanded options and opportunities. And for the final group, it has meant enforced acceptance of nontraditional arrangements. The fact that the group for whom social change has meant fuller lives (within this study) is the largest by far tells me that, in large measure, the changes can be considered good.

It is society's responsibility to adjust its attitudes such that the role model vacuum encountered by some can be filled by any nurturing person and such that women will enjoy sharing their children with the fathers and the fathers will want that sharing. It is society's responsibility because what affects so many affects us all, and parenting, if nothing else, certainly affects us all—if not as parents, then as those who have been parents or have needed parenting. Even those who find themselves parents in optimum circumstances cannot ignore the fact that their children are affected as much by the rest of society as by their home environments; therefore, no one can rightly or effectively remove himself from the changes that are occurring, nor can he or she really ignore them. We need to face them together if we wish to survive these upsetting times.

Absentee mothers have already begun to deal with their situations by taking part in studies like this, by reaching out to one another through a national organization, and by confronting their emotions in therapy groups which are beginning in many states (often initiated by psychologists who are, themselves, absentee mothers). With the insights gained from this book and other similar projects completed and to come, the relatives, older children, friends, employers, and chance acquaintances of the absentee mother may gain what could be the heretofore missing ingredient for a positive relationship with her: understanding.

Representatives of our religions, educational institutions, and social programs now have sources (although still extremely limited) toward recognition of a new group that needs their attention and assistance. Inhumane, unrealistic, and lopsided expectations of mothers (which contribute to both the creation of absentee mothers and the damaging negative reactions toward them) must be rectified in religious dogma, in educational materials, in social perceptions, and in social policy. Children must cease to be the responsibility solely of women. It is simply and clearly not right and, as we have seen, can be mortally destructive.

Individual men have it in their power and must take the initiative toward more involved parenting with the knowledge that such moves will greatly benefit themselves, the women they love or have loved, and the children they have missed knowing. It will not compromise their masculinity but add an appealing aspect to it.

Employers and government agencies must be poked and prodded until they see their obvious and vital responsibilities to working parents regarding child care, one of the keys to both married and single-parenting success. (Sweden would be an ideal example to hold up to them; there, 89 percent of day-care costs are borne by the government, and people have learned that such support brings practical rewards. One Swedish economist points out that "the lifelong earnings of a woman who is able to work without interruption yield enough tax dollars to pay for more than four places in a quality day nursery."[1] American women average only two children each.)

Even more palatable to the American capitalist sensibility, employers (subsidized in part by parents and government) could provide child care as an employment benefit, something unions could help establish. On-site child care would be extremely convenient for all involved and would allow parents to have lunch with their children or to be readily available if a child became ill. It would benefit the company's needs as well as the family's in that overtime work would cease to be a problem and absenteeism related to obtaining child care would be eliminated. School-aged children could best be accommodated (during the parents' working hours) through open-ended, flexible facilities at their schools.

Society exists at all because human beings realized early on that we need one another. It remains for us to rediscover that truth and to make it an all-pervasive and personal element of our social structures. To the extent that we succeed, the absentee mother's dilemma, and many others like it, will cease to exist. Fewer women would feel the need to become absentee mothers, and those who do will be viewed simply as noncustodial fathers are presently viewed: without judgment or bitterness.

The belief that a mothering instinct exists in every female and that its absence helps define being male is a nineteenth- and twentieth-century myth, a culturally induced creed. In the seventeenth and eighteenth centuries, for instance, French women of all classes above that of peasant routinely sent their newborn infants to the countryside to wet nurses, with whom the babies remained for the first four years of their lives. They were rarely, if ever, visited, yet there is no evidence that they felt rejected. It was merely the way things were done. The biological mothers, as far as anyone can tell, did not experience the practice as personally hurtful. Even in the very common occurrence of children dying during this period, the mothers seem not to have suffered. There existed a quite distinct detachment of mothers from their children.[2]

More currently, surrogate mothers are allowing themselves to be artificially inseminated with the sperm of husbands whose wives are infertile, carrying the pregnancies to term and then relinquishing the babies to the childless couples with seemingly no hesitation and a good deal of joy.

There are many reasons to believe that the "mothering instinct" (a term that has been discarded by psychologists) is not inborn among women. Even among lower mammals, the female and her offspring are totally indifferent toward one another once the nursing period is over, and the nursing period, from what I've observed, appears to be something the mother *tolerates*. Among lower mammals, nursing is a necessity; among human beings, it is not. Among human beings, anyone can take the place of the mother.

There is anthropological evidence of societies in which men have been central as caretakers of children:

As long ago as 1953, Dr. Margaret Mead suggested that any claim for an innate nurturing potential in women, or for a biologically-rooted dependence of children on their mothers alone, was suspect of being "a new subtle form of antifeminism in which men—under the guise of exalting the importance of maternity—are tying women more tightly to their children." Dr. Mead had reason to believe, from her own studies of primitive societies, like the Arapesh of New Guinea, where it was quite normal for men to share fully in the care of infants, that culture, not biology, dictated child rearing practices.[3]

In this light, to charge absentee mothers with being unnatural, to insist that all women are or ought to be "natural" mothers, is not only incorrect but also foolish. As an obvious, self-serving ploy on the part of nineteenth- and twentieth-century civilization, it is failing. The fact that more women are deciding to have no children or to limit themselves to one child or to relinquish or share custody in divorces is proof of that.

I will not repeat the familiar, correct feminist rhetoric that refers to industrialization, capitalism, and patriarchy as having created the unnatural isolation of mother and child: it is *almost* beside the point now. The logical assertion by the absentee mother that what she is doing should not be regarded as wrong for her when it is perfectly all right for men is confronted by the realistic consideration of the fact that, almost invariably, children have come to depend too completely on their mothers for essential emotional closeness as well as day-to-day care. Even those who believe that nurturing can be and ought to be provided by both parents, ask how we can dismiss that serious responsibility, even equipped as we are with humanistic justification and a logical philosophy. How can we do it knowing the situation that exists? The needs of our children, now, surely must supercede our own needs or the changing of society.

My first response to this question is irritation with what I feel to be the stubbornly masochistic determination of even the most aware feminists to continue cooperating in their own oppression. Put a child in front of them, tell them that they will be the sole source of that child's emotional nutrients and physical care, and regardless of the exploitation and oppression they know this represents, they will proceed to do what everyone has come to count on their doing. Many of us feel that the pattern must be broken.

There is no way to accomplish societal change for the better without also experiencing the discomfort of adjustment. And, unfortunately, all of us, including children, experience the discomfort. We have come to accept this about divorce; we no longer remain in bad marriages "for the sake of the children," as we used to say. In order to affect the change to equal nurturing responsibilities for men and women, when it comes to instances of divorce especially, women who feel the need to extricate themselves from the full responsibility of child rearing must be willing to suffer the knowledge that even their children will have to endure the adjustments necessary. There is no reason to believe that this will impose an unbearable existence on them, and there is emerging evidence that it will prove to be less troubling to them than divorce itself. The majority of fathers will soon learn to provide their share of nurturing and physical care. But they will never learn or discover if we continue assuming that they cannot or will not. To be convinced that one is irreplaceable is the most effective form of exploitation, and I believe the time has come for mothers to confront the reality that their children will not die, physically or psychologically, if their needs are fulfilled by a combination of sources rather than the mother alone (witness the children of kibbutzim in Israel). The trouble with this will lie primarily among women who are loathe to relinquish what has become their sole source of identity and self-worth and among men with weak confidence in their masculinity.

Child-care professionals tell us that men are as capable of supplying the things a child needs as are women. They are encouraging men to develop these capabilities and are beginning to see positive responses from the men themselves. It is a philosophy that is on its way (too slowly to be sure) to becoming a widely accepted social good, but much more so for parents within functioning marriages than parents who are divorced. Aside from the scant application and limited possibilities of joint custody, society is proving more reluctant to transfer the identical ideal of shared nurturing or father-nurturing to divorced couples and their children. And the innovation of organizations for fathers who want custody aside (because they represent a minuscule portion of divorced fathers), only 5 to 6 percent of divorcing fathers *ask* for custody. Divorcing mothers continue to have few options.

In addition to our failure to fully embrace the emerging capacities and responsibilities of individuals (male and female), we appear to be very far from recognizing the need for preparation for parenthood in the schools. This preparation ought to include more than learning the physical aspects of conception, pregnancy, birth, care, and feeding. We must begin to teach our children and young adults of the emotional demands involved in parenting. We *must* begin to address the psychological makeup of individuals and its bearing on whether a given person is a good risk for parenthood. Those who find that they are not need not necessarily refrain from having children, but they could postpone it until they are able to address their problematic characteristics. They would at the very least know what to expect and be aware of some methods for coping. I also believe that premarital counseling (not licensing) should be actively encouraged with an eye toward preparing adults to make realistic, well-founded decisions about parenthood. We also need to foster acceptance of those who decide against parenthood. We owe all of this to one another and to generations to come. And we owe people like absentee mothers, who are walking victims of social mistakes, a minimum of dispassionate acceptance.

It all amounts to having the courage to remove the limiting but safe-feeling masks with which we have lived for too long, so that we may see and pursue the selves beneath. And the removal of individual masks carries with it the appeal that our institutions refrain from promoting further harmful mythologies. Absentee mothers have tried unsuccessfully to hide from reality behind assigned masks. We tried believing the myths, but they have proven themselves false "truths." The practice of automatic parenthood and the myth of purely glorious holy motherhood deserve to be abandoned.

Note: Noncustodial mothers now have a national organization available to them as a source of support in their unorthodox situations. For detailed information, write or call:

Mothers Without Custody
Box 76
Sudbury, MA 01776
(617) 443-9681.

Notes

Introduction

1. Froma Sand, *The Life Wish* (New York: Hawthorne Books, Inc., W. Clement Stone, 1974), p. 63.
2. Group for the Advancement of Psychiatry, Committee on Public Education, *The Joys and Sorrows of Parenthood* (New York: Scribner, 1973), p. 81.
3. Ibid., pp. 83–84.

Chapter 1

1. Names used throughout this book are fictitious.
2. Many of the shorter quotes herein have been slightly edited to facilitate reading.
3. Avery Corman, *Kramer vs. Kramer* (New York: New American Library, 1977).
4. Susan Dworkin, "Meryl Streep to the Rescue!," *Ms.*, February 1979.
5. Margaret Trudeau and Caroline Moorehead, *Beyond Reason* (New York: Pocket Books, 1979), p. 234.
6. Leo N. Tolstoi, *Anna Karenina*, trans. Nathan Haskell Dole (New York: Thomas Y. Crowell & Co., 1886).
7. Curtis Cate, *George Sand, A Biography* (New York: Avon, 1975).
8. Ingmar Bergman, *Autumn Sonata, A Film*, trans. Alan Blair (New York: Pantheon Books, 1978).

Chapter 2

1. All statistics from U.S. Bureau of Census, current population reports; Special Studies, Series P-23, No. 106 and No. 107, as reported in *Ms.*, April 1981, p. 86.
2. The discrepancy between the number of absentee mothers referred to and the

number of fathers to whom children were relinquished (eighteen mothers, seventeen fathers) is due to the fact that two mothers relinquished custody to someone other than the fathers of their children, and one mother relinquished custody of two sons, one each, to their different fathers.

3. One of the nine lost custody to her parents; in one other case, it was the child's wish to live with his grandfather; two of these nine absentee mothers gave up their children out of emotional problems of their own (one through adoption to a cousin and her husband, one through legal custody to her own parents); one woman's grandmother kidnapped her child, and the mother did not attempt to regain custody; another mother allowed herself to be influenced by her second husband into giving her child up for adoption; the ninth absentee mother gave custody to her parents simply because she wanted to be free. That amounts to six cases in which the children were with other relatives, three in which they were with strangers. In the cases involving care by strangers, the fathers were not fit for custody: one was a permanent welfare recipient; one had never married the mother and his whereabouts were unknown; the third was a mental patient.

4. The extent to which any mother has the option of relinquishing custody of her children to their father is referred to in the Epilogue.

5. See my definition of *absentee mother* in the Introduction; it does not exclude former absentee mothers from participation. Former absentee mothers were included because my primary interest has been in the experience of absentee motherhood; and, obviously, former absentee mothers have had that experience.

6. This amounts to six women (37%) of the sixteen in the group for whom the question of permanancy of absentee motherhood is relevant. It is not relevant for one woman in the group because her children are already adults.

7. One participant in the study refused to divulge her sexual activity, past or present; no sexual activity information was available for three of the earliest additional participants, because that line of questioning was not included in the initial questionnaires.

8. Harold T. Christensen, "Scandinavian and American Sex Norms: Some Comparisons, with Sociological Implications," in *Sex and Society*, ed. John N. Edwards (Chicago: Markham Publishing Company, 1972), pp. 31–32.

9. John N. Edwards, "Unmarried Heterosexual Relations," in *Sex and Society*, p. 18.

10. As noted in the Before Marriage section, two of the hundred absentee mothers in the study never married. Of the four in the Before Marriage section for whom there is no relevant information, one is an early participant for whom there is relevant information relating only to her sexual activity during marriage.

11. Robert R. Bell, Stanley Turner, and Lawrence Rosen, "A Multivariate Analysis of Female Extramarital Coitus," *Journal of Marriage and the Family* 37 (May 1975): 375–84.

12. Among the women in the Bell study, the rate of extramarital coitus among women twenty-five years and younger was 17 percent; among women between twenty-six and thirty, the rate was 34 percent; among women thirty-one to fifty, the rate was 29 percent; and among women past age fifty, the rate was 16 percent. To quote the study, "The key group age may be that of 26 to 30, and as they move to age 40 their rate will continue to increase as will the 25-year-old-and-younger group coming behind them. Ultimately, the rate of extramarital coitus for the current 30 years of age and under cohort may reach between 40 and 50 per cent."

13. Paul Gebhard, "Postmarital Coitus Among Widows and Divorcees," *Sex and Society*, pp. 142–54.

14. Morton M. Hunt, *The World of the Formerly Married* (New York: McGraw-Hill Book Co., 1966). One hundred percent male postmarital coitus rate as stated by Hunt is cited in footnote of Gebhard, "Postmarital Coitus," p. 153.

15. The number of absentee mothers being considered in the postmarital section is ninety-four. Six were removed from consideration because two of them had never married, and no postmarital data was available for the other four.

Chapter 3

1. In Chapter 2, the twenty-five absentee mothers who had noncustodial status imposed upon them by the court or by their children were considered separately from the seventy-five absentee mothers who, technically, had chosen to relinquish custody. That procedure was appropriate to the process of sorting participants' manifest noncustodial positions; however, to the extent that one cooperates with or influences or presents fertile ground for outside forces, it is necessary to include even the "unwilling" absentee mothers in considerations of predisposition to absentee motherhood.

2. Rollo May, *The Meaning of Anxiety*, rev. ed. (New York: W. W. Norton & Co., 1977), pp. 358–59.

3. Judith S. Wallerstein and Joan B. Kelly, "California's Children of Divorce," *Psychology Today* 13, no. 8 (January 1980); "The Children of Divorce," *Newsweek*, February 11, 1980, pp. 58–63.

4. U. S. Bureau of the Census, *Historical Statistics of the United States, Colonial Times to 1970*, Bicentennial Edition, part 2 (Washington, D.C.: Government Printing Office, 1975), p. 62.

5. Walter Toman, *Family Constellation: Its Effects on Personality and Social Behavior* (New York: Springer Publishing Co., 1969), p. 91.

6. Florence O. Keller, "The Childless Mother: An Evaluation of Deviancy as a Concept in Contemporary Culture" (Ph.D. dissertation, California School of Professional Psychology, San Francisco, 1975). University Microfilms International, Ann Arbor, Mich., 1981.

7. U.S. Bureau of the Census, *Historial Statistics*, p. 61.

8. The specific distribution of the hundred participants' relationships to their parents is as follows:

Mother	Participants
Positive	27
Mixed or neutral	34
Negative	35
Nonexistent	4
Total	100
Father	
Positive	25
Mixed or neutral	23
Negative	38
Nonexistent	14
Total	100

Note: All participants who categorized their parental relationships as either very warm and close or somewhat warm and close were included under *positive*. All participants who categorized their parental relationships as somewhat tense and strained or very tense and strained were included under *negative*.

9. M. A. Isenhart, "Divorced Women: A Comparison of Two Groups Who Have Retained or Relinquished Custody of Their Children," *Dissertation Abstracts International*, 1980, 5628-A; J. L. Fischer and J. M. Cardea, "Mothers Living Apart from Their Children: A Study in Stress and Coping," *Alternative Lifestyles* 4, no. 2 (1981), pp. 218-27.

10. U.S. Department of Health and Human Services, *Vital Statistics of the United States 1977*, vol. 3, "Marriage and Divorce" (National Center for Health Statistics, Hyattsville, Md., 1981), section 2, table 2-1.

11. Parents of twenty-three of the hundred participants divorced while they were children. Divorce statistics are stated as number per one thousand married females, a base ten times larger than my own. In order to extrapolate my study group for comparison, I multiplied both the base of one hundred participants and the number of participants with divorced parents by ten.

12. The childhood religious makeup of the study group:

Religious upbringing	Participants
Protestant	41
Catholic	28
None	16
Jewish	10
Other	5
Total	100

13. U.S. Bureau of the Census, *Statistical Abstract of the United States: 1980*, 101st ed. (Washington, D.C.: Government Printing Office, 1980), p. 56, table 82, gives number of Catholics in 1950; idem, *Historical Statistics*, p. 8, gives total resident population in 1950.

14. Among the twenty-three participants whose parents divorced or separated during their childhoods, the nature of their relationships with their parents are the prime reasons to suspect Oedipal strivings:

Mother	Participants
Positive	4
Neutral	1
Mixed	4
Negative	13
Nonexistent	1
Total	23

Father	Participants
Positive	5
Neutral	1
Mixed	2
Negative	5
Nonexistent	10
Total	23

The reader will note that there are two-and-a-half times as many negative relationships with mothers than with fathers and that the level of missing fathers is ten times that of missing mothers.

15. Keller, "The Childless Mother."

16. The specific distribution of parenting possibilities among the eighteen participants who relinquished custody as a result of emotional problems is:

M+ F+	M− F+	M+ F−	M− F−
6	3	3	6

17. The specific distribution of parenting possibilities among the twelve participants who lost custody in court is:

M+ F+	M− F+	M+ F−	M− F−
3	5	0	4

18. The specific distribution of parenting possibilities among the thirteen participants whose children decided to live with their fathers is:

M+ F+	M− F+	M+ F−	M− F−
4	4	0	5

19. The specific distribution of parenting possibilities among the four participants who relinquished custody because they felt their husbands to be the more nurturing parent is:

M+ F+	M− F+	M+ F−	M− F−
3	0	0	1

20. The specific distribution of parenting possibilities among the fourteen participants who relinquished custody due to intimidation is:

M+ F+	M− F+	M+ F−	M− F−
7	2	2	3

21. The specific distribution of parenting possibilities among the seventeen participants who relinquished custody in order to better pursue self-realization is:

M+ F+ 7	M− F+ 1	M+ F− 4	M− F− 5

22. The specific distribution of parenting possibilities among the eighteen participants who relinquished custody due to financial realities is:

M+ F+ 2	M− F+ 3	M+ F− 8	M− F− 5

Note: The only category of absentee mother not referred to in the text regarding distribution of parenting possibilities is the group of four participants who relinquished custody due to problems in a second marriage. This is because there is a totally even distribution displayed among them, and it is therefore not possible to make any connection in this group between parental attitudes and reason for relinquishing custody:

M+ F+ 1	M− F+ 1	M+ F− 1	M− F− 1

23. Blair Justice and Rita Justice, *The Broken Taboo: Sex in the Family* (New York: Human Sciences Press, 1979), p. 96.

24. Ibid., pp. 15–17.

25. U.S. Bureau of the Census, *Historical Statistics*, p. 8.

26. Maya Pines, "Only Isn't Lonely (or Spoiled or Selfish)," *Psychology Today* 15, no. 3 (March 1981): 15.

27. As cited in ibid.

28. Judith L. Fischer, "Childfree Relationships: Mothers Living Apart from Their Children," paper presented at the Groves Conference on Marriage and the Family, The Poconos, Pennsylvania, 1981.

29. Isenhart, "Divorced Women."

30. Toman, *Family Constellation*.

31. Billie Rosoff (Voluntary Sterilization Program at Preterm Clinic, Brookline, Mass.), "Childless by Choice," *Newsweek*, January 14, 1980, p. 96.

32. U.S. Department of Health and Human Sciences, *Vital Statistics of the U.S. 1959*, vol. 2 (National Center for Health Statistics, Hyattsville, Md.), table 77-A.

33. Erwin Stengel, *Suicide and Attempted Suicide*, rev. ed. (Baltimore: Penguin, 1969).

Chapter 4

1. The median educational level of the absentee mother at the point of marriage was the completion of 12 years; that is, she had graduated from high school. The average educational level of her groom was 13 years, only one year higher in spite of the fact that he was usually four years older. For comparison, the median school years completed among women at large in 1964 was 11.8 and among men was 11.5. Thus, the participants in my study were representative of the degree to which women at large were educated, and the men they married were somewhat more educated than the male population in general by one-and-a-half years.

2. The number of participants mentioned here $(4+42+53=99)$ do not include one participant who failed to respond to the question involved.

3. Of course, among the children who made the custodial decision themselves, the median age was much higher—thirteen.

4. U.S. Bureau of the Census, *Historical Statistics of the United States, Colonial Times to 1970*, Bicentennial Edition (Washington, D.C.: Government Printing Office, 1975), p. 42.

5. Although families containing stepchildren have most recently been dubbed "reconstituted" families, and, I believe, would normally be included where the term *nuclear family* is used, I find it impossible to consider the dynamics of the two situations as being identical. Therefore, I have placed stepchildren in the category of extended family here.

6. U.S. Bureau of the Census, *Historical Statistics*, p. 414.

Chapter 5

1. Froma Sand, *The Life Wish* (New York: Hawthorne Books, Inc., W. Clement Stone, 1974), p. 45.

2. U.S. Bureau of the Census, *Statistical Abstract of the United States*, 100th ed. (Washington, D.C.: Government Printing Office, September 1979); National Center for Health Statistics, *Annual Summary: Vital Statistics* (Hyattsville, Md., 1979), p. 77.

3. One absentee mother of the hundred who completed questionnaires committee suicide before the research period of one year had ended. (I learned of this suicide only incidentally; it is not impossible that other suicides have occurred without my knowledge.) Since the hundred absentee mothers in my study are one-thousandth of the Census Bureau's base of 100,000, I multiplied the 100 participants times 1,000 to create an equal base. As the occurrence of one suicide among the one hundred participants represents 1 percent of the participants, I multiplied 1 percent of 100,000, which results in the extrapolation of 1,000 absentee mothers committing suicide for every seven other American women who commit suicide.

4. Missouri is the only state that keeps a record of custody disposition, so there are no existing statistics on numbers of women who have lost or relinquished custody in the divorcing process. Neither can the U.S. Census Bureau supply the existing number of absentee mothers. The closest it comes to doing so is the number of children living with a currently divorced father, which in 1979 stood at 493,000. Since the average number of children involved in a divorce is one, we can equate the number of children with the number of fathers. However, we cannot equate the number of divorced fathers living with their children to the number of absentee mothers. This would not take into account those fathers with custody who have

remarried (who are believed to be plentiful). Neither would this take into account the absentee mothers who have never married the fathers of their children, those who have relinquished custody to parties other than the fathers, and those who have relinquished custody only unofficially.

5. Bureau of the Census, *Statistical Abstract*, 100th ed., p. 181, p. 29.

6. Carol B. Stack, *All Our Kin* (New York: Harper and Row, 1974).

7. Erwin Stengel, *Suicide and Attempted Suicide,* rev. ed. (Baltimore, Md.: Penguin Books, 1969), p. 52.

8. Ibid., pp. 52–53.

9. Ibid., p. 89, and Froma Sand, *Life Wish*, p. 151. For my purposes, this is a misleading way to state the attempted suicide rate, because it does not differentiate between male and female suicidal behavior. There is a significantly different rate of both suicide and attempted suicide between men and women. Whereas 20 of every 100,000 men commit suicide, only 7 of every 100,000 women do so. Conversely, a good many more women than men attempt suicide. According to a two-year study conducted in England by Parkin and Stengel and published in the *British Medical Journal* 2 (1965): 137, females account for an average of 63% of all attempted suicides. If this finding is applied to the total suicide attempts among the 200,000 men and women just mentioned (that is, 27 suicides x 10 attempted suicides, for a total of 270 estimated suicide attempts), one gets a different, and probably more accurate, picture of attempted suicide rates (270 x .63 = 170 female attempts, leaving 100 male attempts) because they are differentiated by gender. Done in this way, one arrives at the proposition that five times the number of men who commit suicide attempt it (20 male suicides x 5 = 100 attempted suicides) and that twenty-four times the number of women who commit suicide attempt it (7 female suicides x 24 = 170 [in round figures] attempted suicides). The 170 in 100,000 females attempting suicide gives us the attempted suicide rate among the general female population of 0.17%.

10. The U.S. and Great Britain exhibit similar suicide rates, so it is reasonable to use a British study for comparison to an American segment of the population.

11. Stengel, *Suicide*, pp. 94 & 98.

12. Virginia Woolf, *Orlando* (London: Hogarth Press, 1928), p. 64.

13. Stengel, *Suicide*, p. 13.

14. Ibid., p. 56.

15. Lloyd Shearer (*Parade Magazine* staff writer), referring to Donald T. Lunde's book *Murder and Madness* (San Francisco, Calif.: San Francisco Book Co., 1976) on the jacket of that book. Dr. Lunde is an American criminal psychiatrist.

16. Sand, *Life Wish*, p. xvi.

17. Stengel, *Suicide*, p. 53.

18. Ibid., p. 43.

19. Ibid., p. 87.

20. Ibid., p. 117.

21. Gloria's story is not presented verbatim, but has been minimally edited without changing any facts.

22. KRON-TV (NBC), Channel 4, San Francisco, six o'clock news, October 15, 1979.

23. Ibid., early February, 1980.

24. Ibid., October 15, 1979.

25. WTVH-TV (CBS), Channel 5, Syracuse, New York, six o'clock newscast, December 26, 1982.

26. Adrienne Rich, *Of Woman Born* (New York: Bantam, 1977), pp. 260–61.
27. Ibid., p. 35.

Chapter 6

1. The new credit laws, by the way, have not completely changed this situation in practice. Large, sophisticated retailers and banks have been forced to comply due to their high visibility and, thus, vulnerability. However, landlords and smaller retailers and utilities still discriminate against divorcing women with no credit histories in their names.

2. These numbers do not add up to 48 (6 + 15 + 26 = 47) because one participant did not answer the relevant question.

3. The total number of former husbands referred to here (62 + 37 = 99) does not add up to 100. Two of the "husbands" are not included here because they were never legally married to my participants. There are 101 "husbands" in this study, although there are only 100 "wives" (one woman relinquished two children to two different fathers).

4. Angus Campbell, "The American Way of Mating: Marriage Si, Children Only Maybe," *Psychology Today*, May 1975, Reprint No. P-295.

5. One participant cannot be considered in this context because she is no longer living, as referred to in Chapter 5.

6. Among the seventeen women who resumed custody, thirteen (76%) lived with both parents for their entire childhood; among the rest of the study group, only fifty of the eighty-three (60%) have that stabilizing factor in their background.

7.

Parental Attitude Combinations in the Childhood Backgrounds of Two Different Groups of Absentee Mothers

100 Absentee mothers	M+ F+ Number	%	M– F+ Number	%	M+ F– Number	%	M– F– Number	%
17 women who resumed custody	5	29	3	18	6	35	3	18
Remaining 83	28	34	16	19	12	14	27	33

8.

Birth Order among Two Different Groups of Absentee Mothers

100 Absentee mothers	Only Number	%	Oldest Number	%	Middle Number	%	Youngest Number	%
17 women who resumed custody	2	12	7	41	7	41	1	6
Remaining 83	11	13	37	45	20	24	15	18

9

**Quality of Relationship with Sister Closest in Age
among Two Different Groups of Absentee Mothers**

100 Absentee mothers	Positive		Mixed or neutral		Negative		No sisters	
	Number	%	Number	%	Number	%	Number	%
17 women who resumed custody	6	35	4	24	1	6	6	35
Remaining 83	12	14	23	28	11	13	36	43

10. All occupational data from U.S. Bureau of the Census, *Historical Statistics of the United States, Colonial Times to 1970,* Bicentennial Edition (Washington, D.C.: GPO, 1975), pp. 139–40.

11. Dr. Myra Marx Ferree, "The Confused American Housewife," *Psychology Today,* September 1976, Reprint No. P-355.

12. Florence O. Keller, "The Childless Mother: An Evaluation of Deviancy as a Concept in Contemporary Culture" (Ph.D. dissertation, California School of Professional Psychology, San Francisco, 1975), Abstract, p. 3. University Microfilms International, Ann Arbor, Mich., 1981.

13. For further observations regarding self-identities of noncustodial mothers, see M. A. Isenhart, "Divorced Women," *Dissertation Abstracts International,* 1980.

14. The thirty-eight women who want their custody arrangement to be only temporary represent 44 percent, and the twenty-two who are ambivalent about it represent 26 percent of the study group *in relation to this issue:* for fourteen participants the issue is moot. Their children have either become adults or have already returned to their mothers' custody (38+22+14=74). The remaining twenty-six participants definitely want their custody arrangement to be permanent.

15. One participant of the fourteen in the "intimidation" relinquishing group need not be considered because her son is now an adult.

16. One participant of the eighteen in the "emotional problems" relinquishing group is ineligible for consideration because she was hospitalized after attempting suicide before she completed the relevant part of the questionnaire; she withdrew from the study at that point.

17. Zbigniew Bujak, head of the Warsaw Chapter of Solidarity referring to collaborators, "Life Under Jaruzelski's Law," *Newsweek,* January 25, 1982, p. 37.

18. There is a factor that tends to diminish the meaning of the average visiting days in the two groups of absentee mothers discussed. Unfortunately, eighteen participants among the forty "happy" absentee mothers responded to the relevant question too vaguely to allow accurate determinations. They were, thus, excluded from consideration, as were sixteen additional participants among the sixty "unhappy" absentee mothers for the same reason. Therefore, my conclusions in the area of visiting frequency are based on a total of sixty-six participants.

19. Albert Camus, "Love of Life," *Lyrical and Critical Essays,* edited and with notes by Philip Thody, translated from the French by Ellen Conroy Kennedy (New York: Vintage, 1970), p. 56.

20. Judith S. Wallerstein and Joan B. Kelly, "California's Children of Divorce," *Psychology Today* 13, no. 8 (January 1980). In an in-depth study of sixty divorcing families over a five-year period, 34 percent of the children were "happy and

thriving," 29 percent "were doing reasonably well," but 37 percent were depressed. Ninety-two percent of the children lived with their mothers.

Epilogue

1. Letty Cottin Pogrebin, "A Feminist In Sweden," *Ms.*, April 1982, p. 84, referring to Swedish economist Siv Gustafsson.
2. Elisabeth Badinter, *Mother Love: Myth and reality*, foreword by Francine du Plessix Gray (New York: Macmillan, 1981).
3. James A. Levine, *Who Will Raise the Children?* (Philadelphia: Lippincott, 1976), p. 25.

Appendix

Table 1   Years Since Participants' Separation/Divorce

Years elapsed	Number of participants in grouping	Total years in grouping
1	2	2
2	13	26
3	7	21
4	9	36
5	9	45
6	10	60
7	8	56
8	8	64
9	9	81
10	5	50
11	3	33
12	1	12
13	2	26
14	4	56
15	1	18
16	2	44
23	1	23
24	1	24
25	1	25
26	1	26
30	1	30
31	1	31
Total	99	789

Average years elapsed: 8
Median years elapsed: 6.5

Note: Years elapsed are computed from point of separation/divorce to point of completing questionnaire in 1980. Two participants never married the fathers of their children, and one participant relinquished custody of children from two marriages.

Table 2 Time of Relinquishing Custody in Relation to Dissolution of Marriage Among Eight Specific Categories of Participants and Among Voluntary and Involuntary Absentee Mother Participants

Absentee mother participants	Retained custody initially		Median length of custody	Average length of custody	Simultaneous end to custody and marriage	
Category[a] and number	Number	Percentage	Years	Years	Number	Percentage
Emotional problems (18)	9	50	1.00	2.25	9	50
Financial realities (18)	8	44	1.25	2.20	10	56
Self-realization (17)	6	35	1.00	3.10	11	65
Intimidation (14)	6	43	2.25	1.82	8	57
Children's decision (13)	10	77	1.50	3.91	3	23
Lost custody (12)	10	83	1.25	1.56	2	17
Father more nurturing (4)	2	50	2.50	2.50	2	50
Problems in second marriage (4)	4	100	4.00	3.89	0	—
Overall (100)	55	55	1.25	2.65	45	45
Voluntary (75)	35	47	1.75	1.17	40	53
Involuntary (25)	20	80	1.37	2.19	5	20
Overall (100)	55	55	1.25	2.65	45	45

[a]Motivation or causation for relinquishing custody.

Note: Voluntary absentee mothers are those who technically made the decision to relinquish custody of their children. Many of these participants, however, feel that they had no viable options and that they had absentee motherhood imposed upon them by circumstances. Involuntary absentee mothers are those who had either the courts or their children impose absentee motherhood on them.

Table 3   Educational Levels among One Hundred Absentee Mothers

Years of schooling completed	Number of participants in grouping
9	1
10	1
11	2
12	24
13	13
14	20
15	6
16	18
17	5
18	8
21	2
Total	100

Median years schooling: 14
Average years schooling: 14

Table 4   Generalized Educational Comparisons: Average Years of Schooling Completed

Absentee mothers	At time of divorce	To date	Improvement
Entire study group (100 women)	12.50	14	1.50
"Financial realities" group (18 women)	12.50	14	1.50
"Personal freedom" group (17 women)	13	15	2

Table 5 Specific Educational Comparisons

Absentee mothers	Never finished high school		High school diploma		Some college		Bachelor's degree		Some graduate study		Master's degree		Ph.D.	
	No.	%	No.	%	No.	%	No.	%	No.	%	No.	%	No.	%
Entire study group (100 women)	4	4	24	24	39	39	18	18	5	5	8	8	2	2
"Financial realities" group (18 women)	2a	11	3	17	7	39	3	17	1e	5	2e	11	0	0
"Personal freedom" group (17 women)	0b	0	4	24	5	29c	6d	35	0	0	2	12	0	0

aThe two women in the "financial realities" group who did not finish high school account for half the women in the entire study who never finished high school, in spite of the fact that the "financial realities" group represents less than one-fifth of the entire group in numbers.

bEveryone in the "personal freedom" group had at least a high school diploma.

cAmong the women who relinquished custody for financial reasons, 10 percent more have some college than in the group of women who relinquished custody for the sake of personal freedom. However, contrary to what one would expect, the group holds a much inferior employment record. Fifteen of its eighteen members are hourly wage workers. All of the other group's seventeen members are salaried. I therefore consider the seventeen women in the group who relinquished custody for the sake of personal freedom to be high achievers.

dOne-third of the women in the study as a whole who have bachelor's degrees are found in the "personal freedom" group, although their numbers constitute less than one-fifth of the whole study.

eThe three women in the "financial realities" group with graduate studies to their credit are the three teachers in the group.

Table 6 Marital Situations That Contributed to Extramarital Affairs among Absentee Mother Participants

Mitigating Factor	Number of women to whom it applies
Husband's disinterest/low sex drive	8
Husband's infidelity	7
Husband's incompetence as lover	6
Unpleasant/inadequate sexual intercourse with husband due to strains of deteriorating relationship	5
Husband's consenting knowledge/encouragement (swinging or open marriage)	3
During separations from husband only	1
Total	30

Table 7 Pertinent Facts Related to Six Participants Without Mitigating Factors in Their Extramarital Sexual Behavior

Absentee mother involved	Number of consorts	Duration of liason/extramarital sexual activity	Duration of marriage
First of six	1	1 month	10 years
Second of six	1	9 months	7 years
Third of six	1	1 year	6 years
Fourth of six	1	4 years	22 years
Fifth of six	"A few"	1 year	16 years
Sixth of six	Unspecified but numerous	2 years	9 years

Table 8 Participants Who Worked Outside Their Homes or Attended School While Married (for at least portions of their marriages)

Extent of involvement	Outside employment	School attendance
Full time	56	12
Part time	21	37
None at all	21	49
Total who married	98	98

Table 9 Overall Effect of Extended Household on Participants' Marriage and/or Parenting

Participants' assessment of effect	Percentage of group who lived within extended household
Negative	54
None	20
Some good, some bad	14
Positive	12

Note: Very few participants felt their extended households affected their parenting. For the most part, then, these assessments apply to the effects their extended households had on their marriages.

Table 10 Remarriage—Women

	Among absentee mothers			Among other divorced women		
	Number remarried	Median time lapse	Rate[a]		Median time lapse	Rate[a]
	50	2 years	62.5		1.7 years	104.0
	Number unmarried					
	48	4 years.				

[a]Per thousand per year.

Table 11 Remarriage—Men

	Among custodial fathers			Among other divorced men		
	Number remarried	Median time lapse	Rate[a]		Median time lapse	Rate[a]
	62	1.5 years	77.5		1.5 years	165.6
	Number unmarried					
	37	3.5 years				

[a]Per thousand per year.

Table 12 Summary of Postdivorce/Relinquishing Educational Activity

Types of diplomas or degrees earned	Number of degrees	Number of women
High school	10	
Bachelor's	19	
Master's	1	
Total	39	
Caveat: Women who have earned two degrees	(5)	
Those who have earned any number or kind		34
Those who have earned college credit toward degrees		25
Total educationally active		59

Table 13 Absentee Mother Participants with Professional or Management Occupations, Compared with Active Labor Force as a Whole

	Absentee mothers SO employed		Male population SO employed	Female population SO employed	Combined population SO employed
	Number	%[a]	%[a]	%[a]	%[a]
Professionals	22	27	14	15	15
Management	24	29	11	4	8
Overall total	46	56	25	19	23

[a]Percentage of economically active, which excludes students, housewives, children, unemployed, and retired persons.

Note: Data for the labor force as a whole is for 1970, which is within two years of the average year of divorce (1972) in this study.

Table 14   Absentee Mother Participants with Clerical or Service Occupations, Compared with Active Labor Force as a Whole

	Absentee mothers so employed		Male population so employed	Female population so employed	Combined population so employed
	Number	%[a]	%[a]	%[a]	%[a]
Clerical	24	30	8	34	25
Service workers (except private household)	11	14	8	17	11
Totals	35	44	16	51	36

[a] Percentage of active labor force, which excludes students, housewives, children, unemployed and retired.

Table 15   Remarriage among Happy and Unhappy Absentee Mothers

	Remarried?					
	Yes			No		
Absentee mothers	Number	%	After Avg. of	Number	%	After Avg. of
60 with emotional problems	32	53	3 years	28	47	5 years
40 free of emotional problems	18	45	3 years	22	55	6 years

Table 16   Social Responses Experienced by Happy and Unhappy Absentee Mothers

Happy or unhappy absentee mothers	Positive responses		Negative responses		Degree of negative prevalence
	Number	%[a]	Number	%[a]	
60 with emotional problems	58	97	108	180	(83%)
40 free of emotional problems	53	133	71	178	(45%)
Difference		36		2	

[a] Percentage of total responses as measured against number of women in group. The social responses were measured in the following manner: Each absentee mother participant was asked to classify persons' responses to her noncustodial status into the categories of relatives, friends, employers, and strangers. Her answers were translated into either a negative or a positive rating, with the understanding that one could experience *both* in any given category. Each response was given one point, so each participant could produce eight points: positive or negative under each of the four categories (4 points) or both positive *and* negative under each category (8 points). Some participants considered the reactions in any given group to be neutral; for others a given social group did not exist; and some failed to answer the question. Neutral responses (and failure to respond) were not included. The positive and negative responses elicited were measured in terms of the whole group (either the 60 with emotional problems or the 40 free of emotional problems) since they are the total responses forthcoming from the group. The percentage figures used in this chart indicate the proportion of social responses in relation to the number of participants in the group.

Table 17　Specific Social Responses Experienced by Happy and Unhappy Absentee Mothers

Happy or unhappy absentee mothers	Relatives Number	%a	Friends Number	%a	Employers Number	%a	Strangers Number	%a
				Positive responses				
60 with emotional problems	11	19	26	45	7	12	14	24
40 free of emotional problems	18	34	20	38	8	15	7	13
Difference		15		7		3		11
				Negative responses				
60 with emotional problems	39	36	27	25	10	9	32	30
40 free of emotional problems	27	38	18	25	5	7	21	30
Difference		2		Ø		2		Ø

aPercentage of total responses measured against number of women in group. For the method of measuring social responses, see note to Table 16.

Table 18　Distribution of Participants from the Various Relinquishing Categories (between "happy" and "unhappy" absentee mothers)

Reasons for relinquishing custody; number of absentee mothers	60 "unhappy" mothers (with emotional problems) Number in group	%	40 "happy" mothers (with no emotional problems) Number in group	%	Difference
Emotional problems (18)	12	20	6	15	(5%)
Financial realities (18)	12	20	6	15	(5%)
Self-realization (17)	10	17	7	18	1%
Intimidation (14)	6	10	8	20	10%
Children's decision (13)	10	17	3	8	(9%)
Lost custody (12)	7	12	5	13	1%
Father more nurturing (4)	2	3	2	5	2%
Problems in second marriage (4)	1	2	3	8	6%

Note: Percentage differences inside parentheses represent a negative difference: an absentee mother in that relinquishing category is more likely to be an "unhappy" absentee mother than a "happy" one by the degree of the figure. The percentage figures in both the "happy" and "unhappy" categories add up to more than 100. This is due to the practice of raising each individual computation to the next highest whole number when the fraction in the computation equals .50 or more.

Table 19   Children Who Exhibit or Exhibited Symptoms of Emotional Distress
            Following Divorce and/or Relinquishment by Mothers

Category of absentee mother and number	Children with symptoms[a] Number	Percentage
Custodial (Wallerstein and Kelly study) (60)	N.A.	37
Noncustodial with knowledge of symptoms and/or treatment (33)	57	27
Noncustodial who do not know whether children have required or obtained treatment (11)	19 (possible)	9
Total Noncustodial	76	36

[a] Serious enough to require professional treatment.

N.A. Number of children involved is not cited in article, but sixty families participated in the five-year study.

Note: There are 212 children involved in this study.

Demographics

Table A   Geographic Residence of Participants

East: New York, New Jersey, Ohio, Pennsylvania, Virginia,
         West Virginia, Connecticut, Kentucky, Massachusetts   27

South and Southwest: Florida, Georgia, Texas, South
         Carolina   5

Midwest: Illinois, Minnesota, Indiana, Kansas, Michigan,
         Mississippi, Wisconsin, Oklahoma   34

West: California, Oregon, Utah, Idaho, Nevada, Washington   30
Canada   3
England   1

Note: Although four participants live in foreign countries, three of them are U.S. citizens, one a Canadian citizen.

242

Table B   Distances Participants Live from Their Children

Distance from children	Number of participants
Same city	10
2–23 miles	23
25–50 miles	13
60–100 miles (100 = median distance)	5
115–300 miles	7
350–1000 miles	20
More than 1000 miles	23

Note: Distance cited applies to the period during which participants lived apart from their minor children. One participant is counted twice because she relinquished two children to their two different fathers.

Table C   Years Since Participants Relinquished Children

Years elapsed [a]	Number of participants in grouping	Total years in grouping
1	5	5
2	15	30
3	8	24
4	14	56
5	9	45
6	10	60
7	5	35
8	9	72
9	8	72
10	4	40
11	1	11
12	3	36
13	1	13
14	1	17
22	1	22
23	2	46
24	1	24
25	1	25
30	1	30
31	1	31
Total	100	694

Average years elapsed: 7
Median years elapsed: 5

[a] From relinquishment of custody until completing questionnaire in 1980.

Table D Participants' Ages at Marriage

Age	Number of participants in grouping
15	2
16	6
17	8
18	21
19	20
20	12
21	14
22	6
23	4
24	1
25	2
27	1
28	1
Total	98[a]

Median age: 19

[a] Two participants never married.

Table E Participants' Current Ages

Age	Number of participants in grouping	Age	Number of participants in grouping
23	2	38	4
24	1	39	6
25	4	40	5
26	3	41	3
27	2	42	2
28	4	43	3
29	5	44	3
30	6	45	3
31	6	47	4
32	5	48	1
33	4	50	2
34	5	53	1
35	3	60	1
36	5	63	1
37	6	Total	100

Median age: 35.5 years

Table F   Duration of Participants' First Marriages

Duration (years)[a]	Number of participants in grouping	Duration (years)[a]	Number of participants in grouping
1	3	14	5
2	5	15	5
3	9	16	4
4	6	17	1
5	11	18	2
6	6	19	3
7	5	20	1
8	5	21	1
9	5	22	2
10	6	26	1
11	3	Total	98[b]
12	4	Median duration 8.5 years	
13	5		

[a] Up to point of separation, not necessarily legal finality.
[b] Two participants never married.

Table G   Number of Children from Participants' First Marriages

Number of children	Number of participants in grouping	Total children in grouping
1	33	33
2	38	76
3	18	54
4	8	32
5	1	5
6	2	12
Total	100	212

Median number of children: 2
Average number of children: 2

Note: Included as "marriages" are all relationships that produced children who were eventually relinquished.

Table H   Participants' Current Religion

Religion	Number and percentage of absentee mothers	Percentage of population at large[a]
Protestant	24	61
Catholic	14	27
Jewish	8	2
Other	11	3
None	43	7
Total	100	100

[a] 1977–78 Gallup Poll.

Demographics Note: Childhood and marital religion, educational levels, occupations, marital status, race, and sexual orientation among the hundred participants are outlined within the body of this book: see Index.

Index

Abandonment, 10, 16, 93, 146
Absentee mothers, 3; with absentee mothers, 91–99, 110; adopted, 94; age, 5, 99; attitudes toward parents, 105–11, 225–26n8, 226–27n14; and career, 23–24, 45, 60, 80 (*see also Autumn Sonata;* Self-realization); childhood, 4, 33, 46, 77, 91–119, 180, 204; and childless women, 11; children's reactions, 210–13; and custody, 177–79, 181, 193, 200 (*see also* Denial; Noncustodial mothers); and death of parent, 93, 94, 98, 99–103; defined, 5; and divorce, 169–74, 219 (*see also* Self-realization); and divorce of parents, 93, 96, 97, 98, 101, 102, 103–5, 116; education, 2, 15, 53, 56, 61, 75, 171, 181, 182–83, 190 (*see also* Self-realization); and employment, 16–17, 21, 22, 34–35, 54, 60, 110, 124, 147–48, 149–50, 154, 171, 183–85, 217; and extended households, 139–42; and first pregnancy, 126, 131; and guilt, 18, 69, 77, 146, 152, 170, 189, 207, 215 (*see also* Denial; Suicide); and handicapped children, 135–37; husbands and remarriage, 172–73, 179; husbands as fathers, 137–38, 202, 216; image as, 190–93, 208–9 (*see also* Denial); and incest, 111–13; loneliness, 208–9; and male children, 134–35, 178, 212; marriage, 4, 121–44, 153–54; and mothering, 77–80, 92, 107, 108, 116–17, 125–34, 174–81, 209, 216, 218–19, 221, 227n19; national or-

ganization (*see* Mothers Without Custody); and Oedipal strivings, 101–3, 105, 135, 226–27n14; as oldest children, 114–17, 137; as only children, 112, 113–14; perfection syndrome, 157–58, 217; and public perception of, 6, 9–11, 12, 17, 24–25, 36–37, 39–40, 145–46, 149–50, 155–56, 196–97, 198–200, 215, 217; questionnaire, 4–5, 89, 152–53; race, 5, 147; and religion, 5, 63, 79, 104, 115, 125, 126, 179, 217, 226n12; and remarriage, 5, 37, 38, 39, 55, 58, 64, 67, 74–77, 89, 129, 154, 163, 166, 171–73, 175, 201, 209, 228n22; self-image, 112, 113, 148–49, 158, 170, 185; and sex, 17, 21–23, 24, 45, 82–86, 88, 89, 95, 166, 186, 187–88 (*see also Anna Karenina;* Homosexuality); and single life, 172, 205; social status, 99; study sample, 4–5; *see also* Aggression; Emotional illness; Intimidation; Money; Noncustodial mothers; Self-realization; Suicide
Adoption, 57, 76, 93, 167
Adoptive mothers, 5, 6–7
Adultery, 83, 84–85
Aggression, 156–59, 168, 215; *see also* Suicide
Alcoholics Anonymous, 152
Alcoholism, 18, 46, 49, 92, 94, 116, 138–39, 151, 152
Alimony, 53, 171
Andergast, Charlotte (*see Autumn Sonata*)